TEACHING AND TECHNOLOGY FOR HUMAN DEVELOPMENT

TEACHING AND TECHNOLOGY FOR HUMAN DEVELOPMENT

Editor
Prof. Ramesh Chandra

Publications

KALPAZ PUBLICATIONS
DELHI-110052

Teaching and Technology for Human Development

ISBN: 81-7835-233-8

This book is Vol. No. 5 of Universal Education and Technology in 21st Century (Set)

Published in 2005 in India by
Kalpaz Publications,
C-30, Satyawati Nagar, Delhi-110052
E-mail : Kalpaz@hotmail.com

Laser Typesetting at : Master Computers, Delhi
Printed at : Rajdhani Printers, Delhi

Contents

Preface

Technological advance has contributed greatly to the acceleration of human progress in the past several centuries. The information and communications technology can be a tremendous force for human development for all those connected-by providing information, enabling empowerment and raising productivity. Technology may be globalizing communications, but globalization—and its new rules—is also shaping the path of new technologies.

The last 20 years have seen some remarkable innovations in the delivery of education. The technologies available today, and those about to emerge, have the potential to transform the business of education. Some nations may decide to invest in technology for education for the "glitz factor": the technology is there; it is fashionable to have the latest and the best, and it gives a sense of progress to use state-of-art-technology.

The demand for more open and accessible learning has continued to increase since the early 1950s, but even more so following the World Conference on Education for All in Jomtien, Thailand, in 1989. Many factors are contributing to this changing educational culture, the most important of which are economic, social, and technological forces. These forces are worldwide in scope and power, and have had a profound impact on business practices, manufacturing processes, financial services, government policies, and, more recently, teaching practices and learning behaviours.

The challenge of providing education and training to a huge and diverse population with a variety of learning goals and styles, at an acceptable cost, will require new forms of global educational delivery. The emergence of new technologies may have something to do with the push to make drastic changes in the nature of the learning environment. There is also a change in the nature of those requiring education and training. Communities no longer are content to limit access to education and training to the fortunate few who are able; literate; live in urban communities; have access to communications, infrastructure, and classrooms; are knowledgeable about learning opportunities and options; and have the resources to pay for them.

Editor

1

Introduction

The last 20 years have seen some remarkable innovations in the delivery of education. Nevertheless, many would argue that, as remarkable as these innovations are, they are no more than a beginning. The technologies available today, and those about to emerge, have the potential to transform the business of education. However, what may be impeding that potential is our academic culture and traditions. Nine centuries of organized education have generated strong views and deep-seated beliefs about what is best and what is not. diverse needs, clients, demands, goals, and objectives of nations and communities-particularly during a period of transition of societies and economies from an industrial base to one that is knowledge and information-centered. This chapter raises a number of policy considerations and outlines a series of strategic options that could facilitate an effective role for ICT.

Some nations may decide to invest in technology for education for the "glitz factor": the technology is there; it is fashionable to have the latest and the best, and it gives a sense of progress to use state-of-art-technology. This can be described as the technology for its own sake rationale. Other nations may base their investment decisions on the genuine case for improving the efficiency of their education systems or for some other benefits intrinsic to education. For instance, databases and computerised records in education systems have clear advantages and benefits. This is the "technology for educational benefits" rationale. A third rationale may be external to education and concerned with developing skills for the labour market.

The demand for more open and accessible learning has continued to increase since the early 1950s, but even more so following the World Conference on Education for All in Jomtien, Thailand, in 1989. Many factors are contributing to this changing educational culture, the most important of which are economic, social, and technological forces. These forces are worldwide in scope and power, and have had a profound impact on business practices, manufacturing processes, financial services, government policies, and, more recently, teaching practices and learning behaviors. It would not be an exaggeration to say that as embark on a new century, moving irrevocably in the direction of changing the way, think about information, knowledge, and learning. Individuals and governments are beginning to recognize that planning for "competitive advantage" will require a labour force that has literacy and numeracy skills beyond three to six years of primary schooling.

Globally, some 2 billion people who are in today's workforce will continue to be there well into the first quarter of this century. Their knowledge and skills will need continuous renewal. Added to this, need one billion more young children and adults who will require initial education and training. The challenge of providing education and training to a huge and diverse population with a variety of learning goals and styles, at an acceptable cost, will require new forms of global educational delivery. Notwithstanding the skepticism of many in the academic community, recent reports from agencies such as UNESCO, the Organisation for Economic Cooperation and Development, and the World Bank seem to say as much.

In some ways, the emergence of new technologies may have something to do with the push to make drastic changes in the nature of the learning environment. There is also a change in the nature of those requiring education and training. Communities no longer are content (nor should they be) to limit access to education and training to the fortunate few who are able; literate; live in urban communities; have access to communications, infrastructure, and classrooms; are knowledgeable about learning opportunities and options; and have the resources to pay for them.

A fairer, kinder, and more concerned humanity requires that the education it provide must be made available to a broader range of historically underserved groups, including:

— *Functional illiterates*: Apart from about 900 million illiterates globally, there are almost half as many adults who cannot cope with the demands of daily life because they lack literacy.

— *Physically disabled*: Annually, in Asia alone, about 15 million people become disabled as a result of war, diseases, accidents, and malnutrition.

— *Long-term unemployed*: Long-term unemployment is a debilitating pathology; training people in such situations poses special challenges to delivery and pedagogy.

— *Out-of-work youth, especially boys*: This group is highly vulnerable to socially disruptive behaviors. Youth need vocational training, including apprenticeship and self-education, to be part of a productive economy.

— *Women and girls*: In many parts of the world, women and girls still find themselves marginalized in education and training; ways may have to be found to circumvent the social, cultural, and economic impediments they face.

— *Refugees, recent immigrants*: Today, roughly 125 million people live outside their countries of origin, and this number is ever increasing. This flow of people for political, social, or economic purposes is not expected to slow down. To help these people resettle, educational programs, language teaching, and training for social and job skills must be designed and delivered.

In contrast with this escalating demand is the lack of preparedness of a vast majority of our education systems to deal even with existing demand, under circumstances that, in the words of one activist group, "violate the rights of children" through dilapidated schools, inadequate facilities, poorly trained and under trained teachers, inadequate supplies of learning materials, irrelevant curricula, disregard for minority cultures and languages, gender bias and instructional methods which undermine, rather than nourish the potential of children.

World over, the arrival of newer technologies certainly seems to have stimulated a resurgence of interest in diversifying methods of knowledge delivery.

Almost daily, yet another Web-based course becomes available from one university or another. Smart schools are springing all over the richer world, and virtual learning, online learning, and other, newer forms of educational delivery are becoming part of the educational jargon of the new century. Even before the arrival of the newer technologies, institutions such as the Correspondence School of New Zealand; the National Open School of India; the Open Universities of Sri Lanka, Hong Kong, and the UKOU; and the Indira Gandhi National Open University of India were providing good-quality, mass, flexible, and lower-cost education for remote learners from basic to university-level education using the older analog technologies of print, audio, video, and radio and television.

The experience and successes of these institutions around the world are testimony to the effectiveness of technologies to reach individuals and large communities simultaneously. They have transformed the delivery of education and, in the process, also transformed the business of education. In addition, full-time study within the timetabled constraints of the classrooms is only accessible to a few; for many who wish to study, learning has to occur at a time and place of their choice. The growth of open schools, polytechnics, and universities, as well as the numerous suppliers of correspondence and online education, are all manifestations of peoples' desire to learn at their own convenience rather than at an institution's call.

Information Explosion

It is estimated that the total amount of information

doubles every four to five years. Stated in another way, the total of information available to an undergraduate in 1997 was less than 1% of what will be available to a student in 2050. Teachers have to become expert in helping learners to navigate through this sea of information rather than attempt to be effective transformers of that information into knowledge for the learners. Students must be trained to bring about this transformation, during and beyond the school years. ICTs are crucial in coping with the explosion of knowledge over the lifetime of the learner; otherwise, people's knowledge becomes obsolete, and countries become marginalized.

The structure and content of learning activities should equip all children, youth, and adults with the knowledge, skills, values, and attitudes they need to survive, to improve their quality of life, to empower them to participate fully and responsibly in the life of their communities and nations. This education also should help them to initiate and adapt to the changing circumstances of their environment, and to continue learning according to their individual needs and interests. Clearly, any strategy to engage all citizens in lifelong learning will require application of technologies, especially mass media. For the first time in the history of humankind, communication technologies enable us to reach millions of people across continents simultaneously. At the same time, variations of these modern technologies allow educators to tailor content to suit a narrow local audience to respond to individual learning needs. Satellite, community, and Internet-based (through telecenters) delivery of content all enrich the environment for learning. Agriculture, farming, health, market conditions, maternal care, and reproductive sciences all being delivered today through ICTs. Local community radio and telecenter facilities are extremely versatile tools and are used effectively and imaginatively around the world today.

A key feature of the modern global society is the primacy associated with the exchange over computer-communication networks of intangibles such as knowledge, ideas and intelligence, rather than tangible goods that have long been the basis of human interaction.

It is also becoming fairly clear that the power of the computer chip will continue to increase while the cost of building it decreases; bandwidths will broaden and convergence heighten; and the penetration of the Internet will continue to rise while the lack of connectivity drops. Acquisition of up-to-date knowledge, skills, and education will determine the success of individuals and democratic societies both economically and socially. It is not surprising, therefore, that an ever-increasing number of countries wish to see their citizens technologically literate. From 'telecenters' to "smart schools" the push to make every child computer, Internet, and Web-savvy has fast become an overriding concern for education ministers of developed and developing countries.

Illiteracy

Despite the knowledge explosion and advances in information and technologies, in many countries, there are significant numbers of people who cannot read, let alone enjoy the benefits of a technological society. Every country in the world has committed to decreasing drastically the number of illiterate citizens. Mass media, especially print, radio, and, to a certain extent, television, has played a significant role in adult literacy programs. In some parts of the world, newer technologies have been applied, albeit in a modest way. An increase in the use of ICTs seems to be constrained by financial resources, shortage of literacy workers skilled in using technologies, and lack of technical support for a well-functioning technology environment. However, ongoing developments using online resources to train literacy workers and create literacy products seem to demonstrate significant results. ICTs have the potential to:

— reduce the isolation many adult literacy providers and students experience;

— facilitate communication among staff and students within and between programs;

— increase access to high-quality materials and emerging research;

— streamline administrative and reporting processes; and

— help to provide the delivery vehicle for innovative instructional and staff development approaches.

On one hand, the planet is filled with highly skilled and talented people in all fields of human endeavour. On the other, critics of global educational systems constantly bemoan the fact that, by and large, the academic talent needed in schools, colleges, and universities to enhance the quality of the learning environment beyond perceived levels of mediocrity is in short supply. It need excellence in teaching, and need to obtain teachers from the best in the local community and distribute them to the whole learning community.

The Western Governors Virtual University initiative among the northwestern states in the United States is in fact an attempt to do this. This attempt envisages going beyond campus walls to obtain academic 'teaching' talent. Contributors to courses will come from business, commerce, industry, and government, and those who take the courses will include ordinary people, along with thousands of college and university students.

Planning for effective use of ICTs in education necessitates understanding the potential of technology to meet different educational objectives and, consequently, deciding which of these objectives to pursue. This decision affects the choice of technologies and the modalities of use. This section structures the discussion around four objectives that may be enhanced by ICTs:

— expanding access to all levels of education;
— improving the quality of education;
— enhancing lifelong learning; and
— facilitating nonformal education.

In most developing countries, full-time study within the time constraints of classrooms is only accessible to a few; for many who wish to study, learning will have to take place at a time and location of their choice.

Either synchronously or asynchronously, barriers such as time, distance, and social and cultural constraints must be overcome. At the same time, rapid changes taking place in the workplace will require training to be delivered quickly. Such training must be high-speed, low-cost and capable of reaching small and large groups. As a policy consideration, the application of ICTs to enhance access to learning must receive the highest priority. ICTs in their many forms have been applied in a variety of contexts, including:

Reaching learners in remote communities: Provisions have to be made to reach, in particular, children in many parts of the developing world where formal schooling is likely to account for less than 1,000 days in their entire lifetime. Fewer than half of primary-school-age children actually are enrolled in school, and more than two-thirds of those who do manage to enter school fail to complete three years of schooling. While it will take a massive effort to change this situation, as an interim measure, ICTs can be employed in formal and informal settings to deliver essential knowledge and information. The National Open School in India, using print, audio, local tutors, and ICT-based assessment and testing system on-call, provides postprimary education to remote villages throughout India. About 400,000 children have access to education up to grade-12 equivalence, and lessons prepared by teams of highly qualified teachers are made available to students free or at very low cost.

Taking education to girls: Gender disparity in educational access is a major challenge in many communities because of family and social circumstances. Inequalities between women and men extend from literacy classes to access to formal schooling and prospects for completing school. Social, cultural, religious, and economic factors all combine to create barriers and place girls and women at a serious disadvantage. While such barriers will take time to remove, ICTs provide one way to circumvent them. Learning and training will have to find their way to girls and women where they are located, rather than expecting them to come to places where teaching is conducted.

Though all the technologies used were analog, the opportunity to digitize this effort and deliver it through local telelearning centers offers immense opportunities, in both qualitative and quantitative terms, to scale-up the effort.

Providing learning opportunities for individuals in challenged circumstances: Increasingly, ICTs are being recognized and used to bring education and training to those individuals who are challenged in one way or another. These tools include digital voice control software, audio to visual conversions for the hearing impaired, electronic text, and digital audio. The technologies, either stand-alone or as part of integrated systems, help to overcome barriers such as instruction based only on print and dependent on sight, audio dependent on hearing, and video requiring vision. The systems themselves have to be developed for individual use, so they require careful study of individual students' needs.

Providing education for out-of-school youth : Education of out-of-school youth, especially beyond the basic level, can benefit from the application of ICTs. Vocational and trade skills, competency-based training, and alternate entry paths to higher education can be achieved through creation of knowledge products for a variety of situations, from self-learning to flexible learning environments. Multimedia commercial training products are becoming increasingly available for training in vocational skills. Governments can play an important role in enabling vocational training institutes, encouraging nongovernmental organizations (NGOs) engaged in supporting youth development, and prodding media outlets to use ICTs for youth training and personal development.

Creating open and virtual learning environments: Smart schools, online education, and virtual universities are labels that have been attached to institutes applying a new set of strategies to deliver education using digital networks either synchronously or asynchronously. The technologies are used to deliver instruction, to manage the system's administrative services, and to provide support for learners. The last four decades have seen the emergence of colleges and universities dedicated to delivering tertiary-level education off-campus to learners, especially in those countries where the gap between the supply of and demand for tertiary-level education is huge and largely unmet. These universities apply open learning principles and distance education practices to deliver learning. They are generally universities with big student populations comprising mature and mostly part-time learners. Ten of the largest universities in the world are open universities, and all but one of them is located in developing countries. In total, they may have as many as 2 million students enrolled in their programs. ICTs have always played an important role in managing and administering these universities, and older analog technologies such as radio and video also have been used to enrich the learning environment of the open universities. With the arrival of the newer digital technologies, ICTs also have begun to figure much more intensely in this role.

Improving the quality of learning: One of the most powerful reasons for considering using ICTs in an educational system is that they put learning in the hands of the user. They facilitate individualizing curriculum, permit learners to dictate the pace of learning, and widen sources of information. ICTs also promote active learning and allow for interaction between and among peers and mentors. Many would say as well that the quality and effectiveness of learning is enhanced many times through the use of ICTs. The technologies allow faculty to incorporate new information and update learning materials, and they enable immediate and rapid transfer of information pertaining to the administration of a course or program of study. Of these many educational objectives, the five below stand out as extremely important.

The need to reform curriculum at all levels of education to prepare citizens for the new millennium. Learning to know, learning to do, learning to be, and learning to live together are all ideals that are achievable within the framework of basic and postbasic education. These recommendations recognize that today's learners, young and old, will spend their lives in a century that is information-rich, knowledge-dependent, and global. They need the skills to cope with this dynamic period. The growth of online library systems, easy access to expert knowledge through the Web, the variety of sources of learning, and frequent change of careers and location of residence during a person's productive lifetime will necessitate learning new skills and refreshing old skills. The curriculum should reflect these concerns and will include:

— The ability to frame problems when facing unfamiliar situations. Tomorrow's problems may be similar to yesterday's once they are well understood. But these present themselves in new forms. Once a problem has been framed, it must be solved and, often, both framing and solving problems will require powerful information technologies. Framing and solving problems sometimes will be simpler, but they often are likely to · be more difficult than before.

— The ability to communicate, including with people from other groups. Nations' ethnic composition is becoming more diverse, and increasing globalization has meant having frequent contact with people of other nations and cultures. All of this requires sensitivity to numerous cultures, and some common and shared values and insights, if political and social tensions are to be avoided and conflicts minimized.

— The ability to work in, form, and lead teams and coalitions, including involving people of other cultures. This vital skill is seldom taught comprehensively in schools, and, as global interdependence increases in importance, so, too, does collaboration.

— The ability to identify what needs to be learned, and then learn it efficiently. ICTs often will furnish the means for learning. Every educated person will need to spend a certain fraction of his or her life keeping up with changes in that technology.

In all these areas, ICTs are an extremely invaluable asset. The Web, more than any other tool we know of, has the power to make enormous amounts of information from their original source available at the click of a button. This information, in its multimedia form, provides teachers and learners with information to support and enrich curriculum in the modern classroom. Subscriptions to digital libraries, collaborative programmes with peers outside of one's own classroom, and access to remote knowledge and expertise make lessons richer in content and, in the process, learning more exciting.

The time-driven, rigid organizational structures of our institutions of learning, our assumptions of learning, and our traditions of teaching, as well as the urban location of teaching institutions, have combined to present barriers of one kind or another to learning for all but a small proportion of citizens. The new ICTs provide enormous flexibility of use unlike older technologies, which required learners to be assembled in a controlled environment at a specific time and location. Radio and television had to be tied rigidly to schedules developed centrally. On the other hand, the new technologies are available for use 'anytime, anywhere.' The emergence of virtual education is very much a reflection of this versatility: Learners can access their education or training at the workplace, home, library, or anywhere connection to a telephone and power supply is available. Transformation in the Teaching/Learning Process Learning technologies can affect education in systemic and structural ways.

The challenge for educators is to bring about a balance among content learning, technology learning, and social experience. This balance depends on instructional strategies that accommodate individual learning styles and, at the same time, provide for effective assessment. Successful introduction of ICTs into the learning environment also includes support for interdisciplinary interaction with peers and instructors and among groups. This arrangement allows learners to interact with their institutions and their communities.

The newer technologies can change the relationship between teachers and learners to improve the learning process and learning experience. Traditional teaching and learning habits always have favoured a certain passivity. Professors lectured and students listened and took notes; sometimes they asked questions, but they seldom contributed to knowledge. That was also true for the older technologies of print, radio, and television, despite the hype given them. Though active and independent learning were aspired to, they were hard to achieve, given the limitation of the technology.

New ICTs make it possible for students to be active learners. Both teachers and students can control, manipulate, and contribute to information and knowledge generation. Using ICTs, students not only make choices about the pace and order of a presentation, but also may choose topics for explorations; take notes; answer questions; explore virtual landscapes; simulate experiments; enter, draw, or chart data; create and manipulate images; make their own PowerPoint presentations; and communicate with others. ICTs have great capacity to facilitate the educational transaction between providers and users. For instance, ICTs can be used to:

— Keep students well informed about the courses that are available to them.

— Enhance teacher-learner contact, an essential part of a good educational environment, through e-mail, chat sessions, etc.

— Encourage active learning. Students do not learn much from memorizing facts and reproducing set answers; they derive greater benefits by being active in their learning.

— Facilitate peer support in learning. Sharing one's ideas and responding to the ideas of others improves thinking and increases understanding.

— Provide immediate feedback and encouragement.

— Encourage paced learning through tools such as

assignments, tutorials, broadcast programs, computers, etc.

— Allow for effective mapping of learning pathways, which facilitate different styles of learning.

Professional Development

Like all other professions, teachers need constant and continuous renewal to be effective, motivated, and up to date in their knowledge and skills. While this is not a mandatory requirement in many national jurisdictions, those that do have such requirements use and see ICTs as important vehicles to provide continuing professional development to teachers. The use of ICTs, especially in support of distance education activities, adds enormous value to the training. Where the infrastructure exists, and connectivity costs are subsidized, the opportunity to create virtual online learning communities of teachers within nations and across regions exists. Such learning communities enable and empower trainee and practicing teachers to share experience, curriculum, learning materials, lesson notes, and collaborative programmes.

Resource sharing

The arrival of the computer, sharing knowledge, an important basis of education, was more wishful than real. With ICTs, sharing knowledge resources is enhanced many times over. Putting information on the Web makes it available immediately to anyone in the world with a suitable connection. Teachers can share lesson plans with their colleagues in their own jurisdictions and with those far removed from their jurisdictions. Students from all over the world can undertake joint programmes, exchange findings, analyze data collectively, and draw reasoned conclusions. Knowledge about and of interest to minority groups, languages, and interests can enjoy the same opportunity to publish and share.

Enhancing lifelong learning

Lifelong learning is a necessity in a world that changes and renews itself so rapidly. Such dynamism makes demands on individuals to update themselves constantly in the context of their workplace, social life, and participation in healthy and vibrant democracies. Two broad categories of individuals use lifelong learning opportunities. The first group refers to those who are underrepresented across a whole range of postbasic education and includes, among others, illiterate and neoliterate populations engaged in unskilled work; ethnic, marginalized, and minority groups; people with learning difficulties; and the physically challenged. These learners face such obstacles as lack of learning skills, confidence, money, counseling and advice, and personal support, and they require active intervention by the state, the business sector, and voluntary organizations. The second group refers to those who have had the benefit of some form of postbasic education but are not equipped to deal effectively with the technology-driven environment in which they find themselves. This group includes out-of-school youth, employees in workplaces, individuals with basic training, professionals needing continuing education, and older adults seeking personal enrichment.

These people are expected to know their needs, but they face challenges such as inadequate supply of learning opportunities, inflexibility of learning systems, lack of money, and inadequate supply of information. There is increasing evidence that ICTs are beginning to play an effective role in promoting lifelong learning. Supported by a greater bandwidth capacity, digital and interactive radio and television, and multimedia, pathways are extending the speed with which learning products can be delivered to learners over large catchment areas. However, to make this happen, some basic conditions need to be met, including regulatory frameworks, infrastructure, affordable cost structures, public access to multimedia facilities, skills training in ICT use and employer support, and institutional commitment of learning providers.

Facilitating nonformal education

ICTs are being used to make information and knowledge available in nonformal contexts. The demand for enrichment learning is on the rise, particularly in countries experiencing an increase in aging populations and in populations with more leisure time who want to use it in intellectual pursuits. These are learners for pleasure, and, for them, activities in a classroom are not the ideal solutions. ICTs offer a convenient solution, but only if the individual has the skills needed to use the appliances and navigate through the millions of Web pages and is able to pay for the cost of the digital connection.

Besides structured learning for enrichment purposes, unstructured learning opportunities are increasingly available through zoos, museums, planetariums, research institutions, professional societies, interest groups, commercial companies, and national agencies, among others. The knowledge to be gained can range from virtual tours of, for example, archeological sites to the epidemiology of HIV/AIDS. It is as possible to learn to cook exotic food as it is to design and make quilts. One can participate in a debate on the World Trade Organization organized by supporters or detractors or engage in a discussion with a Nobel laureate on rain forest exploitation. All of these learning opportunities inform citizens, enrich their lives, enable them to share indigenous knowledge, and empower them to participate in functioning democracies. The British government, for example, plans to connect all of the country's libraries to the Internet through a National Grid for Learning.

Even as recently as 10 years ago, the choice of technologies for delivering education was somewhat limited, partly because they were expensive, analog stand-alones with limited versatility, and they required skilled technicians to create and deliver the product. Radio and television are prime examples of the demand these technologies made on educational systems.

Today the picture has changed almost completely. Technology application in education no longer is limited by the versatility, convenience, cost, and potential of the technology but, rather, only by our imagination in the way technology can be applied. Through integration, convergence, miniaturization, and intelligence, technologies have become friendly. The question is no longer whether technologies are useful in the teaching and learning environment but which technologies are best suited for a particular purpose. Digitization of many information and communication technologies has made it possible to design, develop, deliver, manage, and assess the learning and training process. The new digital technologies are not single technologies; they are combinations of hardware and software, media, and delivery systems. They are evolving and converging rapidly, as seen in PCs, laptops, notebooks, and digital cameras that are both video and single-image; local area networking; the World Wide Web; CD-ROMs and DVDs; application software, such as word processing, spreadsheets, and simulations; e-mail; digital libraries; and computer-mediated conferencing, videoconferencing, and virtual reality. They also have a capacity to integrate with older analog technologies from print, and through audio and video, make it possible to retrieve information stored in older technologies and to develop synergies between the old and the new. There are excellent reviews of the older analog technologies, which still have tremendous value, especially in many developing countries and their educational systems.

ICTs for teaching and learning range from those that rely on ubiquitous low-cost technology, such as the stand-alone PC, to those deployed for specific purposes at higher cost, such as the electronic classroom. Decisions on the choice of technologies are subject to many considerations and constraints, ranging from constancy of power supply to availability of skilled technical and managerial support to maintaining the technological infrastructure. Assuming these are available, then questions of pedagogical strategies of the system, accessibility, scale, and cost will play a role in the choice. Some of the newer IC technologies available and used today are discussed below.

E-mail: Increasingly, e-mail is becoming the most widely used medium, ranging in function from exchange of gossip, to serious dialogue and collaborative research. It also has become an important supplement to classroom teaching. Bulletin board services extend the classroom beyond fixed timetables; listservs bring communities of learners together; and assignments and term papers are beginning to be channeled routinely through e-mail. On-campus education is being enriched by e-mail facilities, and off-campus education is made more personal and interactive. In economically developed countries, e-mail is almost as common as the telephone. In many cases, connections are free of charge, appliances are provided at low or no cost, and training is available for neophyte users. In poor economies, e-mail has yet to make its presence felt throughout society, but is increasingly available at community service centers such as libraries, telelearning centers, and "cyber cafes."

Presentational software: PowerPoint and similar programs are already commonplace among academics and other professionals. While a simple slide presentation requires little skill to develop, the increasing sophistication level of such a presentation requires higher-level training.

World Wide Web: Many on-campus instructors are beginning to use the Web to make their lecture notes available to students at any time. The Web also has the advantage of providing access to primary sources of information in most media through streaming. This technology requires good organizational and pedagogical skills to profit from its enormous potential, and faculty training in its use will be essential. The Web to be a low-cost technology for several reasons:

— The existence of simple computer languages such as HTML and intermediary course authoring systems such as the WebCT and Blackboard;

— It uses the Internet as a transport vehicle that involves no direct charge for independent packets of information, and pricing is by volume and not by time or distance;

— The Web's ability to combine media, thereby increasing its range of applications;

— Access to high-quality learning resources inexpensively;

— It allows asynchronous interpersonal communication through e-mail, bulletin boards, and discussion forums;

— It enables cross-cultural, international, collaborative learning.

Multimedia, CD-ROM, DVD: Multimedia, CD-ROMs, and DVDs are very exciting learning tools. Their development costs can be very high, especially those at the very high end that can carry large quantities of data in a variety of formats, such as audio and video clips, Internet connections to other databases, large amounts of information, and built-in simulation and other enrichments. Putting all these together in user-friendly packages will require teams of experts, from media producers to content experts. The reproduction cost of CD-ROMs can be reduced considerably if large numbers are 'burned.' Consequently, this medium is a consideration only when enrollments are large enough to justify the development expense. However, there is a strong case for developing the medium when the course can be used by a consortium of institutions working together.

Satellite broadcasting: Satellite broadcasting for educational purposes has a long history. Countries such as India and China, and such regional universities as the University of the West Indies and University of the South Pacific have long used satellites to deliver audio- and video-based lectures to all corners of their region. Satellites serve as good vehicles to carry lessons, and, by marrying satellites to ground facilities, it is possible to build a two-way learning environment. In addition, their digital technologies allow for further sophistication to be built into the learning systems. However, because of their high start-up cost, satellites' value for educators is limited.

Recent developments sponsored by private enterprises such as World Space have combined satellite technologies with digital ones to broadcast voice and data directly to specially designed digital receivers over very large geographic areas. While this venture is driven by and for commercial interests, special provision for educational purposes allows educational providers to reach very remote and isolated parts of the world. World Space eventually expects to reach an audience of some 3 billion people. While satellite technology has some significant advantages in terms of reach and low unit cost, for it to be truly effective as a learning technology requires extensive local support on the ground, either on an interpersonal basis or through telephony, the Internet, etc. Ground support will cause costs to increase considerably, thereby reducing the economic benefits.

Videoconferencing: In the late 1970s, multicampus postsecondary institutions began experimenting with videoconferencing to distribute their education and training services and lectures in real time. With the decreasing costs of telephony, videoconferencing has become relatively popular, especially in Australia and the United States. This technology, an amalgam of telephony and computer-compressed technologies, reduces the amount of time instructors and students spend travelling from campus to campus to deliver and receive lessons. It also saves instructors from having to repeat lectures. The traditional culture of classroom teaching is preserved, and no new skills have to be learned by students or teachers. It is not a flexible system of learning, however. New innovations incorporating videoconferencing technologies with the Internet and Web technologies offer new opportunities, notwithstanding some concerns about the visual and voice quality of such arrangements.

Broadly speaking, ICTs can be used for either one of two purposes, or, in some cases, for both purposes simultaneously. The first purpose is to enhance the richness and quality of education on-campus and in the classroom; the second is to distribute campus-developed knowledge products off-campus through distributed learning, distance education, and open flexible learning. In either case, the selection of technological tools will depend on costs, the technology infrastructure of the learning system, learner access to the technology, the support personnel and facilities available to create digitized knowledge products, and the institutional commitment to sustaining the venture. Based on an extensive survey of European universities, and embedded in a few assumptions relating to the use of technologies, the Association of European Universities-under the sponsorship of the European Union's Socrates program-developed a set of guidelines for using ICTs. Under the right conditions and used properly, the technologies can be highly effective as both teaching and learning tools. The challenge for institutions is to develop the knowledge and skills to exploit the technologies' full potential.

At the heart of all learning that uses ICTs are materials specially designed to exploit the full potential of the available technologies. These materials normally include content in the form of texts, special "books of readings," specially developed study or learner's guides, assignments and assessments pads, and instructor's or tutor's guides. These resources, along with appropriate learner support systems, complete the educational or training environment. There are two ways by which institutions acquire these learning and teaching resources: they design and develop them either by themselves or in partnership with like-minded collaborators, or they purchase, lease, or acquire-through other arrangements-materials already developed and adapt them for their unique needs.

Developing interactive multimedia learning materials is an exceedingly interesting challenge. They can be constructed from a combination of media, sometimes quite modest in cost and sophistication, such as a combination of computer- aided instruction (CAI) and print, and at other times very expensive and elaborate, using a combination of DVD, CD-ROM, hypermedia, and virtual reality.

For well over three decades now, and long before the arrival of the newer technologies, dedicated distance teaching institutions such as the open universities of the UK, Canada, India, Thailand, Turkey, Israel, South Africa, and other countries have been developing courses using a variety of media. The experience gained through these institutions is just as relevant in today's technology-rich environment, where digitization allows for totally seamless integration, as it was then in an analog world. Unlike face-to-face teaching, the design and development of interactive multimedia materials involves the knowledge, skills, and expertise of a number of individuals.

Therefore, assembling a team to undertake the task

is almost a prerequisite if a high-quality product is the ultimate objective. The size of the team, and the skills of the individuals who make up the team, will depend on the sophistication of the product to be developed. It is possible, though not advisable-as is often the case in many small operations-for one person to create the learning materials. At a minimum, the course team should have a content expert and an instructional designer. In addition to content experts and instructional designers, complex course team composition may involve audio and video producers, editors, ICT specialists, publishers, and programme managers. The team approach will require a totally different work culture from what is normally associated with academe.

Digitization of knowledge products opens up unprecedented opportunities for their portability. CD-ROMS, DVDs, and other multimedia have the capacity to carry entire courses on a single disc. Furthermore, granulation of knowledge allows for greater manipulation of the content to suit particular needs and clients. There are also economies to be gained. However, acquiring knowledge products from other sources for local use requires careful consideration of many issues and factors, besides intellectual property rights and economic concerns; sometimes it is cheaper to produce courses in house than to purchase and adapt them. These factors apply to all materials that are moved from the originating location to a new location for possible use. They include such items as:

Contextual—the cultural, learning, and teaching traditions and the location of learners require consideration. In cultures where traditions of learning and teaching are more didactic, enquiry-based approaches to learning may not be a suitable fit. This is especially so at lower levels of study. Also important is the tone and simplicity of the language used.

Disadvantaged learners-individuals from minority groups, as well as physically, aurally, and visually challenged individuals, may require special attention when materials are adapted for their purpose. Instructor skills-using the imported multimedia material skill of instructors has to be taken into account; provisions need to be made to train such teachers in new skills. Professional human assets-to enable local professionals to adapt the imported materials for local needs, all of the professional skills needed to create the original material need to be assembled and trained for purposes of adaptation.

Certain factors specific to a lesson or a course have implications for repackaging imported multimedia materials for local use. These include:

— Suitability of purpose-materials produced for a particular group of learners in a specific learning location may not be a total fit in a different location for another group of learners; extensive adaptation may be necessary.

— Suitability of aims-aims of a learning experience vary from context to context. Context-sensitive materials may require major adaptation if the context of the new user is different.

— Relevance of learning objectives-objectives often are defined generally or specifically, and they focus on precise learning outcomes. If the objectives of an imported knowledge product are not sufficiently specific or relevant for the needs of a local course, revisions become mandatory.

- — Match between syllabus and content-seldom does an imported multimedia package meet all of the needs of a local syllabus; amendments and supplementary materials may be necessary.
- — Potential for adaptation-digitized materials do allow for manipulation of text, graphics, visuals, and audio; however, such adaptation requires skilled technicians, content experts, and resources.
- — Promotion of active learning—the new technologies allow for extensive active learning opportunities; in selecting multimedia material from external sources, attention to this requirement is useful. As an alternative, such interactive learning can be incorporated during the process of adaptation.

Funding for E-learning

In some ways, school Internet capital expenses are equivalent to the expenditures a district makes in purchasing a fleet of school buses. After the initial cost of the purchase, the school buses require fuel, maintenance, trained drivers, parking lots to house them, insurance, and upgrades to keep the fleet current. It is the same with technology. The continuing operational costs of maintaining and using the technology dwarf initial purchase and installation costs. These costs include: payments to utility and Internet service providers; technical support; instructional content; renovations to the physical plant; trained educators and administrators; and upgrades as newer equipment comes on line.

Too often educational institutions have focused on startup costs without planning for the substantial and continuing costs of operation. When this occurs, technology, like unused buses, is relegated to the 'garage' and has little value to anyone. Schools and colleges are beginning to adopt 'total cost of ownership' (TCO) models that have been used for years by the business community. This approach breaks down into component parts each of the expenses involved in using technology so they can be more clearly analyzed. For example, Quality Education Data (QED), K-12 schools spent an average of $122 per student on technology support during the 1998-99 school year.

The amount that K-12 districts spend on school technology and Internet access varies. A 1998 survey 3 of 29 large urban school districts found that technology budgets ranged from $22 per student to $584 per student. The average hovered in the $120 to $130 range per student. Most financing models indicate that the initial costs of hardware purchases and installation, along with retrofitting of old buildings to support an upgraded infrastructure, represent the bulk of costs when amortized over five years. It is assumed that costs then shift to non-capital, or operating expenses. But in reality, K-12 technology expenditures skew heavily on the side of hardware. A survey of 400 district and school level officials found that schools were spending 55 percent of total costs on hardware, 16 percent on networking, 9 percent on software, and only 6 percent on training, with another 6 percent on service and support, 5 percent on supplies, and 1 percent on online services. What seems clear is that schools are under-investing in the personnel and support needed to make their technology investments most useful.

In some ways this is a result of the way technology is funded in schools and colleges. Technology startup costs have often been funded with capital dollars raised by bond issues and special grants that may be easier to raise than the continuing operating funds required for ongoing costs. Yet it is these continuing service and personnel costs that are often most critical to technology integration in an educational environment.

Education for America's elementary and secondary schools is primarily the responsibility of states and localities. The funding follows this pattern. States provide approximately 44 percent and localities close to 40 percent of the nation's expenditures for elementary and secondary education, while foundations, in kind activities and others sources provide 10.2 percent of funding. The federal government currently contributes only 6.1 percent of all elementary and secondary education funds.

The federal share of education funding overall has declined, from 13.9 percent in fiscal 1980 to 6.1 percent in fiscal 1998. This declining federal funding share is also true for higher education, where the federal share was 18 percent in fiscal 1980 and dropped to 12.1 percent in fiscal 1998.

Nonetheless, there are areas where federal dollars have a major impact. The federal government has made a large-scale investment in the future through its support of technology at the K-12 level. Estimates place the current federal share of education technology investment at about $1.5 billion, or between 20 percent 7 and 35 percent of all elementary and secondary technology outlays.

The $1.5 billion federal funding for education technology comes from both targeted programs for technology as well as via core or traditional federal programs. In the former category of direct education technology programs are the Technology Literacy

Challenge Fund funded at $425 million in fiscal 2000 as well as the Technology Innovation Challenge Grant program for stimulating technology- supported high performance learning environments, funded at $146 million in fiscal 2000. Other specialized technology programs include:

— Preparing Tomorrow's Teachers to Use Technology (PT3)-funded at $75 million in fiscal 2000

— Community-based Technology Programs-$32.5 million

— Stars School Program-$50.5 million

— Learning Anytime, Anywhere Partnerships-$23.3 million

— Technology and Media Services-$36 million

— Assistive Technology for the disabled learner-$34 million

An even greater portion of federal education technology funding support comes through core federal programs which have made school hardware and software acquisition, as well as staff development for technology, a greater priority in recent years. These include:

— Basic and advanced skills—Approximately $500 million of this $8 billion annual program is used by schools to support technology investment. All software and hardware used in basic skills instruction in schools.

— Innovative Education Strategies—Approximately $125 million to $150 million a year is spent on upgrading technology in schools.

— Professional Development—With total funding in fiscal 2000 of $335 million, this program places a priority on teacher training with technology, and allows low-income schools to use all Eisenhower funds for hardware and software purchases.

— Goals 2000 Educate America Act—Fiscal 2000 funding is $491 million. A large portion of these funds is spent by states and school districts on technology planning.

— Vocational and Adult Education—School districts use approximately $250 million for technological capacity building.

In addition to the federal investment in education technology, states and school districts contribute another $5.4 billion for instructional technology via a myriad of district-wide programmes and competitive grants.

Missing from these amounts, however, is funding for telecommunications access made possible through the E-rate program. Enacted as a part of the Universal Service Program of the Telecommunications Act of 1996, the E-rate program provides discounts to public and private schools, libraries, and consortia on the costs of telecommunications services, internal access, and internal networking. In the program's first two years, tens of thousands of public and private elementary and secondary schools, and thousands more libraries received a total of $3.66 billion in discounts on connectivity and telecommunications services. In the Spring of 2000, the Federal Communications Commission announced that the third year of the program would be funded at $2.25 billion, the maximum allowed, based on requests submitted by schools and libraries around the country.

Telecommunications and education policy present an intersection of state and federal responsibility. The federal telecommunications funding mechanism that provides universal service offers a basic level of service to individuals regardless of where they live. This subsidy is in effect an 'equal opportunity access guarantee' that applies equally to individuals wherever they live.

The E-rate sits at the intersection of this juncture, as it was developed on the belief that the Internet should provide a place where all learners can find information and opportunities for anytime, anyplace learning. The funding subsidy it provides is levelling the Internet playing field for education. In this new environment, two things are clear: funding must be sustained, and new approaches must be considered. Old models do not meet new realities. It makes little sense to use 30-year bonds to purchase equipment that should be replaced in 3 years. Schools should examine how technology costs in one area can be offset by efficiencies in other areas. The productivity gains found in business through investments in technology took 3 decades to emerge.

Today these investments are considered a foundation of the US economy, accounting for a third of our growth. Similar growth in educational productivity might be derived through technology, but only if other changes are adopted that support more productive educational environments. Streamlining administrative procedures is an obvious example. Web-based test administration could bring significant cost savings in assessment expenditures. Likewise, savings in textbook and instructional materials budgets may be achieved if the licensing, distribution, and updating of these are made less expensive online. Teacher training online may be a more efficient use of time and resources than paying for substitutes when teachers are pulled away from their classrooms. But if technology is used as an add-on to existing activities, rather than as a means to reshape education, then it will simply add to the total cost of operations and few savings will be realized. Business has learned that productivity gains and cost savings come only when old ways of doing business are abandoned and technological solutions replace them. For example, when universities can reach students through online courses, they can re-evaluate their budgets for building more 'bricks and mortar' campuses. There is nothing magical about traditional classroom practice. Educationally, students require a mix of pedagogical support, guidance, and supervision, which can be provided in a myriad of ways. The U.S. classroom is a 150 year-old, relatively low-cost technology, worn out by time and changed conditions for meeting these requirements. Perhaps the much sought after Internet 'killer' application for education is not an application at all, but the potential for reorganizing education and for connecting communities of students, teachers, parents, and highly qualified volunteer experts. While do not suggest replacing the classroom teacher with technology, consider how could do more with the teachers have.

Investing in the development and support of skilled teachers, and supplementing the expertise of a given teacher with the distributed expertise of the broader education community, offers great promise. The possibility of making 'the best and the brightest' of the teaching profession available to learners in places where accidents of geography and economics have led to lower quality educational experiences suggests that the Internet can impact the economics of education in ways have only just begun to imagine. A number of witnesses 16 offered a range of funding model proposals that might address the continuing technology requirements of the education sector. These suggestions fall into the following categories:

— Tax incentives to encourage educational investments in areas of high cost and high need

— User taxes on corporate technology purchases

— Public and private partnerships in building and renovating schools to provide high tech centers an entire community can use during non-school hours, supported through user fees

— Increased federal and state appropriations for technology and web-based learning opportunities

— A learning technology trust fund that could combine these models to help sustain long-term school technology investment momentum Good Education is Good Business. Business should play a much larger role in helping schools make technology support their educational needs. Business depends upon the graduates of our nation's educational system. The strongly on annual increases in the number of visas granted to highly skilled technology workers to supply the US workforce. All businesses-not just high tech companies—have a substantial stake in this area. Banks and retailers, food and beverage companies, and clothing manufacturers all need employees with greater technical capabilities than our schools are currently providing to fill the high-skilled jobs necessary in today's economy. Isolated donations of hardware or software, while potentially helpful, are simply not enough.

Content, equipment, and services costs associated with web-based technologies can be brought down in several ways. Aggregated purchasing would enable suppliers to lower their per unit prices. Many states already purchase technology by aggregating demand, and some state and district education systems are joining in. But more could be done to capture potential economies of scale throughout the education sector.

The development of standardized education technology packages (e.g., hardware, software, training, service support, online content, and Internet services) helps build significant volume to purchases. By making these packages modular and scalable, schools could select appropriate technology and network components at the lowest cost and most effective price point. Other costs include time spent in planning, installing, managing, and upgrading systems. Some institutions have found that hardware, software, and services integrated into packages suitable for different needs and circumstances takes much of the complexity out of planning multimedia network computing installations. Remote management of local school networks can ultimately remove the need for expensive onsite technical personnel, as well as provide higher quality service.

The use of existing internationally recognized standards such as Internet protocols, and the development of additional standards, have the potential of creating packages with enormous market demand, attracting suppliers to the education market, and promoting competition in price and capabilities. This type of standardization, quite common in other areas served by technology, could help lower prices and improve performance in education as well. The development of an efficient network architecture can also help build economies of scale. Designing multi-user/use platforms means that more value can be obtained from hardware and service configurations. Careful network and communications backbone architecture is critical to lowering communications costs. The backbone architecture issues go beyond the design and management capabilities of any school district, but collaborations could be as cost-effective for education as such networks are in other areas. State networks that are in place and ready to link to the Internet2 backbone could offer the most technology access for the dollar.

In many cases, the use of networked computing will enable schools to significantly revamp and modernize their educational programs. Opportunities to expand individualized learning, provide access to a much broader and richer set of educational materials and human resources, and promote 'learning-to-learn' skills will often require changes in how our educational institutions are organized and funded. If schools and universities are to be held accountable for improving educational outcomes based on the investments made using technology, they will need help from government, business, and public sector partners at all levels. There are no technical reasons why cannot make the benefits of web-based education available to everyone; it is simply a matter of our will. The terms of organizing and funding will determine who benefits and how quickly. As a nation, goals of making web-based education networks quickly and universally available, affordable, practical, and effective in improving educational outcomes.

2

Technology Towards Human Progress

The fusion of computing and communications has broken the bounds of cost, time and distance, launching an era of global information networking. Communications change economic competition, empowerment and culture, inspiring global conversation. Genetic engineering leads to complex links between farmers and indigenous people in biorich countries and the multinational pharmaceutical and agricultural industries.

Writing computer programmes and revealing genetic codes have replaced the search for gold, the conquest of land and the command of machinery as the path to economic power. Knowledge is the new asset: more than half of the GDP in the major OECD countries is now knowledge-based. With such importance placed on these technologies, the new rules of globalization-liberalization, privatization and tighter intellectual property rights-are shaping their control and use, with many consequences for human development.

Globalization's rules have set off a race to lay claim to knowledge. A global map for the new technologies is being drawn up faster than most people are able to understand the implications-let alone respond to them-and faster than anyone's certainty of the ethical and developmental impacts.

Bringing together computers and communications unleashed an unprecedented explosion of ways to communicate at the start of the 1990s. Since then tremendous productivity gains, ever-falling costs and rapidly growing networks of computers have transformed the computing and communications sector. If the automobile industry had the same productivity growth, a car today would cost $3. In the early 1990s the Internet shifted from a specialized tool of the scientific community to a more user-friendly network transforming social interaction. The number of Internet hosts-computers with a direct con-nection-rose from less than 100,000 in 1988 to more than 36 million in 1998. More than 143 million people were estimated to be Internet users in mid-1998 and by 2001 that number is expected to be more than 700 million.

The Internet is a centreless web of computer networks-was funded by the US Department of Defence in the late 1960s as a strategy for communicating during a nuclear attack. Soon it was used to link technically skilled science and university communities. In the early 1990s user-friendly innovations—the creation of the World Wide Web, the distribution of free browsers turned the arcana of computer language into the simple point and click of a mouse, making the Internet more widely accessible. At the same time computers became much cheaper, and the network took off. Even people in the industry did not foresee the revolution. In 1977 a computer industry executive said "there is no reason why anyone would want a computer in their home".

Today more than 50 million households in the United States and almost 50 million in Europe have at least one computer at home-and many have two. The Web began as a free-for-all, an unregulated domain, with a spirit of exploration and spontaneity. Now that it is of commercial interest, laws and regulations are needed in areas of privacy, liability, censorship, taxation and intellectual property.

The Internet is the fastest-growing tool of communication ever. Its speed and cost advantages are clear. Network communications connect everything to everything else, creating a network society that forces complex and contradictory shifts:

Decntralisation versus recentralisation: Old economic boundaries around nations have given way to new centres of power in the private sector. Multinational corporations have spread their activities around the world thanks to fast and cheap communications, computer-aided design and the standardization of tasks-yet they can still coordinate and control their worldwide operations as a unit. They operate in an arena beyond the jurisdiction and accountability of any one country, in a global context that does not yet have an adequate framework for regulating them. At the same time network communications have been a tremendous levelling force for small businesses, enabling them to compete-and succeed-in lucrative niches of the global market.

Frágmentation versus integration: Cutting across the tradition of national communities is the rise of on-line communities, drawn together by politics, ethnicity, interests, gender, work or social cause. Using the network, they fire up debates and rally instant responses, bringing a new lobbying power to previously silent voices on the global stage. At the same time network communications can forge closer local communities, providing community information and making local government more transparent.

Homogenization versus diversity: The global entertainment and media industry-spreading opinion, culture and politics-is dominated by a handful of major companies. They control both distribution networks and the programming, including news and films, sent by cable and satellite television into households across the world. At the same time the declining costs of technology have allowed a diversity of voices and cultures to be aired. Multilingual Internet sites and radio programming in local languages reach out to minority groups. Programmes on satellite television bring news and culture from home to many diasporas around the world, including Chinese, Indian and Korean communities.

These changes are still in flux. But information and communications technology can be a tremendous force for human development for all those connected-by providing information, enabling empowerment and raising productivity.

Developing countries suffer many of the world's most virulent and infectious diseases, yet often have the least access to information for combating them. A US medical library subscribes to around 5,000 journals, but the Nairobi University Medical School Library, long regarded as a flagship centre in East Africa, now receives just 20 journals, compared with 300 a decade ago.

Distance learning, through teleconferencing and, increasingly, the Internet, can bring critical knowledge to information-poor hospitals and schools in developing countries. The potential is great-but technology alone is not a solution. There are three cautions are given below:

— Information-poor schools and hospitals are often poorly connected. In South Africa, the best-connected African country, many hospitals and about 75% of schools have no telephone line. Even at the university level, where there is connection, up to 1,000 people can depend on just one terminal. A single computer is not enough: an entire telecommunications infrastructure is needed.

— Equipment is a necessity, but to be part of a solution distance learning requires institutions, skills and good management. Distance learning technology is of little use without relevant course content and strong staff support. Zambia saw an exodus of 7,000 teachers between 1986 and 1990, largely due to a shrinking education budget. Technology cannot work where there are no support staff to help pupils get the best from the network.

— Information is only one of many needs. Email is no substitute for vaccines, and satellites cannot provide clean water. High-profile technology projects risk overshadowing basic priorities.

Communications technology opens new opportunities for small players to enter the global marketplace and political arena.

— *Giving voice to NGOs:* The heat of the moment will not wait for a letter to travel halfway around the world: people's movements must respond fast to have an impact. Instant network communications have brought this power to NGOs, creating a tremendously important countervailing force out of previously silent voices in the global arena.

In India DATPERS, the Dalit and Tribal People Electronic Resource Site, exposes the exclusion of 250 million low-caste people, coordinating international human rights campaigns and keeping the community in touch. During the Indonesian riots of 1998 the ethnic Chinese minority used the Web to draw the attention of the world to their plight. Women have been innovative in using global communications for their needs. In Mexico City an NGO called Mujer a Mujer—Woman to Woman—emailed contacts in California for assistance when plans for a new textile factory were announced in their community. The women went to meet the management with a bulky portfolio detailing the company's practices, profits and ownership—information impossible to find in Mexico City, and even on the Web, but available in the United States for a small database access fee. And one inspired group used the Internet to build community across the lines in war-torn former Yugoslavia in 1994, creating the Electronic Witches to link women from different ethnic groups. Gathering at Internet-linked computers around the country, often in universities, groups of women sent messages to one another, sharing their concerns, their grief over the bombing of the city of Tuzla and their survival strategies. One message advised that burning just one running shoe would be enough to bake a loaf of bread.

— *Creating commerce for small businesses:* Telephone, email and the Internet give small businesses access to markets and bring much-needed savings in cost and time. A study in Ghana found that workers in small-scale industries without telecommunications can waste up to half their work time travelling from place to place. Starting from a small base, electronic commerce is booming. The market was valued at $2.6 billion in 1996, and by 2002 it is expected to be more than $300 billion, promising to transform the way business is done around the world.

The potential is not limited to companies with sophisticated Websites, or to customers with credit cards and electronic banking. There are many ways of using the Internet to do business—from making contacts and checking prices to displaying goods and entering into contracts. Small businesses everywhere are exploiting the opportunities. PEOPLink is a fair trade organization selling crafts over the Internet, linking the work of more than 130,000 artisans across 14 countries of Africa, Asia and Latin America. By recording their work with a digital camera, the trading partners can display their products on the Internet and receive orders from around the world.

— *Empowering governments of poor countries:* In 1990 more than 90% of data on Africa were stored and managed in the United States and Europe, inaccessible to African policy-makers and academics. The Internet is bringing the data back home. Policy-makers can also gain access to international expertise and ongoing debates, strengthening their negotiating positions for a much-needed greater presence in international forums. The Small Islands Developing States Network, SIDSNet, is a forum for its 42 member nations-from Malta and Mauritius to Cuba and Comoros-to share data and experience on common concerns: energy options, sustainable tourism, coastal and marine resources and biodiversity.

— *Informing remote specialists:* Isolated academics and scientists can take part in Internet conferences, keeping up to date on discussions and developments in their fields. Contacts made can become technical support groups, which are of tremendous value to remote specialists. By allowing participants to share and discuss papers on-line, Internet conferences can easily involve more than 1,000 people worldwide, without any of the costs of travel.

With the knowledge sector at the forefront of global economic opportunity, getting into knowledge production can be a fast track to growth. By creating a basic capacity to operate imported technology, countries can progress, climbing the rungs of the ladder, by learning to duplicate, to adapt to their own needs and, finally, to innovate. The Eastern Caribbean has seized the opportunity to step onto the first rung, using its low-cost, semiskilled labour to export data processing services. In Sweden, too, remote communities have specialized in data processing, airline ticketing and hotel reservations, creating productive employment to keep young people from heading for the cities. India has forged ahead, specializing in software programming for export. Japan and the first tier of newly industrializing countries have climbed the furthest-they focused their industrial strategies on creating knowledge-intensive industries and have built up strong national capacities in research and development. Indeed, Japan is perhaps the ultimate proof that comparative advantage is not a fixed given, but can be created in the information economy.

Many governments recognize the tremendous potential of the Internet and use it to provide public information: from the Indian Ministry of Finance to the

Malaysian Ministry of Agriculture, government agencies are using Websites to increase the transparency of their operations. Several countries, however, have attempted to censor and control this popular empowerment. Some monitor Web searches and have blocked access to sites providing foreign news or airing political criticism. Others have even made use of the Internet a punishable crime. But censoring the Internet is difficult, ultimately impossible, since it was designed by the US Department of Defence to operate even if under nuclear attack and to hunt for ways around obstacles when access is blocked.

Web discussion groups write the equivalent of thousands of broadsheet newspapers every day-an impossible volume to oversee. The Global Internet Liberty Campaign brings together civil liberties groups, journalists and NGOs to persuade national governments not to restrict access to the Internet because of its tremendous potential for human development. Compared with most traditional tools for development, information and communications technologies can reach many more people, go geographically deeper, work faster and at lower cost.

Information Access

The information revolution has only just begun on a worldwide scale, and its networks are spreading wider every day. But they are heavily concentrated in a very few countries. In Cambodia in 1996, there was less than one telephone for every 100 people. In Monaco, by contrast, there were 99 telephones for every 100 people. A widely accepted measure of basic access to telecommunications is having 1 telephone for every 100 people-a teledensity of 1. Yet as we enter the next century, a quarter of countries still have not achieved even this basic level. Many of those countries are in Sub-Saharan Africa and among the least developed countries. Beyond basic landline connections, the disparities are even more stark.

In mid-1998 industrial countries-home to less than 15% of people-had 88% of Internet users. North America alone-with less than 5% of all people-had more than 50% of Internet users. By contrast, South Asia is home to over 20% of all people but had less than 1% of the world's Internet users. Thailand has more cellular phones than the whole of Africa. There are more Internet hosts in Bulgaria than in Sub-Saharan Africa. The United States has more computers than the rest of the world combined, and more computers per capita than any other country. Just 55 countries account for 99% of global spending on information technology.

Most telephones in developing countries are in the capital city, although most people live in rural areas. Connections are often poor in the rainy season, and the costs of calls are very high. In several African countries average monthly Internet connection and use costs run as high as $100-compared with $10 in the United States. Yet even if telecommunications systems are installed and accessible, without literacy and basic computer skills people will have little access to the network society. In 1995 adult literacy was less than 40% in 16 countries, and primary school enrolments less than 80% in 24 countries. Even for the newest and most advanced technologies, the most basic and long-standing policy lies at the heart of the solution: investment in education.

Within each region it is only the tip of each society that has stepped into the global loop-worldwide, just 2% of all people. What sets these people apart from the rest? Current access to the Internet runs along the fault lines of national societies, dividing educated from illiterate, men from women, rich from poor, young from old, urban from rural. National Internet surveys in 1998 and 1999 revealed that:

— *Income buys access:* The average South African user had an income seven times the national average, and 90% of users in Latin America came from upper-income groups. More than 30% of users in the United Kingdom had salaries above $60,000. Buying a computer would cost the average Bangladeshi more than eight years' income, compared with just one month's wage for the average American.

— *Education is a ticket to the network high society:* Globally, 30% of users have at least one university degree-in the United Kingdom it is 50%, in China almost 60%, in Mexico 67% and in Ireland almost 70%.

— *Men dominate:* Women accounted for 38% of users in the United States, 25% in Brazil, 17% in Japan and South Africa, 16% in Russia, only 7% in China and a mere 4% in the Arab States. The trend starts early: in the United States five times as many boys as girls use computers at home, and parents spend twice as much on technology products for their sons as they do for their daughters.

— *Youth dominate too: The* average age of users in the United States was 36; in China and the United Kingdom, under 30.

— *Ethnicity counts*: In the United States the difference in use by ethnic groups widened between 1995 and 1998. Disparity exists even among US university students. More than 80% attending elite private colleges used the Internet regularly, compared with just over 40% attending public institutions, where African-American students are more likely to enrol.

— *English talks:* English is used in almost 80% of Websites and in the common user interfaces—the graphics and instructions. Yet less than 1 in 10 people worldwide speaks the language. Geographic barriers may have fallen for communications, but a new barrier has emerged, an invisible barrier that, true to its name, is like a world wide web, embracing the connected and silently-almost imperceptibly-excluding the rest.

The typical Internet user worldwide is male, under 35 years old, with a college education and high income, urban-based and English-speaking—a member of a very elite minority worldwide. The network society is creating parallel communications systems: one for those with income, education and literally connections, giving plentiful information at low cost and high speed; the other for those without connections, blocked by high barriers of time, cost and uncertainty and dependent on outdated information. With people in these two systems living and competing side by side, the advantages of connection are overpowering. The voices and concerns of people already living in human poverty-lacking incomes, education and access to public institutions—are being increasingly marginalized. Determined efforts are needed to bring developing countries—and poor people everywhere-into the global conversation.

The past decade has proven the tremendous potential of global communications to provide information, enable empowerment and raise productivity. But it has also exposed the risks of dividing and polarizing societies, threatening greater marginalization of those left out and left behind. What lies in between is proactive policy. The greatest danger is the complacent belief that a profitable and growing industry will solve the problem by itself. But the market alone will make global citizens only of those who can afford it. Fulfilling the potential of global communications for development demands relentless effort in reaching out to extend and enhance the loop. Seven goals on the road to an information society:

— *Connectivity*—setting up telecommunications and computer networks.

— *Community*—focusing on group access, not individual ownership.

— *Capacity*—building human skills for the knowledge society.

— *Content*—putting local views, news, culture and commerce on the Web.

— *Creativity*—adapting technology to local needs and constraints.

— *Collaboration*—devising Internet governance for diverse needs around the world.

— *Cash*—finding innovative ways to fund the knowledge society.

Connectivity: A telecommunications infrastructure is needed, but the infrastructure costs are immense, and many governments are turning to the private sector.

Opening telecommunications and Internet provider services to the market can massively increase connectivity. But schemes are needed to ensure that the market does not focus only on lucrative urban customers. When Senegal privatized telephone services, operators were required under licence to install public telephones in 50% of the rural villages containing more than 3,000 people by 2000. In the Philippines new mobile phone operators usually serving an elite market are also required to install 400,000 landlines serving poor communities within five years.

Computing hardware and software are needed to transform telephone lines into Internet connections, and policies are needed to promote this. To encourage computer ownership, the governments of Bangladesh and Mauritius, for example, eliminated tariffs and taxes on personal computers. The satellite revolution promises greater connectivity, since every point on the globe can be reached instantly without a need for expensive land-based infrastructure. User costs are still very high, but with several major satellite networks due to be launched before 2001, competition could bring rapidly falling prices in the future. Competition is hard to ensure in the telecommunications industry-especially for local calls, as even the most developed countries have seen. Strong regulation and antitrust laws, well implemented, are needed to ensure that private markets are competitive markets and that public needs are met. This will be a challenge for all countries.

Community access: To bring connectivity to people, community access is key, not individual ownership. The concept of one household, one phone is unrealistic in many developing countries, especially in rural areas and among poor communities everywhere. A more appropriate approach is to create multimedia community centres—or "telecentres"—in places accessible to those often blocked out of institutions: poor people and communities, women and youth. From Peru to Kazakhstan, basic telecentres have been set up in post offices, community centres, libraries, video shops, police stations and health clinics, providing local community access to telephone and fax services, email and the World Wide Web. But providing access takes more than providing computers. Telecentres need to become hubs for skills training and capacity building. Egypt is leading the way in this approach.

Capacity: Building people's capacity to use the Internet starts in schools. In Hungary the ambitious Sulinet (Schoolnet) has enabled students in more than two-thirds of secondary schools to browse the Net from their classrooms. The annual NetDay initiative in the United States has used volunteers to connect more than 140,000 schools at a fraction of the commercial cost. Beyond classroom connections, support staff are essential for on-line learning, and teachers need training. In Finland teachers receive more than a month of training in how to use information technology in the classroom. In Lesotho the Technical Enhanced Learning Institutes in Southern Africa (TELISA) were launched in 1998 to renew regional education with professional development for teachers.

Content: The information highway cannot be a one way street. Websites need to be created locally, adding new voices to the global conversation and making content relevant to communities. The first step is language and culture. The government of Tamil Nadu, India, is promoting keyboard standardization, software interfaces and Websites in Tamil, spoken by 75 million people worldwide. In Estonia the highly effective Tiger Leap Programme is developing educational software to teach the Estonian language and the history of the country. Local content can enhance community participation and institutional transparency. In India the state government of Andhra Pradesh is setting up a network to connect telecentre access points with government services and offices.

Creativity: The context for communications varies greatly around the world, yet solutions have focused on industrial countries. Creativity is needed to adapt the possibilities of technology to the needs of poor countries and poor people. In rural Bolivia most farmers have never seen a computer, but they already have access to the Internet. How? Farmers with crop concerns can give questions to a community leader, who relays the inquiry to the radio station, where it is sent to UNDP's communications centre. The question is then posted on the Internet and answers received are emailed back to the radio station and broadcast. In South India, too, creativity has tailored computer technology to local community needs.

Collaboration: The Internet has rapidly become not only a global communications tool but a great source of economic potential. Its evolution, at first ad hoc, is being shaped into a system of governance—with rules on domain names, taxation, privacy and protection of intellectual property rights. But governance should not be framed by the United States, the European Union or the OECD alone. Commercial interests may be at stake—but so is the right of access to communications for all people. Internet and telecommunications need global governance framed by global interests.

Cash: There is an urgent need to find the resources to fund the global communications revolution—to ensure that it is truly global. One proposal is a "bit tax"—a very small tax on the amount of data sent through the Internet. The costs for users would be negligible: sending 100 emails a day, each containing a 10-kilobyte document, would raise a tax of just 1 cent. Yet with email booming worldwide, the total would be substantial. In Belgium in 1998, such a tax would have yielded $10 billion. Globally in 1996, it would have yielded $70 billion-more than total official development assistance that year. How quickly are different countries preparing for global communications? Many factors are involved, and the race to join the information society has set off at a fast pace. It will determine many of the winners and losers in the globalized world.

Current Situation of Human Development

The most basic capabilities for human development are to lead long and healthy lives, to be knowledgeable, to have access to the resources needed for a decent standard of living and to be able to participate in the life of the community. Without these, many choices are simply not available, and many opportunities in life remain inaccessible. This way of looking at development, often forgotten in the immediate concern with accumulating commodities and financial wealth, is not new. Philosophers, economists and political leaders have long emphasized human well-being as the purpose, the end, of development. In seeking that something else, human development shares a common vision with human rights.

Human development and human rights are mutually reinforcing, helping to secure the well-being and dignity of all people, building self-respect and the respect of others. Human development challenges remain large in the new millennium. Across the world, unacceptable levels of deprivation in people's lives. Of the 4.6 billion people in developing countries, more than 850 million are illiterate, nearly a billion lack access to improved water sources, and 2.4 billion lack access to basic sanitation. Nearly 325 million boys and girls are out of school. And 11 million children under age five die each year from preventable causes -equivalent to more than 30, 000 a day. Around 1.2 billion people live on less than $1 a day, and 2.8 billion on less than $2 a day. Such deprivations are not limited to developing countries. In OECD countries more than 130 million people are income poor, 34 million are unemployed, and adult functional illiteracy rates average 15%.

The magnitude of these challenges appears daunting. Yet too few people recognize that the impressive gains in the developing world in the past 30 years demonstrate the possibility of eradicating poverty. A child born today can expect to live eight years longer than one born 30 years ago. Many more people can read and write, with the adult literacy rate having increased from an estimated 47% in 1970 to 73% in 1999. The share of rural families with access to safe water has grown more than fivefold. Many more people can enjoy a decent standard of living, with average incomes in developing countries having almost doubled in real terms between 1975 and 1998, from $1,300 to $2,500.

The basic conditions for achieving human freedoms were transformed in the past 10 years as more than 100 developing and transition countries ended military or one-party rule, opening up political choices. And formal commitment to international standards in human rights has spread dramatically since 1990. These are only some of the indicators of the impressive gains in many aspects of human development. Behind this record of overall progress lies a more complex picture of diverse experiences across countries, regions, groups of people and dimensions of human development.

All regions have made progress in human development in the past 30 years, but advancing at very different paces and achieving very different levels. East Asia and the Pacific has made rapid, sustained progress in most areas, from expanding knowledge to improving survival to raising standards of living. South Asia and Sub-Saharan Africa lag far behind other regions, with human and income poverty still high. The adult literacy rate in South Asia is still 55% and in Sub-Saharan Africa 60%, well below the developing country average of 73%. Life expectancy at birth in Sub-Saharan Africa is still only 48.8 years, compared with more than 60 in all other regions. And the share of people living on less than $1 a day is as high as 47% in Sub-Saharan Africa and 40% in South Asia, compared with 15% in East Asia and the Pacific and in Latin America.

The Arab States also lag behind in many indicators, but have been making the most rapid progress. Since the early 1970s life expectancy at birth has improved by 14 years and the infant mortality rate by 85 per 1,000 live births, and since 1985 the adult literacy rate has risen by 15 percentage points faster progress than in any other region. Differences among regions and countries are particularly marked in economic growth, which generates public resources to invest in education and health services and increases the resources people have to enjoy a decent standard of living and improve many other aspects of their lives. In 1975 -99 per capita income quadrupled in East Asia and the Pacific, growing 6% a year.

The growth rate in South Asia exceeded 2%. Two countries that together account for a third of the world population did well: per capita income in China grew at an impressive 8% a year, and in India at an average rate of 3.2%. OECD countries had average growth of 2% a year, raising already high incomes to an average of more than $22,000. But in the Arab States and Latin America and the Caribbean growth has been slower, averaging less than 1%. Most devastating has been the performance of Sub-Saharan Africa, where already low incomes have fallen; in 1975 -99 GDP per capita growth in the region averaged 1%. Since 1990 per capita incomes have declined in 16 countries in 4 by more than half.

The course of human development is never steady. The changing world always brings new challenges, and the past decade has seen serious setbacks and reversals. At the end of 2000 about 36 million people were living with HIV/AIDS -95% of them in developing countries and 70% in Sub-Saharan Africa. More than 5 million became newly infected in 1999 alone. In Sub-Saharan Africa, mainly because of HIV/AIDS, more than 20 countries experienced drops in life expectancy between 1985 -90 and 1995 -2000. In six countries -Botswana, Burundi, Namibia, Rwanda, Zambia and Zimbabwe -life expectancy declined by more than seven years. The spread of HIV/AIDS has multiple consequences for development. It robs countries of people in their prime, and leaves children uncared for. By the end of 1999,13 million children were AIDS orphans. In Eastern Europe and the CIS the disruptive impact of the transition has exacted a heavy toll on human lives, with adverse effects on income, school enrolment and life expectancy, particularly of males. Personal security continues to be threatened by crime and conflicts. Globalization has created many opportunities for cross-border crime and the rise of multinational crime syndicates and networks.

In 1995 the illegal drug trade was estimated at $400 billion, and an estimated 1.8 million women and girls were victims of illegal trafficking. And because of conflict, the world now has 12 million refugees and 5 million internally displaced people.

The human development index (HDI) for 162 countries, as well as trends in the HDI for 97 countries having data for 1975 -99. The results show a substantial shift of the world's people from low to medium levels of human development and from medium to high levels. As a summary measure of human development, the HDI highlights the success of some countries and the slower progress of others. Rankings by HDI and by GDP per capita can be quite different, showing that countries do not have to wait for economic prosperity to make progress in human development. Costa Rica and Korea have both made impressive human development gains, reflected in HDIs of more than 0.800, but Costa Rica has achieved this human outcome with only half the income of Korea. Pakistan and Viet Nam have similar incomes, but Viet Nam has done much more in translating that income into human development. So, with the right policies, countries can advance faster in human development than in economic growth. And if they ensure that growth favours the poor, they can do much more with that growth to promote human development.

The HDI measures only the average national achievement, not how well it is distributed in a country. Disaggregating a country's HDI by region and population group can spotlight stark disparities, and in many countries the results have sparked national debate and helped pol-icy-makers assess differences in human development between rural and urban areas and among regions and ethnic and income groups. In South Africa in 1996 the HDI for the Northern Province was only 0.531, compared with 0.712 for Gauteng. In Cambodia in 1999 the HDI for the poorest 20% was 0.445, well below the national average of 0.517 and, more important, nearly one-third less than that for the richest 20%, at 0.623. In Guatemala in 1998 the rural HDI, at 0.536, was well below the urban HDI, at 0.672. In the United States in 1999 the HDI for white Americans was 0.870, ahead of the 0.805 for African Americans and well ahead of the 0.756 for people of Hispanic origin.

The HDI for untouchables in Nepal, at 0.239 in 1996, was almost half that for Brahmins, at 0.439. Another way to look at the distribution of national achievements in human development is to estimate the human poverty index (HPI), a multidimensional measure of poverty introduced in 1999. The United Republic of Tanzania and Uganda, for example, have very similar HDI rankings (140 and 141), but Uganda has higher human poverty. Similarly, the 17 OECD countries for which the HPI has been estimated have nearly identical HDIs, yet their HPIs range from 6.8% in Sweden to 15.8% in the United States. Disaggregating a country's HPI by region can identify concentrations of impoverishment.

In the Islamic Republic of Iran in 1996 the disaggregated HPI showed that human deprivation in Tehran was only a quarter that in Siṣtan and Baluchestan. The HPI for urban Honduras in 1999 was less than half that for rural areas. For English speakers in Namibia in 1998 the HPI was less than one-ninth that for San speakers. Similar differences exist in the developed world. In the United States the HPI for Wisconsin in 1999 was less than half that for Arkansas.

Because the HDI assesses only average achievements, it masks gender differences in human development. To reveal these differences, the gender-related development index (GDI), introduced in 1995, adjusts the HDI for inequalities in the achievements of men and women. This year the GDI has been estimated for 146 countries. With gender equality in human development, the GDI and the HDI would be the same. But for all countries the GDI is lower than the HDI, indicating the presence of gender inequality everywhere. The extent of the inequality varies significantly, however. For example, while in many countries male and female literacy rates are similar, in 43 countries including India, Mozambique and Yemen -male rates are at least 15 percentage points higher than female rates. And while there has been good progress in eliminating gender disparities in primary and secondary enrolments, with the ratio of girls to boys in developing countries 89% at the primary level and 82% at the secondary level in 1997, in 27 countries girls 'net enrolment declined at the secondary level between the mid-1980s and 1997.

The gender empowerment measure (GEM), also introduced in 1995, helps to assess gender inequality in economic and political opportunities. This year it has been estimated for 64 countries.

Income is a very important means of enlarging people's choices and is used in the HDI as a proxy for a decent standard of living. Income growth has varied considerably among countries in recent decades, more so than trends in many human development indicators. The distribution of the world's income, and the way this is changing, are thus a vital issue deserving special consideration. Income levels across countries have been both diverging and converging -with some regions closing the income gap and others drifting away. In 1960 there was a bunching of regions, with East Asia and the Pacific, South Asia, Sub-Saharan Africa and the least developed countries having an average per capita income around 1/9 to 1/10 of that in high-income OECD countries. Latin America and the Caribbean fared better, but still had just 1/3 to 1/2 of the per capita income of these OECD countries. The impressive growth in East Asia and the Pacific is reflected in the improvement in the ratio of its income to that of high-income OECD countries, from around 1/10 to nearly 1/5 over 1960 -98.

The relative income in Latin America and the Caribbean stayed about the same. Income in South Asia - after worsening in the 1960s and 1970s, then improving significantly in the 1980s and 1990s -remains about 1 /10 of that in OECD countries. In Sub-Saharan Africa the situation has worsened dramatically: per capita income, around 1/9 of that in high-income OECD countries in 1960, deteriorated to around 1/18 by 1998. Despite a reduction in the relative differences between many countries, absolute gaps in per capita income have increased. Even for East Asia and the Pacific, the fastest growing region, the absolute difference in income with high-income OECD countries widened from about $6,000 in 1960 to more than $13,000 in 1998.

Also important is income inequality within countries, which may affect long-term prosperity. Although there are reasonable data on within-country inequality for points in time, the data are not based on uniform surveys across countries and so comparisons must be treated with care. But even very rough comparisons reveal a lot about within-country inequality.

In the remaining 16 countries either no clear trend emerged or income inequality initially declined, then levelled off. Latin American and Caribbean countries have among the world's highest income inequality. In 13 of the 20 countries with data for the 1990s, the poorest 10% had less than 1 /20 of the income of the richest 10%. This high income inequality places millions in extreme poverty and severely limits the effect of equally shared growth on poverty. So Latin America and the Caribbean can reach the Millenium Declaration's development target of halving poverty by 2015 only if the region generates more growth and that growth disproportionately benefits poor people. All five South Asian countries with data have fairly low Gini coefficients, in the 30s.

China and India two countries with low but rapidly growing per capita incomes and large populations deserve special consideration. In China inequality has followed a U-shaped pattern, with inequality falling until the mid-1980s and rising since. The story is better in India, with inequality falling until recently, and then coming to a halt. Many countries in Sub-Saharan Africa have high levels of income inequality. In 16 of the 22 Sub-Saharan countries with data for the 1990s, the poorest 10% of the population had less than 1 /10 of the income of the richest 10%, and in 9 less than 1 /20. Despite the pressing need to understand what is happening to income in equality over time in this poor region,trend data on income distribution remain too limited to draw conclusions.

Changes in inequality during the transition were modest in Eastern European countries such as Hungary and Slovenia, but much more dramatic in countries of the former Soviet Union. Russia saw its Gini coefficient jump by an astonishing 24 points, Lithuania by 14. Among OECD countries there is also diversity in income inequality, from the low levels in Austria and Denmark to the relatively high levels in the United Kingdom and the United States. Still, in global terms income inequality among these countries is relatively low. What about trends over time? Results from a variety of country and cross-country studies suggest that income inequality increased in many OECD countries between the mid-to late 1980s and mid-to late 1990s. While data for earlier periods are more limited, these countries seem to have experienced a U-shaped change in inequality, with declines in the 1970s changing to increases in the 1980s and 1990s. The constant level in Canada and slight improvement in Denmark are exceptions to the apparent trend.

Another measure of inequality looks both between and within countries lining up all the world's people from richest to poorest (in real purchasing power) regardless of national boundaries. A recent study by Milanovic compares the poorest and richest people across the globe, giving a much more complete picture of world inequality than a simple comparison of country averages would. Based on household surveys for 1988 -93, the study covers 91 countries (with about 84% of the world's population) and adjusts income levels using purchasing power parity conversions. The disadvantage is that the study relies entirely on household budget survey data that are not necessarily comparable and are limited in their scope. Nevertheless, the study produced some powerful results; World inequality is very high. In 1993 the poorest 10% of the world's people had only 1.6% of the income of the richest 10%. The richest 1%of the world's people received as much income as the poorest 57%. The richest 10% of the US population (around 25 million people) had a combined income greater than that of the poorest 43% of the world's people (around 2 billion people). Around 25% of the world's people received 75% of the world's income.

Two societies with the same income inequality could differ greatly in the mobility and opportunity facing individual members and in the mobility and opportunity that children have relative to their parents. A focus on mobility helps to identify the factors that block the opportunities of poor people and contribute to the intergenerational transmission of poverty. This approach is well suited to evaluating the effects of policy changes on poverty and inequality. The problem is that mobility is difficult to measure accurately. Still, the few studies that examine it are suggestive. In South Africa 63% of households in poverty in 1993 were still there in 1998, while 60% of households in the highest income category in 1993 were still there in 1998, indicating limited income mobility. In Russia downward mobility was extreme in the late 1990s. Among households in the top income quintile in 1995, nearly 60% slid to lower quantities by 1998 -and 7% fell to the bottom quintile.

In Peru there has been a great deal of movement up and down the income ladder. Opportunities are increasing with market reforms, but so are insecurities. Between 1985 and 1991, 61% of households had income increases of 30% or more and 14% had income drops of 30% or more. Overall, downward mobility dominated in 1985-91, and upward mobility in 1991-97. In every country family background significantly influences the length of children's schooling. Children with wealthier, better-educated parents are always likely to do better. But there is substantial variation across countries and periods, depending on macroeconomic conditions and public education policies. An emphasis on basic schooling in public spending enhances intergenerational mobility in Latin America. There, a person needs at least 10 years of schooling to have a 90% or higher probability of not falling into poverty or of moving out of poverty. And having just 2 years less schooling means 20% less income for the rest of a person's active life.

More than 360 national and subnational human development programmes have been produced by 120 countries. The human development concept into national policy dialogues -not only through human development indicators and policy recommendations, but also through the country-led process of consultation.

How HIV/AIDS is reducing economic growth and increasing poverty, and provides policy guidance for political action at the highest levels. The public discussion on the accessibility of antiretroviral drugs and whether the government should be responsible for providing them. Botswana's minister of health then asked the Bank of Botswana to explore the financial viability of such an approach. Meetings were convened at UNDP with key stakeholders, including the National AIDS Coordinating Agency, the ministries of health, finance and development and major insurance companies. Those consultations led to a decision in March 2001 by the president of Botswana to provide antiretroviral drugs for free to the 17% of the country's people with HIV.

Many of India's 25 states rival medium-size countries in size, population and diversity. The government of Madhya Pradesh was the first to prepare a state on human development, in 1995, to bring the subject to political discourse and investment planning. By 1998 social services accounted for more than 42% of planned investment, compared with 19% in the previous plan budget. Human development, have also been prepared in Gujarat, Karnataka and Rajasthan and are under way in Arunachal Pradesh, Assam, Himachal Pradesh and Tamil Nadu. The states 'preparation of the development has made human development priorities an important part of political discourse and development strategies. Kuwait's first human development, in 1997, raised awareness of the human development concept and its relevance to the country's struggle to shift from dependence on oil towards a knowledge-based economy.

The Ministry of Planning has started to monitor human development and to incorporate the human development approach in its indicators for strategic planning. The ministry is following up with a second. Colombia's 2000, looks at human rights as an intrinsic part of development and shows how they bring principles of accountability and social justice to the development process. Exposing weaknesses in the interpretation and implementation of some constitutional rights, debates and dialogues on human rights to a new level, with a vigorous focus on economic, social and cultural rights.

The stresses basic social services, discusses social exclusion and revisits labour rights under globalization, providing a new lens for viewing development in Colombia. Bulgaria's 2000 programmes, analysing the socioeconomic situation in each of the country's 262 municipalities, initiated a healthy competition among neighbouring municipalities to do better in human development. Determining the target locations for a large government programme for small-business job creation. It has also sparked constructive debates, in the media and among mayors, governors and ministers, about such issues as decentralization, municipal budgets and educational attainment and subsidies.

Technologicies and human devlopment

Technological advance has contributed greatly to the acceleration of human progress in the past several centuries. Those contributions have the promise of even greater acceleration. The information and communications industry could provide entry points for developing countries into producing for the knowledge-intensive economy. Yet the path of technology is not predetermined—many avenues of research could be pursued, but only a few are followed.

Technology may be globalizing communications, but globalization—and its new rules—is also shaping the path of new technologies. Over the past 20 years increasing privatization of research and development, ever-growing liberalization of markets and the tightening of intellectual property rights have set off a race to lay claim to knowledge, and this has changed technology's path. The risk is that poor people's and poor countries' interests are being left on the sidelines.

The knowledge sector is a fast-growing area of the global economy: between 1980 and 1994 the share of high-technology products in international trade doubled, from 12% to 24%. Yet in the 1990s, with many governments facing a squeeze on budgets, the proportion of public funding for research and development in science and technology has fallen around the world, to be replaced by private industry. Research and development has also shifted away from developing countries. Their share in the global total dropped from 6% in the mid-1980s to 4% in the mid-1990s. The trend has been particularly strong in agriculture and biotechnology. In the early 1980s most crop and seed development in the United States was under public research. Patents were rarely sought and rarely enforced; saving and trading of seed was commonplace. This changed when new legislation encouraged closer cooperation with the private sector, enabling companies to profit from products developed largely with public funds.

The intellectual property of public and university research was increasingly passed over to private industry: the portion of public sector patents in biotechnology sold under exclusive licence to the private sector rose from just 6% in 1981 to more than 40% by 1990. With increasing privatization of research and rising costs for risky innovations, the 1990s have seen a boom in the number and value of mergers and acquisitions. The biggest year ever was 1998, especially for biotechnology, telecommunications and computing industries.

As a result economic power has consolidated among a very few players. By 1995 the world' stop 20 information and communications corporations had combined revenue of more than $1 trillion-equivalent to the GDP of the United Kingdom. In biotechnology genetic engineering underlies the new direction of pharmaceuticals, food, chemicals, cosmetics, energy and seeds. This is blurring the boundaries between the sectors, creating mega "life sciences" corporations. Indeed, across all knowledge-intensive industries, a select group of corporations controls ever-growing shares of the global market. In 1998, how much of the global market did the top 10 corporations in each industry control? In commercial seed, 32% of a $23 billion industry; in pharmaceuticals, 35% of $297 billion; in veterinary medicine, 60% of $17 billion; in computers, almost 70% of $334 billion; in pesticides, 85% of $31 billion; and in telecommunications, more than 86% of $262 billion. The lesson is clear: privatization does not automatically lead to competition.

At the creation of the World Trade Organization in 1994, the most far-reaching multilateral agreement on intellectual property was drawn up: Trade-Related Aspects of Intellectual Property Rights, or TRIPS. The past two decades have seen a huge rise in patent claims. The World Intellectual Property Organization's Patent Cooperation Treaty accepts a single international application valid in many countries. The number of applications made annually soared from less than 3,000 in 1979 to more than 54,000 in 1997-and those applications in 1997 were equivalent to nearly 3.5 million individual national applications.

According to the director of research and development at one of the largest biotechnology corporations, "the most important publications for researchers are not chemistry journals but patent office journals around the world." Yet the claims to intellectual property are concentrated among very few countries. Industrial countries hold 97% of all patents worldwide. In 1995 more than half of global royalties and licensing fees were paid to the United States, mostly from Japan, the United Kingdom, France, Germany and the Netherlands. Indeed, in 1993 just 10 countries accounted for 84% of global research and development, controlled 95% of the US patents of the past two decades and captured more than 90% of cross-border royalties and licensing fees-and 70% of global royalty and licensing fee payments were between parent and affiliate in multinational corporations. By contrast, the use of intellectual property rights is alien to many developing countries. More than 80% of the patents that have been granted in developing countries belong to residents of industrial countries. These new rules of globalization-privatization, liberalization and tighter intellectual property rights—are shaping the path of technology, creating new risks of marginalization and vulnerability:

— In defining research agendas, money talks louder than need-cosmetic drugs and slow-ripening tomatoes come higher on the list than a vaccine against malaria or drought-resistant crops for marginal lands. Tighter control of innovation in the hands of multinational corporations ignores the needs of millions. From new drugs to better seeds for food crops, the best of the new technologies are designed and priced for those who can pay. For poor people, the technological progress remains far out of reach.

— Tighter intellectual property rights raise the price of technology transfer, and risk blocking developing countries out of the dynamic knowledge sector in areas such as computer software and generic drugs.

— New patent laws pay scant attention to the knowledge of indigenous people, leaving it vulnerable to claim by others. These laws ignore cultural diversity in creating and sharing innovations-and diversity in views on what can and should be owned, from plant varieties to human life. The result is a silent theft of centuries of knowledge from developing to developed countries.

— Despite the risks of genetic engineering, the rush and push of commercial interests are putting profits before people.

Genetic engineering is largely the product of private commercial research in industrial countries. The top five biotechnology firms, based in the United States and Europe, control more than 95% of gene transfer patents. It can take 10 years and $300 million to create a new commercial product-so, not surprisingly, companies want to protect their innovations and ensure that they reap profits. But this approach focuses research on high-income markets. In 1998, of the 27 million hectares of land under trans-genic-genetically altered-crops, more than 95% was in North America and Europe. Research has focused on the wants of rich farmers and consumers: tomatoes with longer shelf lives or herbicide-resistant soyabeans and yellow maize to be used mainly for poultry feed.

Seed varieties are engineered to be suitable for mechanized mass production with labour-saving techniques, designed for industrial and intensive farming conditions. Far less time and money have been given to the needs of farmers in developing countries: increasing nutritional value, disease resistance and robustness. Similarly, research is lacking on water-saving plant varieties for smallholders. Instead, many major corporations are seeking patents for the innovation of linking genetic characteristics to chemical triggers. What for? One likely use is to create seeds that will germinate and bear fruit only when used with the company's brand of fertilizers or herbicides-increasing sales through dependency on inputs. With agrochemical, plant breeding and seed distribution companies merging into megacor-porations, farming communities risk becoming caught in a chain of biological and licensing controls.

Local plant breeding is essential for adapting seeds to the ecosystem and maintaining biodiversity. The 1.4 billion rural people relying on farm-saved seed could see their interests marginalized. With increasing control and homogenization of the market by major agribusinesses, the competitiveness of alternative varieties and the scope for producing alternative crops will most likely decline, depleting local genetic diversity. In the pharmaceutical industry private interests cannot be expected to meet all public needs. Almost all research on diseases in developing countries has been done by international organizations or the military in industrial countries.

Of the annual health-related research and development worldwide, only 0.2% goes for pneumonia, diarrhoeal diseases and tuberculosis-yet these account for 18% of the global disease burden. In the United States between 1981 and 1991, less than 5% of drugs introduced by the top 25 companies were therapeutic advances. Some 70% of drugs with therapeutic gain were produced with government involvement. Vaccines are the most cost-effective technologies known in health care, preventing illness in a one-time dose. But they generate smaller profits and have higher potential liabilities than treatments used repeatedly. As a result a consortium of US pharmaceutical companies has united to develop antiviral agents against HIV, but not to produce a vaccine against AIDS.

The costs of industrial catch-up for Japan and the first-tier newly industrializing economies in East Asia were greatly reduced by the weak enforcement of intellectual property rights in the region before the mid-

1980s. Tighter control under the TRIPS agreement has closed off old opportunities and increased the costs of access to new technologies. In the pharmaceutical industry, prior to the TRIPS agreement, countries such as China, Egypt and India allowed patents on pharmaceutical processes but not final products. This approach supported the development of domestic industries using different methods to produce mainly generic drugs, similar to but far cheaper than the original brand names.

The difference is highlighted by contrasting drug prices in Pakistan, where there are patents, to India, where there are none. When Glaxo Wellcome launched AZT as an inhibitor of AIDS, it cost $10,000 per patient each year. As sales increased, the price fell to $3,000-still far out of reach for most people in developing countries. An Indian company then produced a generic-Zidovir 100-and exported it to Belgium, Tanzania and Uganda at less than half the price. The TRIPS agreement requires 20-year patents on both processes and products, so India and others must change national patent laws, making such opportunities impossible in the future. As gene therapy comes to dominate the pharmaceutical industry, this will significantly limit the industry's potential in developing countries.

Countries can choose to require patent holders to give licences to competitors—but the process is long and the fees may be prohibitive. Imposing price controls on industry, calculated as a mark-up on costs, is another option, but multinationals often avoid low prices by using loopholes in transfer pricing-artificially inflating the cost of inputs transferred from country to country within the multinational's domain. In India multinational companies have sometimes charged 2, 4 or even 10 times the prices they would charge for inputs in Europe and the United States in order to avoid controlled low prices. They have little interest in pricing drugs for the market in developing countries because they are maximizing global, not national, profits and do not want to set a low-price precedent.

In the computer industry, software is one of the fastest-growing areas and can be a way for new countries to get into producing for the knowledge sector. In 1994 the global market for final, packaged software was $79 billion, of which OECD countries accounted for 94%. With a small but growing number of developing countries entering the competition, it is not surprising that the battle over intellectual property rights for software is a fierce one. Protection is certainly needed: programmes are expensive to develop, while pirating them is cheap and easy. Many firms have lost billions of dollars of trade in this way. At the same time excessively tight intellectual property rights would eliminate competition and innovation in this industry underlying global communications. A careful balance needs to be struck. The TRIPS agreement followed the United States in placing software, like music and novels, under copyright law, with strong and universal protection. The United States has started to grant patents on software in addition to copyright, creating stronger control over programme interfaces and tightening control over the industry. But there is leeway.

The TRIPS agreement does not prohibit making copies for reverse engineering-a process of unravelling computer programmes to see how they work, generating ideas and innovation. With programmes such as Word and Excel becoming computing standards, reverse engineering is essential for smaller producers to create software that is compatible and competitive, and it must be protected in future reviews of the agreement. If it were forbidden, the development of competitive products would be drastically limited. And different computers around the world would not be able to interact with one another-defeating the aim of connecting the network society.

Biodiversity is of great importance to drug development, and developing countries are the source of an estimated 90% of the world's store of biological resources. More than half of the world's most frequently prescribed drugs are derived from plants or synthetic copies of plant chemicals-and this trend is growing. Plant-based drugs are part of standard medical treatment for heart conditions, childhood leukaemia, lymphatic cancer and glaucoma, with a global value over the counter of more than $40 billion a year. In the same way that many Arab states benefited from industrialization's thirst for the petroleum that lay beneath their land, so now biorich countries could have the chance to benefit from biotechnology's demand for the rare germ plasm found on their land.

Many indigenous communities have a further claim to biotechnology's bounty because they have been the cultivators, researchers and protectors of their plants-indeed, it is their long-acquired knowledge of nature's potential that is valuable to pharmaceutical companies today. Bio-prospectors have for many years taken samples of plant material and documented their traditional medicinal uses. Without the consent of local people, this knowledge has been used to develop highly profitable drugs. In any other situation this would be called industrial espionage-theft of both the genetic materials and the long-acquired knowledge of using them to develop medicines.

Plant material was once treated as common property, but a landmark US legal case in 1980 awarded a patent on a genetically altered organism, launching the first step in the race to patent life. Yet patent laws were drawn up in 19th-century Europe during the industrial revolution; their legal frameworks have been extended to cover global markets during the information revolution. Three fundamental concerns:

— The inventions born of genetic engineering bring radically new characteristics. Can a framework of property rights first designed to protect industrial machinery really cope fairly and effectively with the complexities of genetically manipulated organisms?

— Scientific research now takes place under a regime based on ownership and control. It rewards research according to short-term profitability, not according to the needs to protect biodiversity, ensure sustainable and ethical use of genetic resources or meet the essential needs of people.

— The attempt to create a global market in property rights imposes one conception of ownership and innovation on a culturally diverse reality, benefiting private industrial research but not public institutes or farming communities.

Policies are urgently needed to turn the advances in the new technologies into advances for all of humankind—and to prevent the rules of globalization from blocking poor people and poor countries out of the knowledge economy.

Intellectual property rights were first raised in GATT in 1986 to crack down on counterfeit goods. Their reach has gone far beyond that into the ownership of life itself. As trade and intellectual property law increasingly come to determine the path of nations—and the path of technology questioning present arrangements is not just about economic flows. It is about preserving biodiversity, carefully considering the ethics of patents on life, ensuring access to health care, respecting other cultures' forms of ownership and preventing a widening of the technological gap between the knowledge-driven global economy and the rest trapped in its shadows. At a time of such dramatic breakthroughs in new technologies, it is indefensible that human poverty should persist as it does. What is more startling is that the current path could be leading to greater marginalization and vulnerability of poor people.

The relentless march of intellectual property rights needs to be stopped and questioned. Developments in the new technologies are running far ahead of the ethical, legal, regulatory and policy frameworks needed to govern their use. More understanding is needed in every country of the economic and social consequences of the TRIPS agreement. Many people have started to question the relationship between knowledge ownership and innovation. Alternative approaches to innovation, based on sharing, open access and communal innovation, are flourishing, disproving the claim that innovation necessarily requires patents.

Broader governance is also needed in the communications industry. Governance of the Internet has until recently been ad hoc and largely biased towards the needs of high-tech countries. Debates over taxing electronic commerce, allocating domain names and creating privacy laws need to be opened up to include the needs and concerns of developing countries, which have an equal interest in the evolution of this tremendous tool. Participation in the governance of technology must also be widened. Race car drivers would not be the best advisers on public transport, and scientists at the cutting edge of the technological revolution cannot alone decide its path. This calls for collaboration—in national and global forums—between industry, independent scientists and technicians, governments, regulators, civil society organizations and the mass media.

The path of technology must be reshaped if developing countries are to see an advance in sustainable agriculture, wide access to global communications and improvements in the health of their populations. The new structure of science requires new initiatives. New technologies promise many advances for human development, but public institutions cannot afford them alone and private industry will not develop them alone. Jointly they can. Innovative policy is needed to ensure that much-needed solutions for human development are pursued. Incentives are needed to turn research towards the pressing needs of the world, not just of those who pay. One proposal is for the Consultative Group on International Agricultural Research (CGIAR) to reroute genetic research to wider needs.

A representative group of independent scientists is needed to identify the critically important technological challenges-those that, if solved, would substantially improve the human development of the world's poorest people and address the global challenges to human security faced by all. Every five years the group could offer financial incentives and public recognition to researchers, public and private alike, for innovations that would be used for global public interests. What would be high on the list? In agriculture, sustainable, robust and biosafe crops. In medical research, vaccines for malaria and HIV.

In communications technology, personal computers powered by solar strips and wind-up or dynamo drives, resistant to sand and humidity; software for touch screens; and prepaid chip card software for electronic commerce without credit cards. In environmental science, diverse sources of renewable energy. What would fund such initiatives? A levy on patents registered under the World Intellectual Property Organization is one possibility. A levy of just $100 on each patent would have raised $350 million in 1998 alone, equivalent to the annual budget of the world's largest international research organization in agriculture, the CGIAR. Alternatively, funding could be reallocated from the research subsidies, grants and tax breaks now given to industry.

The WTO is planning a review of the TRIPS agreement. But these discussions must not simply push into new issues. Intellectual property rights agreements were signed before most governments and people understood the social and economic implications of patents on life. They were also negotiated with far too little participation from many developing countries now feeling the impact of their conditions. There is a clear need for a full and broad review of existing legislation, not an additional, unsustainable burden of new conditions.

The review needs to ensure that the room for manoeuvre granted in the TRIPS agreement is respected in practice. Interpretation of the agreement is obviously not a unilateral matter, and proposals by developing countries have often been rejected by G-7 countries keen to maintain their industrial interests. In the event of disagreement, dispute resolution mechanisms involve intense negotiating among lawyers—expensive and complex. The advantage in costs and expertise clearly does not lie with developing countries.

To strengthen their bargaining positions in pushing for change, countries need to present frameworks that provide alternatives to the provisions of the TRIPS agreement. Work is already well under way. Many countries are exploring possible sui generis legislation for plant varieties to protect farmers' rights. The difficulty is the need for legislation to meet many diverse interests within each country. One strong and coordinated international proposal is the Convention of Farmers and Breeders (CoFaB). It offers developing countries an alternative to following European legislation by focusing legislation on needs to protect farmers' rights to save and reuse seed and to fulfil the food and nutritional security goals of their people. For indigenous people's interests, too, open debate is needed across countries to bring together the most up-to-date thinking for use by negotiators and policy-makers.

Some initiatives have already been taken. Indigenous people's organizations around the world such as the Indigenous Peoples Biodiversity Network are seeking guidelines for legal recognition of their intellectual property. Thailand, the Philippines and Australian aboriginal groups have all taken steps to protect indigenous knowledge. Developing countries facing similar challenges can benefit from consultation and co-operation to create model laws, collaborate in training public officials and devise strategies to help industries adversely affected by the new regime. Spreading awareness of the issues at stake is important in building coalitions among national interest groups, regional organisations and international civil society campaigns. Presenting counterproposals as a united negotiating bloc would greatly strengthen the possibility for change.

In March 1999 the International South Group Network drew together representatives from 17 southern and East African countries to discuss a joint position on the upcoming World Trade Organization round and the review of the TRIPS agreement, greatly strengthening the clarity and force of the message to be delivered from countries in the region. The TRIPS agreement was drawn up with remarkably little analysis of its expected economic impacts. The costs of implementation-revising laws, training officers, testing and enforcing patents-are high, yet the benefits are unclear. If the agreement is to be reviewed, then let it be a review in everyone's interests. A transparent cost review mechanism should be established within the World Trade Organization, to track the costs of implementing the TRIPS agreement, the effects on consumer prices, the cost of anti-competitive effects and the impact on technology flows. And most important, it should examine the impact on biodiversity, on farming communities and on access to medical resources and scientific information.

The potentially great benefits of the new biotechnology come with risks attached: national and international guidelines are urgently needed as transgenic crop production grows. Each country needs to draw up biosafety measures, to monitor changes in biodiversity, demand transparency and labelling of products, consider the social, economic and ethical impacts and promote research into areas of national need. Regional coordination is needed for sharing data and experience, for sharing in the costs of training officials and for developing rules of trading. Much greater attention must be given to understanding the potential environmental and health hazards of genetically altered crops-an especially important task in countries where the science base and media coverage are narrow and there is extensive fragmentation of the food chain into many smallholders, processors and traders. Participation in the process must be widened. Knowledge is needed not only of the latest technologies but also of local ecosystems and food chains, local culture and systems of exchange, socioeconomic conditions and political and market stability. This calls for broad collaboration.

Some countries are already on this path with established and representative biotechnology advisory groups. France's government has adopted the precautionary principle, promising to survey the development of the genetic revolution and increase public transparency on findings. The European Parliament favours creating a registry of tested and accepted transgenic products, making a database available to the public. Information and communications technologies and biotechnology hold great potential for human development. But strong policy action is needed nationally and internationally to ensure that the new rules of globalization are framed to turn the new technologies towards people's needs.

3

Bridging Technology through Net

Although the personal-computer revolution began only twenty years ago and widespread use of the world wide web (WWW) is even more recent, computer technology has already had a dramatic impact on society and schooling. For example, in United States, between 1984 and 1993, the percentage of people using computers in the workplace nearly doubled from 24.6 percent to 45.8 percent. Similarly, the percentage of people owning one or more computers in their home increased rapidly from 8.2 percent in 1984 to 22.8 percent in 1993 to 33.6 percent in 1997. Although schools have been slower to acquire these technologies, computer use in schools has recently increased rapidly. Not only are more computers in classrooms, but schools are also increasing students' use of computers and access to the Internet.

Although it is unclear how computers are affecting student achievement in schools, there is little doubt that the computer revolution has gone to school. As a result, more and more students are writing and performing school assignments on computers. Meanwhile, many states are increasingly seeking to hold students, teachers and schools accountable for student learning as measured by state-sponsored tests.

According to annual surveys by the US Council for Chief State School Officers (CCSSO), 48 states use statewide tests to assess student performance in different subject areas. Many of these tests are tied to challenging standards for what students should know and be able to do. Scores on these tests are being used to determine whether to:

1) promote students to higher grades;
2) grant high school diplomas; and
3) identify and sanction or reward low- and high-performing schools.

Currently, 32 states control, or plan to control, graduation and/or grade promotion via student performance on state-level tests. Because of the limitations of multiple-choice tests, many statewide tests include sections in which students must write extended answers or written explanations of their work.

As the recent CCSSO, commented, 'Possibly the greatest changes in the nature of state student assessment programs have taken place in the 1990s as more states have incorporated open-ended and performance exercises into their tests, and moved away from reliance on only multiple-choice tests'. In 1996-97, an estimated ten to twelve million students nationwide participated in a state-sponsored testing program that required them to write responses long hand (given a total national K-12 enrollment of about 50 million and open-ended assessments in almost all the states in 3 out of 12 grade levels). For example, students must pass the written portion of the Ohio Proficiency Test in order to graduate from high school. Although many observers have criticized state-sponsored high-stakes tests on a variety of grounds, here direct attention to a widely unrecognized but critical limitation of depending on these tests to drive educational reform: paper-and-pencil written tests yield misleading information on the capabilities of students accustomed to using computers.

Research on testing via computer goes back several decades and suggests that for multiple-choice tests, administration via computer yields about the same results, at least on average, as administering tests via paper-and-pencil. However, more recent research shows that for young people who have gone to school with computers, open-ended (that is, not multiple choice) questions administered via paper-and-pencil yield severe underestimates of students' skills as compared with the same questions administered via computer. In both studies, the effect sizes for students accustomed to working computer ranged from.57 to 1.25. Effect sizes of this magnitude are unusually large and of sufficient size to be of not just statistical, but also practical significance.

Effect sizes of this magnitude, for example, imply that the score for the average student in the experimental group tested on computer exceeds that of 72 to 89 percent of the students in the control group tested via paper and pencil. This topic began with a puzzle. While evaluating the progress of student learning in the Accelerated Learning Laboratory (ALL, USA), a high-tech school in Worcester, MA, teachers were surprised by the results from the second year of assessments. Although students wrote more often after computers were widely used in the school, student scores on writing tests declined in the second year of the new program.

In 1995, a randomized experiment was conducted, with one group of sixty-eight students taking math, science and language arts tests, including both multiple-choice and open-ended items, on paper, and another group of forty-six students taking the same tests on computer (but without access to word processing tools, such as spell-checking or grammar-checking). Before scoring, answers written by hand were transcribed so that raters could not distinguish them from those done on computer. There were two major findings.

— The multiple-choice test results did not differ much by mode of administration.

— The results for the open-ended tests differed significantly by mode of administration.

For the ALL School students who were accustomed to writing on the computer, responses written on computer were much better than those written by hand. This finding occurred across all three subjects tested and on both short answer and extended answer items. The effects were so large that when students wrote on paper, only 30 percent performed at a "passing" level; when they wrote on computer, 67 percent "passed". Two years later, a more sophisticated study was conducted, this time using open-ended items from the new Massachusetts state test (the Massachusetts Comprehensive Assessment System or MCAS) and the National Assessment of Educational Progress (NAEP) in the areas of language arts, science and math. Again, eighth grade students from two middle schools in Worcester, MA, were randomly assigned to groups. Within each subject area, each group was given the same test items, with one group answering on paper and the other on computer. In addition, data were collected on students' keyboarding speed and prior computer use. As in the first study, all answers written by hand were transcribed to computer text before scoring. In the second study, which included about two hundred students, large differences between computer and paper-and- pencil administration were again evident on the language arts tests. For students who could keyboard moderately well (20 words per minute or more), performance on computer was much better than on paper. For these students, the difference between performance on computer and on paper was roughly a half standard deviation.

According to test norms, this difference is larger than the amount students' scores typically change between grade 7 and grade 8 on standardized tests. For the MCAS, this difference in performance could easily raise students' scores from the "failing" to the "passing" level. Recalling that nearly ten million students took some type of state-sponsored written test last year and that nearly half of the students nationwide use word processors in school, these results suggest that state paper-and- pencil tests may be underestimating the abilities of millions of students annually. In the second study, however, findings were not consistent across all levels of keyboarding proficiency. As keyboarding speed decreased, the benefit of computer administration became smaller. And at very low levels of keyboarding speed, taking the test on computer diminished students' performance (effect size of about 0.40 standard deviations). Similarly, taking the math test on computer had a negative effect on students' scores. This effect, however, became less pronounced as keyboarding speed increased.

These studies highlight the importance of the gap between the technology and testing strategies for school improvement. Increasingly, schools are using computers to improve student learning. To measure increases in student learning, states are depending upon tests administered on paper. The open-ended questions on these tests, however, underestimate the achievement of students who regularly use computers. As a result, this mis-match between the mode of learning and the mode of assessment may be underestimating improvements in achievement. This problem is likely to increase as more students become accustomed to writing on computers. There are at least four possible ways to bridge this gap.

— Schools could decrease the amount of time students spend working on computers so that they do not become accustomed to writing on computers. Some schools have already adopted this practice. After reviewing the first study described above and following the introduction of the new paper-and-pencil MCAS test in Massachusetts, the ALL school required students to write more on paper and less on computer. In another Massachusetts school system, the principal feared that students who write regularly on computer lose penmanship skills, which might lead to lower scores on the new state test. This school increased penmanship instruction across all grades while also decreasing students' time on computers. Such strategies, in effect reducing computer use in schools to better prepare students for low-tech tests, may be pragmatic given the high stakes attached to many state tests. But they are also short-sighted in light of students' entry after graduation into an increasingly high-tech world and workplace.

— Bridge the test-technology gap would be to eliminate paper-and-pencil testing and have students perform open-ended tests on computer. This might seem a sensible solution, but it will not be feasible until all schools obtain an adequate technology infrastructure. Moreover, as shown by problems in recent moves to administer some large-scale tests for adults on computers, computerized testing is not the panacea some had hoped. Among other problems, it adds considerably to the cost of testing and creates new test security concerns. But more importantly, as the second study summarized above indicates, administering open-ended tests only on computer would penalize students with poor keyboarding skills.

— Students the option of performing open-ended tests on paper or on computer. On the surface, this seems like a sensible solution. However, it would add considerable complexity and cost to test administration and scoring procedures. Although there has not been a large amount of research on the extent to which computer printing versus handwriting affects ratings of written work, significant effects can occur. Surprisingly, computer printed responses produced by adults tended to receive lower scores than the same responses produced by hand. To control for such effects, in offering tests on paper and computer, handwritten responses would need to be converted to computer text. Surely it will be some years before text recognition software is sophisticated enough to convert handwritten responses into computer text. Thus, for the foreseeable future, the cost of transcription would be prohibitive.

But beyond the need to convert responses to the same medium for scoring, the second study summarized above provides evidence that, when given the choice of using computer or paper to write their tests, many students make poor decisions as to which medium they should use. This was evidenced in two ways.

— The correlations between both students' preference for taking tests on computer or on paper and keyboarding speed and between preference and prior computer experience were near zero.

— Preference was not found to be a significant factor in predicting students performance.

Together, the added complexity of scoring open-ended responses produced in both mediums and students' apparent inaccuracy in selecting the medium that optimizes their performance suggest that simply giving students the option of performing open-ended tests on computer or on paper would do little to reduce the gap between testing and technology.

The most reasonable solution in the short term, is to recognize the limitations of current testing programs. Without question, both computer technology and performance testing can help improve the quality of education. However, until students' can take tests in the same medium in which they generally work and learn, we must recognize that the scores from high-stakes state tests do not accurately reflect some students' capabilities. Reliance on paper and pencil written test scores to measure or judge student and/or school performance will mischaracterize the achievement of students' accustomed to working on computers. Thus, the gap between the use of technology in schools and testing programs serves as yet another reminder of the dangers of judging students and schools based solely on written test scores.

Web-based Teaching: A Case Study

The Center for Research on Learning and Technologies at Indana University conducted an evaluation of four online courses for an academic school at another major university. Four graduate level online courses were evaluated. The course evaluations were over seen conducted by a team of four doctoral students from the Center for Research on Learning and Technology. Each of the four evaluators took a lead role in the evaluation of a different one of the four online courses. The lead investigator for each course evaluation was responsible for gaining a clear understanding the course from a student perspective. This was done by reading all of the course materials available online as well as reading the communication threads in the asynchronous conferencing forums. Hundreds of pages of information and thousands of student and instructor postings to bulletin boards were read by the evaluators.

Periodically during the evaluation process, the entire team would get together to exchange notes, discuss their analyses, and identify trends in the data. Additionally, in three of the four cases, the instructors were interviewed in person by a pair of the evaluators. These interviews helped the evaluators to answer questions that had surfaced in the evaluation process as well as help evaluators understand the design and structure of the course from the instructor's perspective. Finally, it is important to note that students who were enrolled in the courses were not contacted as a part of the course evaluations.

All of the instructors were open and willing to let the evaluators access their course web-pages. Three of the four courses used web-based asynchronous conferencing and the evaluators were given full access to these bulletin board forums to read the postings. The evaluators did not have access to the email correspondence between the instructors and the students. This was a definite limitation in the case of one course because the course primarily depended on correspondence using a listserv and private email. The primary criteria used for the evaluations were the Seven Principles for Good Practice in Undergraduate Education which guide teaching and learning in the School being evaluated:

— Good Practice Encourages Student-Faculty Contact

— Good Practice Encourages Cooperation Among Students

— Good Practice Encourages Active Learning

— Good Practice Gives Prompt Feedback

— Good Practice Emphasizes Time on Task

— Good Practice Communicates High Expectations

— Good Practice Respects Diverse Talents and Ways of Learning

The human computer interface (HCI) designs, including the organization and presentation of online materials, were also evaluated based on the following principles:

— Clear organization and presentation of information

— Consistent and easy to use web site navigation

— Aesthetically pleasing design and graphics

Seven Principles for Good Practice

The Seven Principles for Good Practice in Undergraduate Education as well as several Human Computer Interface design principles as a structure for presenting strengths, areas for improvement, and recommendations to the School regarding their online courses are described below:

(1) Good practice encourages student-faculty contact:

> "Frequent student-faculty contact in and out of classes is the most important factor in student motivation and involvement. Faculty concern helps students get through rough times and keep on working. Knowing a few faculty members well enhances students' intellectual commitment and encourages them to think about their own values and future plans".

Email was the primary form of private communication between instructor and students. Three out of four of the instructors were good at encouraging contact through private email messages. All of the instructors wen tout of their ways to make it clear to students that they could be contacted via email and telephone. A couple of the instructors also invited students to have unscheduled face-to-face meetings with them in order to help students who were struggling with the learning experience done entirely at a distance over the Internet. In fact, one instructor reported such a high rapport among her students that several of them rented a lim to take her to lunch with.

Listservs and class bulletin boards were the main source of public communication between instructors and students. Three of the courses evaluated used the WebCT bulletin board system quite heavily while the fourth class relied primarily on a class listserv for public communication. With a few notable exceptions, instructors were respectful in the ways that they responded to students publicly. There was at least one instance where an instructor publicly confronted a student in a way that the evaluators felt should have been saved for a private dialog between instructor and student.

Building trust with the students enhances student-faculty communication. All of the instructors to one degree or another built trust with their students by providing opportunities for strengthening their relationship. This was done by sharing values, attitudes, and experiences with the students and encouraging them to do the same. One instructor had the students write a short bio and send it to her at the beginning of the semester to help her get to know the students better while another instructor had each student fill in an online survey to help her better understand the students backgrounds. Several instructors also found it helpful to begin the semester with an "ice-breaker" assignment geared entirely towards helping everyone in the class (instructor included) to get to know each other better. One instructor indicated that she even got requests from the students for advice in their personal lives.

While instructors were good at encouraging email contact, none of the instructors clearly and adequately communicated their email response policies to the students. This is an important step in establishing student-faculty contact. The 24-hour availability of email to the students provides a mechanism for contacting faculty unparalleled in the past. Students often assume that instructors have easy, constant access to their email. If they contact an instructor and don't hear back within an expected time frame they may feel that the instructor is ignoring their request. This kind of misunderstanding can be reduced if the instructor communicates to the students a general policy or time line for answering student's email questions. An example of one such policy was an instructor who made it clear to her students that she would be away from her email on weekends. However, this same instructor did not give the students any clear indication of how quickly they could expect her to respond to their email requests during the week.

Because there are not frequent face-to-face meetings, it is easy for students in an online course to fall through the cracks and to be forgotten if they don't participate in asynchronous conferencing or make contact by email. Students who seem to be falling behind or who are not participating regularly in bulletin board discussions should be contacted by the instructor. In the class that used a listserv, the instructor claimed, that she periodically contacted students she hadn't heard from in a while. There was no clear indication beyond that of how well she kept track of who was on task and who was falling through the cracks. The job of keeping track of students' progress in this class was difficult because the majority of the assignments were due all at once in a final portfolio at the end of the course. Thus there was no clear checkpoint for determining if a student was on track.

In the classes that used bulletin boards, there seemed to be some students that participated very actively in the discussions while others rarely contributed. It was not clear to the evaluators if the instructors ever followed-up with the less active students through private email to encourage a greater level of participation in the course.

(2) Good practice encourages cooperation among students:

> "Learning is enhanced when it is more like a team effort than a solo race. Good learning, like good work, is collaborative and social, not competitive and isolated. Working with others often increases involvement in learning. Sharing one's own ideas and responding to others' reactions improves thinking and deepens understanding".

One way that instructors have encouraged cooperation among students is by including group projects and assignments as a part of the course. Two of the four courses required student collaboration on an assignment or project. Another course encouraged cooperation through the use of well designed discussion assignments. Most instructors included some kind of "ice breaker" at the beginning of the course. These were good for helping the distance students get to know each other better. One instructor included a required face-to-face orientation class with the instructor and other class members. While this strategy is not always possible, having the students meet face-to-face once at the beginning of the semester is a positive strategy for building a sense of community. Building a strong sense of community among class members will increase their willingness to interact and cooperate with each other online.

Create activities and assignments that foster a sense of community among the students. It can be much more difficult for students at a distance to gain a sense of belonging or community with each other. One course had virtually no meaningful student-student contact during the semester while the other three classes had varying degrees of student-student contact. The courses could begin with a structured activity in which students are asked to share and find out about each other's interests. In at least two courses students were asked to introduce themselves informally, but participation was not required. Peer interaction was a weak part of most of the courses. One course had virtually no peer interaction and was taught like several independent study courses. Another course had a fairly high volume of peer interaction but many of the interactions were superficial or administrative in nature.

Another course began with a fairly high volume of interaction which dramatically decreased as the semester went on and students began to get busier and only participate in "essential" or required activities. Instructors should develop assignments that require meaningful peer interaction. Peer interaction will help to enrich the learning experience for the students as well as take the responsibility off the instructor for being the only feedback provider. Students might take the leading role in class discussions. For example, a group of students might lead the discussion by coming up with a set of questions while another group summarizes the discussion at the end.

Ask students to evaluate each other's work. Encourage students to praise each other for their accomplishments. None of the courses explicitly encouraged students to critically evaluate each other's work. It is easier for students to evaluate each other's work honestly if doing so is an expected part of the course. If it is not expected in the course, students may not provide critical feedback to each other because they feel like they are overstepping their bounds. Students will learn from each other if they are encouraged to openly evaluate each others work. Instructions to students should help them learn to be tactful in their critiques as well as open in their praise of peers' accomplishments.

Develop a mechanism for evaluating individual participation and contribution to group projects. The courses that were evaluated did not assess individual responsibility on group assignments and projects. If there is a collaborative project as part of the course, it is important that a mechanism be incorporated to encourage individual accountability and responsibility. Determining the level of individual contribution can typically bed one through the process of peer and self evaluations. In these evaluations students who worked with each other on a team are asked to evaluate peer contributions to the team effort. They are also asked to evaluate their own efforts using the same evaluation criteria. Some portion of the student's project grade should be based on the self and peer evaluation.

(3) Good practice encourages active learning:

> "Learning is not a spectator sport. Students do not learn much just sitting in classes listening to teachers, memorizing prepackaged assignments, and spitting out answers. They must talk about what they are learning, write reflectively about it, relate it to past experiences, and apply it to their daily lives. They must make what they learn part of themselves".

Overall, the instructors in all of the courses that were evaluated did a very good job of encouraging students to engage in active learning. They were particularly good at getting students to relate the ideas that they were learning to real-world issues. This was often done by getting students to do real-world projects or authentic assignments. While reading was usually required, assignments were often structured to get the students to do something with that knowledge rather than just regurgitating it.

Students should be asked to present their work to the rest of the class. Class members should also been couraged to give feedback on the projects that are presented. In the online courses evaluated, bulletin board assignments were typically available for all to see while course projects were typically not shared among students. Students will learn from seeing the work of others. While formal synchronous presentations may not be practical in an online environment, the project work can be made available for other students to review. However, in doing so, it is important that specific questions be formulated to help structure a productive asynchronous discussion about the project or assignment work. Without a specific task, it is unlikely that the students will just review the work of others.

Assignments and bulletin board discussions could be structured in a way that enables students to challenge the ideas of the instructor, of other students, or those presented in the readings or other course materials.

(3) Good practice gives prompt feedback:

"Knowing what you know and don't know focuses your learning. In getting started, students need help in assessing their existing knowledge and competence. Then, in classes, students need frequent opportunities to perform and receive feedback on their performance. At various points during college, and at its end, students need chances to reflect on what they have learned, what they still need to know, and how they might assess themselves". There are typically two main types of feedback:

— acknowledgment feedback

— information feedback

Acknowledgment feedback is feedback that confirms or assures the student that some event has taken place. In a face-to-face environment this kind of feedback happens all the time and is often communicated through non-verbal cues. For example, when a student raises her hand to ask a question in class, she knows that the instructor has seen her request because of the eye contact she makes with the instructor. Similarly when a student submits an assignment in class, he gets visual confirmation that the instructor has received the assignment when the instructor picks up the stack of assignments and puts it into a briefcase at the end of class. This kind of feedback is often not readily available to students in an online learning environment. For example, if a student sends an instructor a question via email, she has no way of verifying that the instructor has seen her question. Similarly, when an assignment is submitted electronically, a student has no way of assuring that the instructor has really received his assignment.

Information Feedback is feedback that is informational or evaluative in nature. It is often manifested as the answer to a student question or as an assignment grade and comments. This type of feedback is typically explicitly given in both face-to-face and online environments.With the exception of one course, the instructors were good about giving information feedback on assignments and projects in a timely manner. The turnaround time for giving feedback on assignments in all cases, however, could be improved. A good goal to shoot for is a turnaround time of one week or less. When instructors set student expectations by communicating a clear feedback response policy it reduces student stress.

Strengths in the area of giving information feedback in bulletin board discussions tended to be more course/

instructor specific. Some instructors were good about monitoring group bulletin boards regularly and giving specific information feedback to students. These instructors were typically good about guiding students by asking questions and encouraging them to find their own solutions rather than just giving them answers to their questions. One instructor used the strategy of providing evaluative feedback through summarizing each week's discussion.

While all instructors but one were good at giving informational feedback, improvements could be made in providing more and better acknowledgment feedback. Instructors could alleviate student concerns by sending them a brief note of acknowledgment when they receive an assignment via email. Also, if an instructor is too busy, for some reason, to give a detailed answer to a student question in a timely manner, the instructor should give the student an acknowledgment email stating that they have received the question and will address the question later when they have more time.

All feedback does not and should not necessarily come from the instructors. Assignments and projects should be structured so that students can provide feedback to each other on them. Typically, as the semester progressed and instructors became busier, the amount of instructor feedback decreased. Instructors need not become overwhelmed by the amount of feedback to give the students if they are properly leveraging the capabilities of other students in the class.

(4) Good practice emphasizes time on task:

> "Time plus energy equals learning. There is no substitute for time on task. Learning to use one's

> time well is critical for students and professionals alike. Students need help in learning effective time management. Allocating realistic amounts of time means effective learning for students and effective teaching for faculty. How an institution defines time expectations for students, faculty, administrators, and other professional staff can establish the basis of high performance for all." Part of this has to do with how demanding the task is, part of this has to do with the expectation the instructor sets for working. Among assignments, some tasks require much more time than others.

Strengths were not uniformly found in all evaluated courses but mixed throughout the four courses that were evaluated. Most courses had assignments with specific deadlines that required students to participate in the class on a regular basis. Having regular assignments due throughout the semester helped to encourage students to spend time on the course and not to procrastinate. One course had due dates every week on the same day to help students remember and plan time to participate each week. Another course with a large course project, required students to report on intermediate milestones during the project to ensure that students were remaining on task and not procrastinating.

Overall instructors did a good job of underscoring the importance of regular work, steady application, sound self-pacing, and scheduling. This can be communicated explicitly through email etc. as well as through the structuring and due dates of the assignments. Most of the courses structured their assignments in a way that required students to stay on task and work weekly throughout the semester. Only one of the four courses had a very loose assignment structure in which almost all of the due dates fell at the very end of the semester.

The students should be given a structure with deadlines that are spread throughout the semester. This rule was not followed in one course. The instructor only required all projects to be completed by the end of these mester offering the rationale that this gave students more flexibility in completing the course. While flexibility can be provided by allowing the students to sequence the assignments the way they wish, courses should not allow students to turn in all of their assignments at the end of the semester. This does a disservice to the students by encouraging them to procrastinate and spend time off task because of other commitments in their busy lives.

Asynchronous Conferencing can be a good way to improve student time on task. At least one course required the use of materials found only on campus. If the course assignments need some campus based resources (e.g. CDs, videos, books) instructors should try to make arrangement with the related university department (library, AV center, etc.) for the students' to easily access the resources. It would be preferable if it could be arranged for the resources to be available at a distance.

(5) Good practice communicates high expectations:

> "Expect more and you will get it. High expectations are important for everyone-for the poorly prepared, for those unwilling to exert themselves, and for the bright and well motivated. Expecting students to perform well becomes a self-fulfilling prophecy when teachers and institutions hold high expectations for themselves and make extra efforts".

Strengths were not uniformly found in all evaluated courses but mixed throughout the four courses that were evaluated. Three of the instructors did a great job of setting high expectations to motivate the students. Most instructors clearly listed their expectations from the students on the course Web site. In addition to listing the assignments, due dates, and expectations, often the grading rubrics were provided for the students. Instructors were good at publicly calling attention to excellent performance by the students. Instructors did a good job of balancing the praise given with the advice offered to the students. Giving positive attention to the students provides motivation as well as feedback about the kind of excellence that the instructors are looking for.

Instructors should periodically discuss how well the class and individual groups are doing during the course of the semester. Giving the class feedback as a whole can help to motivate them to reflect on their performance and improve it. Instructors should provide examples of exemplary performance to students. In three of the four classes the instructors did not provide examples of good performance at the beginning of the course for students to use as a guideline. Once course did an excellent job of providing examples of different qualities of student responses. Providing this kind of feedback is especially important when the students are asked to participate in bulletin board discussions as part of their grade. It is helpful for them to have some models to pattern their postings after.

(6) Good practice respects diverse talents and ways of learning:

> "There are many roads to learning. People bring different talents and styles of learning to college. Brilliant students in the seminar room may be all thumbs in the lab or art studio. Students rich in hands-on experience may not do so well with theory. Students need the opportunity to show their talents

> and learn in ways that work for them. Then they can be pushed to learning in new ways that do not come easily".

All of the instructors were conscientious about trying to incorporate diverse viewpoints and methods of learning into their courses. The instructors for the courses that were evaluated used many different methods to bring diverse talents and ways of learning into the course. One method used was to allow students to shape their own course work by choosing project topics. Instructors also attempted to learn about the different backgrounds and interests of the students through online icebreaker activities at the beginning of the semester. Instructors also were good about encouraging students to express their diverse points of view. Additionally instructors often included learning exercises filled with real-life examples that represented diverse, unique perspectives.

Human computer interface design evaluation

Three of the four courses used WebCT, so there are certain aspects of the human computer interface (HCI) design that the instructors did not have control over.

(1) Consistency of web page layout and design.

Consistency in the interface allows people to easily learn and recognize the graphic language of the interface. It also allows them to transfer their knowledge and skills from one application to another. It also makes repeated visits and information retrieval from the same site easier. Three of the four courses had fairly consistent layout designs and did not have any glaring consistency problems. One course needed extensive work to make look more professional and internally consistent. One course had Power Point presentations available for the students on the site. However, the presentations did not look at all consistent. They had different color schemes, fonts etc. This can bedistracting to the students.

A few guidelines for details that can be used to improve the web page layout and design consistency: Include standard information on each page. The following basic information should be included at the bottom of each web page:

— last update date and time of page

— contact information

— copyright information

Pages (and PowerPoint slides) should include consistent/ complimentary backgrounds, font type, font size, icons, logos, banners etc.

(2)Clear organization and presentation of information.

A well-organized interface allows the user to work efficiently. Users benefit from functions that are easily accessible and usable. A poorly organized interface cluttered with many advanced functions distracts users from accomplishing their everyday tasks. Effective categories should be used to describe the information available at the site and the interface should be designed to inform the users about available information. In a well organized site the relationships between elements on the page should be easily understood. Some rules of thumb are:

— Information should be well organized and structured to support scanning and locating.

— Navigational aids should be supplied for users.

— Internal document links should be used for long pages.

This is the area in which there was the most need for improvement in the courses that were evaluated. Additional attention in at least three of the courses could be paid to formatting edits which could make the materials easier for the students to scan through. Instructors could do a better job of breaking up large blocks of text on pages through the appropriate use of headings and other formatting features. Also, the number of accidental postings to incorrect discussion areas in a couple of the courses indicated that the bulletin board discussion structure may have been either too complex or not explained clearly enough. Below are some general guidelines that can be used to evaluate individual course materials.

— Use text formatting to organize information on the page. If a lot of textual information is being presented on a web page, that information should be broken up and organized by the systematic and appropriate use (but not overuse) of bolding, italics, colors, etc. to set off main ideas and important information.

— Ways to limit the amount of scrolling required by the learner will improve the usability of the site. Onemethod for doing this on text rich pages is through the appropriate use of internal hyper links and anchors so that the user can easily jump around within a page.

— Attempting to keep the format of assignments will make the information easier for the students to find and use.

— It is important to clearly specify the difference between group bulletin boards and public bulletin boards as well as information about when students are to post in the public vs. private bulletin boards. Some of the courses had problems with students posting to the wrong forums. In these cases the organization and number of forums should be evaluated to determine the optimal organization.

(2) Consistent and easy-to-use web site navigation.

Navigating hypertext can place heavy mental loads on users. In order to orient users and minimize the disruptive effects of jumping from one place to another, visual support and context should be supplied. Descriptive headings should be supplied in each page. Dead-end pages without navigational options should be eliminated. Standard navigational aids (text and graphic) should be supplied in each page. Users should have more control using the site navigation.

Although the WebCT environment has an inconsistent navigational structure, changes to the standard WebCT navigation may not be possible or practical. However, instructors should keep links up-to-date and replace or remove broken links.

A strength of the School's program is that many of the courses use the same course management tool, WebCT. Three of the four courses evaluated used WebCT. This is good for the students because it decreases the learning curve that must occur when taking a second or third distance course from the school.

Below are some general guidelines that can be used to evaluate website navigation. Standard navigational bars, icons, and links should appear in a consistent location on each page. Navigation icons should be consistent and location of navigational bars or buttons should appear in a consistent spot on each page for ease of use. It is generally a good idea for pages to have a link back to the homepage or the main menu page.

- The look and feel of navigational icons should be consistent.
- Consistent navigation design improves the usability and learnability of the site's navigation.
- Take advantage of web environment to link related information.

The instructor should take advantage of the strengths of the web to link related information so that it is easy for the students to access.

(3) Aesthetically pleasing design and graphics.

Aesthetic integrity means that information is well-organized and consistent with principles of visual design. Users will be more engaged by a task if the information presentation is both well-structured and aesthetically pleasing. Since users spend a lot of their time working while looking at the computer screen, the visual interface should be designed to be pleasant to look at on the screen for a long time. In such an interface the graphics of the display should be kept simple and arbitrary graphic images should not be used.

With the exception of one course there was not a problem with the aesthetics of the course web sites. In the one course mentioned, there were a couple instances in which animated graphics were used that detracted from the professional look and feel of the course.

Icons and images used in the site should all be professional in nature and appropriate to the content of the course. Unrelated and distracting animated images should not appear on the course web site because they make the site look amateur.

Just like students learn from each other, instructors can learn from each other. The School provide opportunities and incentives for instructors to share and discuss with each other what kinds of strategies they are using in their online courses. The following are few ways in which the school might do this:

— Faculty Development Workshops which highlight the work of one or two different instructors and their online courses.

— Brown-bag Lunches in which a faculty member demonstrates his/her online course and faculty can discuss best practices.

— Awards for Innovations in Teaching might be awarded to faculty who are on the forefront in developing and delivering online courses.

— A School Newsletter which highlights a different online course each quarter or semester.

— Faculty Seminars which bring in guest presenters and/or discuss literature in the area of online learning.

(4) Use Asynchronous Conferencing Effectively

One of the key components of an online course is its use of asynchronous conferencing tools. The way in which the asynchronous conferencing tool is used can have a dramatic effect on the student learning in the course. Instructors who will be teaching online courses should be given some guidelines for effectively using asynchronous conferencing in their courses. Some general principles that have been developed at the Center for Research on Learning and Technology for effectively using asynchronous conferencing tools are given below:

If participation is not required, students will generally disregard using the tool for meaningful types of tasks. Atleast a portion of the final grade should be based on the student's participation in the asynchronous discussion. Students need a task to focus their discussion.

A common mistake that is made when using asynchronous conferencing tools is that students are just asked to use the tool to "discuss" a topic. This often results in shallow "talking around" the topic in question. The instructor should provide a specific task to the students to help focus their online discussion.

Instructors should appropriately structure the physical discussion space to facilitate the discussion and minimize potential confusion. In the courses that were evaluated there were some discussion structures that made it very difficult for the students to remember where they were suppose to be posting at which times during the semester. The discussion structure (including public, private, topical, team forums, etc.) should be simple and easy for the students to understand. Multiple postings from students in the wrong discussion space is a clear indication that the discussion structure is too complex.

Discussion must be evaluated based on quality of content and not length of posting or number of postings

Evaluation of postings based on number or length of postings encourages students to contribute trite and thoughtless information to the discussion just to be "counted." Discussion postings should be evaluated based on quality of content. This might be done by evaluating the synthesis or final product developed from the discussion.

Instructors can improve the quality of student discussions by explicitly giving exemplars to the students. For example, in one course students were given example scenarios for three "types of postings". One good example, one from a student who thought she knew everything, and a third from a student who was just agreeing with other posts and not adding anything substantive.

Receiving feedback on the discussions is crucial in helping the students learn. Feedback can come from various sources including instructors and other students.

Experience dictates that if the number of students in a discussion group gets too large that meaningful discussion is less likely. If there is a large number of students in an online course it is more productive to divide them into several smaller discussion groups which work in parallel.

One of the dilemmas that is faced in giving feedback in an online discussion environment is that instructors want to encourage and increase of quality discussion because that increases time on task. At the same time the more discussion that is generated the more difficult it is for the instructor to keep up with it in a timely fashion. This is especially the case if a class is broken up into several small discussion and project groups because the instructor then has to monitor the discussion threads for multiple groups while student group members only have to monitor one group's discussion. The following are a few suggestions of strategies to help in managing online courses:

Increasing the emphasis on peer evaluation does not absolve the instructor from the responsibility of providing feedback in the discussions. However, it can alleviate much of the stress. The more quality feedback students get the better off they are. Peers can provide much of the needed feedback with the instructor monitoring and providing guidance at critical times rather than all of the time. Students can be encouraged to give meaningful feedback by making it a requirement for the grade or by providing other incentives.

Another way to improve the manageability of a course without compromising its effectiveness is to place a greater emphasis on group work. Creating assignments that encourage student collaboration can improve the quality of the learning for the students as well as reduce the number of final products that must be graded.

Another way to maintain a high level of expectation for student participation in discussions without overwhelming the instructor is to selectively evaluate the discussions. There are several possible methods for doing this. First, the students could be informed that they are required to participate actively in all the discussions but that the instructor will evaluate everyone's participation quality for a grade only at a certain number of (unspecified) times during the semester. A second possible method would be assigning a group discussion leader for each topic or assignment and making that person responsible for encouraging and stimulating quality group discussion.

It is important to set clear student expectations from the very beginning about how you plan to provide evaluation and feedback to them in their class discussions. Instructors who do not establish clear expectations often have to deal with a higher level of student stress due to unmet student expectations regarding evaluation and feedback. In the process of evaluation, it was found that not all School's faculty who are developing online courses have access to course development resources such as WebCT. Itwas recommend that all faculty in the School who are teaching online courses be extended access to resources which will increase the likelihood of creating successful online courses. There are three main reasons for this recommendation:

— *Need for asynchronous conferencing*: While faculty may be able to develop web pages on their own, it is beyond the capability of most faculty to develop and support their own system for asynchronous conferencing. This is such a key component insuccessful online courses that the School should do everything it can to facilitate its use.

— *Standard interface*: Allowing all online courses to use the same general interface (WebCT) decreases the learning curve for students who are taking online courses. Instead of having to familiarize themselves with a new interface for each course, students will be able to jump right into learning and participating in the course after taking their first course.

— *Need for technical support*: To overcome the technical problems of the course, strong technical support should be supplied by the School. Instead of dealing with technical problems, the instructors should be able to focus their energies entirely on teaching their courses.

Overall the courses that were evaluated were well done. The key strengths of the courses evaluated are:

— *Encouraging Active Learning*—All courses did an excellent job of encouraging active learning through authentic real-world assignments

— *Encouraging Student-Faculty Contact*—Faculty were good at encouraging students to contact them through email and phone.

— *Respecting Diverse Talents and Ways of Learning*— The faculty did a great job of encouraging students to express their different views in the courses. They also incorporated learning exercises filled with real-life examples that often represented diverse perspectives.

— *Encouraging cooperation among students*— Although there was learner-learner interaction designed into three of the four courses, often times the interaction seemed to be somewhat superficial and students did not really interact to any large degree in any of the courses. Following the guidelines for asynchronous conferencing should help to overcome this problem.

— *Giving prompt feedback*—Instructors did a good job of giving feedback to students about their work, however, feedback typically became more and more delayed as the semester wore on. Instructors should try to get feedback to students within a week of an assignment due date.

— *HCI Design*—Although most aspects of the design were good in most of the classes, there was one class in particular that needed a lot of improvements made to the interface to make it more usable for the students. Additionally most of the courses could use some work in breaking up text heavy pages with appropriate formatting and images if appropriate.

Teacher Community-building

Collaboration among teachers to foster community-building is not a new idea in teacher professional development. In the domain of education, there are a few strands of research that discuss the design and structure of cooperative educational learning experiences using telecommunications as a tool to enhance learning, particularly in teacher education. At present, there is limited research on the impact that cooperative telecommunications network design has on the educational experiences of teachers involved in the process of designing the telecommunications technology that they use. TERC's LabNet telecommunications network serves as a case study for exploring diverse modes of incorporating user participation. The LabNet project began enacting these beliefs by creating a telecommunications network for teachers. After using the Delphi network for three years the LabNet project switched to the America Online (AOL) network in February of 1992. Since switching to AOL, the LabNet team has been engaged in the process of re-designing the LabNetwork. It has undergone three major redesigns and many smaller changes.

The LabNet project was committed to designing, with the users, a network space that reflected an educational purpose: To promote based science learning and reflective practice about teaching as one important component of professional development. By creating a telecommunications network dedicated to teacher professional development it was hoped to entool teachers with the mechanisms for defining and 'growing' their own professional development. TERC's NSF funded LabNet telecommunications network serves as the case study for exploring modes of fostering user participation to encourage community-building. A series of research questions emerge that are related to collaboration as a mechanism for successful teacher professional development. The challenge of the LabNetwork design is to create and support a nationwide community of practice using a telecommunications network. The community's focus is to promote and incorporate teachers' use and development of science projects to enhance students' science learning. In order to promote project based learning teachers share their thoughts about their work. For teachers to grow in their practice there is a need for critical attention to the details of their classroom work, and that the details of practice need to be reflected upon and shared in conversations.

Teachers frequently lack the time and opportunities to reflect upon their work experiences and often, like many other professionals, lack the skills to do so. By sharing and conversing with other professionals on-line, the intention of the community is to create room for cooperative learning experiences to occur. Collaborative learning and reflection rarely occur in the practice of teaching. Therefore, it is not surprising that it rarely happens in the telecommunications medium. Telecommunications could potentially be an effective medium for fostering reflective discourse. Yet, in order to "grow" these experiences, careful consideration needs to be given to the actual design of the network space. Two types of roles the teachers played in the community building process: conceptualizing a community of practice and growing a community of practice.

The LabNet project has involved users and project staff over a sustained period of time to create a telecommunications network. Over the course of two years the LabNet area on AOL has gone through many changes - redefinitions in scope, size and content. Each network change was enacted to support the existing and growing community. The process of shaping the LabNetwork community was a long, complex venture.

A "community of practice" can take many shapes and forms, especially when the community takes place on a telecommunications network. Throughout the design process, it was continually revisited questions about what it could mean to build a community, what kind of community intended to build, and whether the outcomes of the design matched the intentions. The network's conceptual and pedagogical framework was largely defined in October 1991 at a four day LabNet-sponsored workshop. At the workshop there was a group of teacher leaders (teacher moderators—TMs), who were selected from an application process and who worked in consultation with staff on all facets of creating and supporting the network.

The TMs wanted to "test" their design plans with the users. They realized that the LabNetwork needed to reflect multiple viewpoints and accommodate different ways of working. In some ways, the TMs viewed themselves as representative of the community. Given the diversity of work practices, the group strove for the commonalties and created a flexible design. After shaping the design, the group named areas on the LabNetwork, planned what content should fill each area, and chose graphics as physical representations of the areas.

Users can open any of the areas listed on the left to read text files created by project staff. To engage in conversation, teachers need to click on "Teacher Forums." This area is graphically represented on the right hand portion of the screen. Within the Teacher Forums area there are two public bulletin boards - areas for discussions. There is an area for teachers to interact with members of their state and there is an area for science -related discourse. The science topics area is called "Science Teachers' Forum" and is a place for any and all discussions about project based science teaching, teaching issues in general, and community issues.

One of the most critical components of a teachers' network is a place for professional discourse. During the initial phase of the design process collaborating teachers helped to conceptualize and design an area for this discourse. They named it the "Science Teachers' Forum." It was intended to be the primary place for teaching discussions, reflective practice and collaboration around project enhanced science learning (PESL).

Since it was the only place on the network for teachers to talk about their practice, the area was intentionally left undefined. The area for discussion was unstructured, community members would start discussions about their teaching that were of interest to them. It is critical to note that throughout LabNet's history, folders have always been created by members of the community, reflecting their areas of interest.

Some folders created within this space were of an interdisciplinary nature, but most were subject focused. This intention, to create space for discussion, meant that interdisciplinary collaborations could be possible because the network's structural organization was minimal. Teachers of different grade levels and subjects, the group believed, would need to interact in a common space in order to meet each other and form professional collaborations. The first network design met the needs of the community for about seven months. The network so that it could accommodate the users' evolving needs. As the community grew, the discussions around particular teaching disciplines become more frequent and were more diversified. There were many conversations and because of technical constraints the LabNetwork had run out of space for new topics.

The second design occurred in response to the community's growth in number and content shifts toward subject orientation on the network. New topics were being created by teachers around subject areas and members were requesting designated space for discipline specific discussions such as physics, chemistry, biology.

After receiving all of the survey responses, the project staff compiled them into one document. The disseminated to both staff and users so that it could begin to make informed decisions based upon user input and suggestions. Although the 'feedback' offered many viewpoints, there appeared to be consensus that everyone should create subject folders within the larger framework. The team was concerned that subdivisions would fragment the community feeling and inadvertently create isolated sub-communities that were largely defined by subject matter.

The decision to subdivide the network conversations area was not an easy decision. This proposed structural change, potentially yielded both wanted and unwanted outcomes. There was a sense that the community of practice concept could be lost within the restructured framework of the network. The difficulty was that needed to strive for a solution that met most teachers needs while also meeting the specific needs of the PESL membership. The intention was to foster both diversity and community simultaneously. Suggestions were made by teachers and staff to marry these components through structural changes in the design. During this redesign, when the focus was being reevaluated, the level of user involvement took a critical turn. Until this point, the users offered ideas and suggestions only when prompted by staff. From the time of the second design on, the users frequently offered unsolicited suggestions and ideas via electronic mail, folder discussions, and phone conversations.

The shift in dynamics in the level and types of community engagement is an important indicator in the process of entooling teachers to shape their own learning. In many ways, the teachers have formed their community of practice to resemble, ideologically and structurally, the types of professional development experiences they were seeking. By building a community they have created for themselves new and innovative avenues for professional learning. The collaborative efforts described in this case have continued. The LabNetwork is presently in the process of another redesign and the teachers are taking the most active role in redesign yet. This process of "making" a community that design is a human effort and that the factors that contribute to its' making are largely determined by human variables. Design is shaped largely by human invention and interaction.

Designers need to engage their users in the building process if the intention of the network is to foster collaboration. This process has been a complex venture that has attempted to incorporate many social factors within design efforts. Continued research on the educational outcomes of network design should take into account the variations on the purpose as interpreted by the community. Through the collaborative design process the LabNet project has enacted modes of user-designer participation based on the concept that a purposeful network is driven by content that is meaningful to the users. The content and discussions about teaching issues were the force that drove the network design changes. In essence, the community discussions, manifested in network messages, were the catalyst for structural changes on the network. Once structural changes were decided upon by the group and implemented, the shape of the network was altered. This alteration impacted the ways in which the community used the network and worked to diversify the content.

Users reacted to the "openness" of the network structure that they had collaboratively created in two ways: They used the network to discuss teaching practice, and they recruited other members in order to shape a community of teachers. Subsequently, the message content and foci grew. As a result of this growth, the network structure no longer was appropriate; discussions were difficult to return to and different conversations of similar topics were scattered throughout. Through the process of cooperatively designing an educational network space, some socially constructed situations to help inform other on-line communities that are seeking to promote professional dialogue, were identified. These factors, play a critical role in cooperative community building and can work to close the gap between intentions and outcomes.

4

Impact of Technology in Education

As the world becomes more complex, the skills that students need to acquire and master are quickly changing. The rise of the global economy, an increasingly multicultural society, and rapid changes in technology require students to learn and apply new skills in their academic and career endeavors. Students need to learn to communi-cate more effectively, both through speech and the written word. They need to learn how to work with others to find new and better ways to solve problems and meet the challenges of everyday life. They need to develop skills they can use in college or the workforce. Perhaps most important, students need to discover the joy of learning. If students are to function effectively in this ever-changing world, they must continue to learn every day of their lives.

Technology can help instill in students an eagerness to learn that will follow them through-out life and better enable them to reach their goals. The fundamental skills of reading, writing, and arithmetic remain the cornerstones of schooling and student learning. Studies have shown that students with routine access to technology learn these basic skills faster and better when they have a chance to practice them using technology.

One of the reasons cited for this improvement is that students are engaged by the technology. As a result, they spend more time learning and practicing the basic tasks than students who approach the same tasks in a traditional paper-and-pencil manner. Students are more motivated to learn when technology is part of their daily school experience. At-risk students show substantial improvement when technology is introduced into their curriculum. Experts believe the reason for this is that technology provides educators with a way to individualize and customize the curriculum to match learners' developmental needs and also provide a nonthreatening and motivating environment for repetitious learning tasks.

The ACOT studies have revealed that in classrooms where technology is used, students interact more with their peers and teachers than in traditional classrooms. Students change the manner in which they organize and accomplish their work, choosing to work collaboratively to solve complex problems. They routinely employ inquiry, collabora-tion, technology, and problem-solving skills uncommon to graduates of traditional high school programs. Collaboration becomes a learning tool, a means to an end, not just a chance for students to socialize. A research study on learning with laptops showed that the use of lap-tops encouraged even greater collaboration among students. During the study, on average, students with laptops worked in groups several times a week, compared with a few times a month before the laptops were introduced in their classrooms. Technology provides powerful tools for organizing and analyzing information and modeling concepts and underlying structures. Students who have the opportunity to use these tools gain a deeper understanding of complex topics and concepts and are more likely to be able to recall information later in life and use it to solve prob-lems in nonschool situations.

One of the most important contributions technology makes in the classroom is how it affects students' attitudes toward learning. Studies have shown that when technology is a routine part of their school experience, student attendance improves and dropout rates decline. When ACOT students were compared with their non-ACOT peers in the same high school, absenteeism was about half in the ACOT classes compared with the rest of the school.

Over the five years of the study, there were no dropouts in the ACOT program, while 30 percent of the student body dropped out from the regular program. This result is of crucial importance. Research shows that more students finish high school and many more consider attending college when they routinely learn and study with technology. Fewer than half of the students in the ACOT study came into the program with any interest in pursuing college. Overall, in the school where the study took place, only 15 percent of the graduating students went on to college. Not only did 100 percent of the students in the ACOT classroom graduate, but more than 90 percent went on to college.

Studies show that students who participate in student-centered learning programs score consistently higher in every subject are on standardized tests. Teachers with routine access to computers tend to employ teaching practices that put students at the center of learning. They focus their lessons on discussion rather than lecture, encouraging student-led inquiry and emphasizing thinking skills.

In this way, technology offers greater opportunities for learner control and greater connections between class work and the real world. Technology encourages students to take charge of their education. In classrooms where technology is part of the curriculum, students are more likely to initiate learning-based activities, sometimes even directing them. In addition to exploring topics more often on their own, students who regularly use laptops assume a greater variety of roles in the learning process, helping to teach other students and even their teachers.

In general, students respond positively when given the chance to actively participate in the learning process via technology. They come to class eager to learn and take more pride in their work.

By giving students greater control of their education and increasing their motiva-tion to explore and discover, technology plays a major role in instilling in students a love of learning that will help them to reach new heights of achievement not only in school, but throughout their lives. The keys to raising student achievement are to provide students with a solid foundation of basic skills and to motivate them to learn. Technology can help accomplish this goal. It engages stu-dents and fires their imaginations. It helps teachers stimulate young minds in ways that make a profound and lasting difference. Numerous research studies on the impact of technology on student achievement have demonstrated this finding with remarkably similar results.

Researchers found that students who use laptops regularly at school and at home are better writers, outperforming their peers in all four scored areas of writing assessment-content, organization, language/ voice/style, and mechanics. When asked what impact using laptops had on their writing, students answered that computers allowed them to do more extensive editing, which led to better writing. Improvements in student achievement, however, are not limited simply to writing skills. Fourth-grade students who participated in Missouri's eMINTS project (a program that incorporated a wide range of multimedia and computer technologies) consistently scored 10 to 13 points higher on Missouri Assessment Program (MAP) tests than non-eMINTS students. Special education and Title I students enrolled in eMINTS classes scored 10.1 points higher on MAP tests than their non-eMINTS counterparts.

In addition, an eight-year study of SAT I performance involving students at Brewster Academy showed that students who regularly used laptop computers increased their combined SAT performance by an average of 92 points. Research has also shown that the benefits of technology go well beyond the classroom. A study conducted by the U.S. Department of Education revealed that when schools provided students with home computers and modems so they could connect to the schools' networks, students increased the amount of time spent on educa-tional activities outside of school. Furthermore, students with home computers spent less time watching television, enhanced their prob-lem-solving and critical-thinking skills, improved their writing and math skills, and showed greater computer literacy.

Studies show that once students become familiar with technology, they quickly develop proficiency in its use. This opens up an exciting new world of learning possibilities for them, and their potential for achievement skyrockets. Students gain new skills and become familiar with new technologies that will help prepare them for future success in an increasingly technological world. Even the most basic tools can help young learners become more productive. Researchers involved in the Apple Classrooms of Tomorrow (ACOT) project revealed that third-grade students found it easier to write with a keyboard than with a pencil or a pen. Because writing was easier, they wrote more. By writing more, they learned to write better.

Web browsers make it easy for students to find in-depth information on just about any subject, while basic software tools such as databases, spreadsheets, and concept maps help them to organize and evaluate the data they find online. As a result, students express their ideas more clearly and creatively, using a variety of communications media includ-ing words, images, audio, and video. Technology also helps students create work that looks more professional. So when it's time to hand in or publish their work, students take pride in sharing it with their peers, parents, and teachers.

In the classroom, many teachers are turning to digital media to strengthen students' basic skills. Using video and audio technology brings class material to life in a way that stimulates young minds and facilitates learning. By incorporating pictures, sound, and animation, multimedia significantly enhances students' ability to recall basic facts, as well as improving their understanding of complex systems.

One reason for this improvement may be that digital media tools can be used to address each student's individual learning style, thereby empowering all students to achieve their potential. Gaining technological proficiency helps students learn more effec-tively, and it also improves their desire to learn. One study shows that students who have access to laptop computers explore topics on their own and work longer on school projects. In an interesting side note, the same study revealed that students with regular access to laptops are more confident in their computer skills. That confidence often translates into better performance in the classroom.

In United States, the importance of securing an adequate education for children has long been clear, this undertaking has, over the past fifteen years or so, acquired a sense of special urgency. On the one hand, expanded global competition and corporate restructuring have drawn attention to the importance of preparing the next generation of Americans to add value within an increasingly integrated world economy. Over this same period, however, serious concerns have been raised regarding the capacity of the U.S. educational system to meet this challenge. While a number of different approaches have been suggested for the improvement of K-12 education in the United States, one common element of many such plans has been the more extensive and more effective utilization of computer, networking, and other technologies in support of a broad program of systemic and curricular reform.

Such proposals have been motivated in part by specific examples of the successful application of technology to education, and in part by the more general observation that, during a period in which technology has fundamentally transformed America's offices, factories, and retail establishments, its impact within United State's classrooms has generally been quite modest. The Goals 2000: Educate America Act, which was signed into law in 1994, contained a number of provisions designed to foster the application of technology within the nation's elementary and secondary schools. Thethen US President Clinton has since announced several additional programs that aim to establish various forms of cooperative partnerships involving the federal government, the states, local communities, individual schools and school districts, and the private sector, in each case with the goal of mobilizing technology in service of K-12 education.

The Panel on Educational Technology was organized in April 1995 under the auspices of the President's Committee of Advisors on Science and Technology (PCAST) to provide independent advice to the President on matters related to the application of various technologies (and in particular, interactive computer-based and digital-network based technologies) to elementary and secondary education in the United States. The Panel consists of seven PCAST members and five outside experts in the field of educational technology, and has been assisted in its activities by a small research and operational staff.

In the course of its investigations, the Panel reviewed a substantial body of existing written material on the subject of educational technology and solicited additional written input from a number of academic and industrial researchers, practicing educators, software developers, governmental agencies, and professional and industry organizations involved in various ways with the application of technology to education. A smaller group of individuals chosen from each of these categories were invited to meet personally with the Panel's members and staff in briefing sessions conducted at the White House in October 1995. The discussion start with the nature of the problems now facing elementary and secondary education in the United States, and of the role technology might play in helping to solve those problems.

Since the effective utilization of technology within all of America's elementary and secondary schools will require a substantial investment of public funds. While much remains to be learned about the optimal use of technology in K-12 education, the Panel believes the case for educational technology to be a compelling one in view of certain critical economic and social problems now facing US and the weight of the available evidence regarding technology's potential contribution to the solution of these problems. While the continuing expansion of international trade has the potential to confer substantial long-term benefits on American companies and workers, it also presents certain challenges.

As trade barriers fall and cross-border transaction volume increases, children will find themselves competing more directly with the citizens of other countries to provide goods and services within the world marketplace. Indeed, the effects of international competition have already become evident in the (permanent or temporary) loss of U.S. market share to European and Asian economic competitors within certain industries and in competition-induced productivity improvements which, while beneficial in the long term, have been accompanied in some cases by "corporate downsizing" and economic insecurity on the part of American workers. Although it seems unlikely that the

United States could reverse the secular trend toward global economic integration even if it believed this to be in its own interest, there is much we can do to influence the role that Americans play within the integrated world economy of the future.

The Role of Technology in Education

The introduction of technology will not in itself improve the quality of American education, there are several ways in which the Panel believes it can be used as a powerful tool in addressing the problems outlined above. One of the earliest insights into the educational applications of technology was that interactive computer-based systems admit the possibility of individualizing the educational process to accommodate the needs, interests, proclivities, current knowledge, and learning styles of each particular student.

Even the earliest drill-and-practice based computer-assisted instruction systems, in which the student was exposed to successive blocks of textual material and answered a series of questions posed by the computer, typically offered the advantages of self-paced instruction. Among other things, self-pacing obviates the need for teachers to target their presentations to some hypothetical "typical" pupil, leaving part of the class behind while other students become bored, restless and inattentive. In recent years, however, many researchers have begun to focus on the potential of technology to support certain fundamental changes in the pedagogic models underlying the traditional approach to the educational enterprise. Within this "constructivist" paradigm:

— Greater attention is given to the acquisition of higher-order thinking and problem-solving skills, with less emphasis on the assimilation of a large body of isolated facts.

— Basic skills are learned not in isolation, but in the course of undertaking (often on a collaborative basis) higher-level "real-world" tasks whose execution requires the integration of a number of such skills.

— Information resources are made available to be accessed by the student at that point in time when they actually become useful in executing the particular task at hand.

— Fewer topics may be covered than is the case within the typical traditional curriculum, but these topics are often explored in greater depth.

— The student assumes a central role as the active architect of his or her own knowledge and skills, rather than passively absorbing information proffered by the teacher.

Quite apart from its use by students, technology can serve as a potentially powerful tool for teachers, who may use computers and computer networks to:

— monitor, guide, and assess the progress of their students

— maintain portfolios of student work

— prepare (both computer-based and conventional) materials for use in the classroom

— communicate with students, parents, and administrators

— exchange ideas, experiences, and curricular materials with other teachers

— consult with experts in a variety of fields

— access remote databases and acquire educational software over the Internet

— further expand their own knowledge and professional capabilities

Acomprehensive approach to the learning process may also involve the use of technology by parents, and by other (physically proximate or geographically remote) community members. While the Panel has concerned itself only incidentally with the use of information technology in school administration, it should be noted that the effective utilization of technology can yield significant "back office" efficiencies for schools, freeing up resources for application to learning-specific activities.

The effectiveness of various applications of educational technology remains incomplete, such research as is available, combined with anecdotal reports of the positive experiences of a number of schools, suggests that technology may indeed have the potential to play a major role in transforming elementary and secondary education in the United States.

In Californina, Blackstock Junior High School has ten "smart classrooms," including one in which students can use computer-aided design (CAD) software to describe products that are then fabricated using a computer-controlled flexible manufacturing system. Higher test scores and improvements in comprehension, motivation, and attitude have been reported for the predominantly Hispanic student body.

Most researchers and practitioners in the field of educational technology, however, are already convinced that information technologies have the potential not only to improve the efficacy of current teaching methods, but perhaps more importantly, to support fundamental changes in those methods that could have important implications for the next generation of Americans.

Although elementary and secondary schools in the United States have for some time been acquiring new computing and networking hardware faster than they have been retiring old equipment, access to modern hardware remains a significant impediment (though by no means the only impediment) to the widespread application of technology within grades K-12.

The amount of equipment available for instructional purposes remains suboptimal relative to the country's K-12 student population, and a large fraction of the equipment that is available to the schools is obsolete and of very limited utility. This problem is compounded by a lack of appropriate infrastructure for the operation of modern computer and networking equipment, and by a shortage within the schools of trained personnel capable of supporting the use of such equipment.

Over the years since microprocessor-based personal computers first became widely available, this ratio has declined significantly, dropping from 125 in the 1983-84 school year to 10.5 in 1994-95. This figure, however, still falls short of the ratio of four to five students per computer (which has been achieved by only a very small minority of all U.S. public schools) that many experts consider to represent a reasonable level for the effective use of computers within the schools.

Middle and junior high schools have less access to computers than senior high schools on a per-student basis, and elementary schools have an even higher student/computer ratio. As a result of the relative scarcity of computer equipment, most schools locate the majority of their computers not within the individual classrooms, but in specialized computer labs that are shared among all classes. If lab use is carefully scheduled, this approach can offer the potential for certain cost efficiencies through higher equipment utilization.

On the other hand, the sequestration of a school's computers within a computer lab makes it more difficult to use these tools on an intermittent basis as an integral part of various elements of the curriculum. About half of all teachers have at least one computer in their classrooms, but most have no more than two, making student computer use by individuals and small groups impractical within most classrooms. The computer access problem is exacerbated by the fact that most of the computer systems now in use within the public schools would be considered obsolete by private sector standards.

While such machines are able to run certain early educational applications (including some drill-and-practice systems), little or no new software is being written for these platforms, and they would in any case be incapable of supporting much of the functionality incorporated in the most interesting current applications of technology to education. A 1992 survey by the International Association for the Evaluation of Educational Achievement (IEA) revealed that only about 20 percent of all school computers were equipped with hard disk drives, thus further limiting the range of accessible software and databases.

Nearly 90 percent of all printers owned by American schools were then based on dot-matrix technology, significantly limiting both the speed and quality of digital output, and laser printers were exceedingly rare, especially in elementary and middle schools. One measure that has been proposed to ameliorate or eliminate the shortage of computer equipment within the schools is the donation by corporations of used computer equipment at the time it is replaced with newer models.

While it is possible that such an effort could be beneficial under certain circumstances, the Panel believes that this is not likely to have a major effect on the computer hardware problems now facing American schools for several reasons. First, such equipment would generally be at least one generation behind the then-current state of the art as of the time of donation.

Although this might well represent a modest improvement over the current situation in many schools, we believe the "obsolescence gap" between the computers used in American industry and those used in American education should be more aggressively attacked in order to end the technical isolation that has thus far drastically limited the range of software and functionality available to most schools.

However, the net effective life-cycle cost of donated equipment may actually prove to be higher than would be the case with purchased equipment. Unless a given school receives a large number of identical machines, such donations can raise costs substantially by increasing the number of different platforms that must be integrated, administered, and maintained by school- and district-level personnel.

Even in the absence of such considerations, older equipment tends to be more expensive to maintain in usable condition than new machines -- a potentially significant factor, since the average cost of administering and maintaining a computer system over the course of its useful life has been shown to be surprisingly high relative to the value of the hardware itself. When these less visible costs are taken into consideration, the net value of a corporate equipment donation may in some cases actually be negative particularly after accounting for the loss of public revenue attributable to federal and state tax deductions claimed by the donor.

The Panel believes that it would be unrealistic for the Administration to expect such donations to make more than a relatively small contribution overall toward ameliorating the current shortage of modern hardware. It is also important that educators and policy-makers view the purchase of computer equipment not as a one-time expenditure, but as an ongoing cost.

Although technological change in the computer industry is difficult to predict with any certainty, a useful life of between three and five years (which is longer than the typical life cycle in industry) may represent a realistic expectation for schools, assuming that the criteria for replacement include not only age-related malfunction, but also obsolescence and the inability to support then-current software.

The vast majority of all American classrooms, however, are not even wired for telephones, much less local area networks and Internet onramps. To make matters worse, many schools have asbestos within their classroom walls, making an already challenging wiring and cable-routing task even more expensive.

Although volunteer efforts like the NetDay '96 initiative have illustrated the contribution that community members and cooperative unions can make toward outfitting schools with the infrastructure necessary to support modern computer networking, it seems unlikely that such efforts can be relied upon as the sole mechanism for providing universal access to technology throughout the schools. Although wiring once may represent an unavoidable expense, conservative advance planning may at least obviate the need to wire repeatedly to accommodate future growth and unanticipated changes in technology. Although it may be slightly more expensive initially, it is important that resources be made available to allow schools to install the sorts of flexible and capacious conduits, raceways, and wiring systems that will support the later installation of future generations of higher-speed interconnection technologies without the need for extensive surgery on schoolroom walls.

The placement of significant numbers of computers within the same room can result in enough additional heat dissipation to require air conditioning in schoolrooms that do not currently have such facilities, or to require the provision of additional cooling capacity in those that do. Moreover, air conditioning consumes additional electrical power, adding hidden costs to the expense of installing and operating such environmental control systems.

Local Area Networks

Local area networks (LANs) are important not only to connect computers, printers, and other devices together within a given school, facilitating important forms of communication among students, teachers, administrators, and support personnel, but also to provide many or all of these computers with access to systems at remote locations through the Internet or other wide area networks (WANs).

A 1992 study reported that only about 20 percent of all school computers were connected to a LAN, though nearly a third of all elementary schools and one-half of all high schools reported that at least some of their computers were interconnected in this manner. It would appear that the use of locally-networked computers by K-12 schools may be growing at a relatively rapid pace: A survey conducted shortly thereafter by a different organization found that 44 percent of elementary schools and 66 percent of high schools had local area networks.

The use of LANs for instructional (as opposed to administrative) purposes would also appear to be enjoying a period of unusually rapid increase. According to a third source, only 5 percent of all public schools used LANs for instruction during the 1991-92 school year; three years later, this figure had risen to 33 percent.

Wide Area Networks

About half of all public schools had at least one connection to the Internet as of fall 1995, and another 11 percent to a wide area network that was not connected to the Internet. Although it is encouraging that 61 percent of schools are now connected to wide area networks (WANs) allowing at least some form of communication with remote sites, these connections are used only modestly by teachers, and are often unavailable for use by students. While a substantial majority of all schools with Internet connections report that access is available to teachers, for example, a survey commissioned by the National Education Association and other education groups found that only 16 percent of all teachers actually make use of the Internet or online services.

Even among schools having access to a WAN, 72 percent reported that teachers either never used this network or used it only "to a small extent." In cases where WANs are made available for student use, access is often provided only within a centralized library, media center, or computer lab rather than within individual classrooms, where it might be more extensively utilized as part of the process of day-to-day learning. Internet access is more commonly available in secondary schools than in elementary schools, and larger schools are more likely to be connected than smaller ones.

In the vast majority of all schools with Internet access, connections are made through ordinary modems; higher-speed connections are still very uncommon. Until greater external network bandwidth becomes more widely available within the schools, many Internet applications having an extensive audio and/or graphical component (and in particular, those involving the extensive use of three-dimensional renderings or moving images) will remain too slow for practical use. Among the principal determinants of the extent to which American schools are able to make use of the Internet and other wide area networks is the availability of reasonably priced telecommunications services of adequate bandwidth to support the interactive use of network-based applications (including those with a substantial multimedia component).

A sustained federal commitment to the maintenance of a genuinely competitive telecommunications environment -- not only within the long distance market, but among alternative local carriers as well -- should play a major role in reducing the cost of access for schools.

In addition, however, consideration should be given to measures designed specifically to promote affordable Internet access for American schools, with special attention to those in remote rural areas and to those facing resource limitations that would otherwise preclude the possibility of securing and maintaining such a connection.

The purchase price of a computer system represents only 20 to 25 percent of the cost of its operation over the period of its useful life within a typical business; the largest part of the life cycle cost of such a system is actually represented by the cost of installation, training, systems administration, user support, and hardware and software maintenance.

While the Panel was unable to find reliable data that might shed light on any systematic differences between the operating costs reported in industry and those experienced by the typical elementary or secondary school, it seems likely that the effective life cycle cost of operating a computer within a school environment is in fact an integer multiple of its original acquisition cost, particularly in view of the longer service period typical of computers used within the schools. Portions of this effective expense may in many schools be incurred in the form of staff time diverted from other, often unrelated functions.

An analysis of the 1992 IEA survey data found that only six percent of all elementary schools and three percent of all secondary schools have full-time computer coordinators. Indeed, only about 40 percent of all schools have even a single employee who allocates time in an official capacity to the operation of computer systems.

In schools having access to a wide area network, support is most commonly provided by a part-time network administrator associated with the school, although some WANs are administered at the district level. The extent to which limited support for local- and wide-area networks has retarded the widespread utilization of technology within the public schools remains unclear, but experience within the business sector suggests that this may indeed represent a significant obstacle. Of particular relevance to the schools is the fact that the cost of maintaining a given computer system tends to increase over time, especially when measured relative to the functional capacity or market value of the underlying hardware.

While a portion of this increase is attributable to ordinary component- and system-level aging, this effect is exacerbated (again, in value-relative terms) by the use of progressively higher levels of integration within the semiconductor, digital storage, and computer industries. Older equipment uses more integrated circuit chips, more printed circuit boards, and more moving parts to realize the same amount of processing power, data storage, and output capability, and system reliability tends to be inversely correlated with component count and with the number of connections between components.

The federal government is to play a meaningful role in applying technology effectively within the nation's elementary and secondary schools, the deployment of computers and their interconnection within local- and wide-area networks must not be viewed as an end in itself. Indeed, such hardware, while important, is in many ways less central to a discussion of the determinants of favorable outcomes than the educational content, pedagogic models, and organizational framework that define the manner in which it is used.

Computer-Based Tutorial Systems

Among the earliest applications of computer technology within the field of education were systems designed to automate certain forms of tutorial learning. Such systems, which were first deployed on an experimental basis during the 1960s, are commonly referred to using the (now confusingly general) term computer-assisted instruction (CAI).

In a classical CAI application, short blocks of instructional material are presented to an individual student, interspersed with questions designed to test that student's comprehension of specific elements of the material. Questions must typically be posed within a multiple-choice or "true/false" framework, or in such a way as to admit a simple, concrete answer (such as a numerical quantity) that can be interpreted by the system in a straightforward manner. Feedback is generally provided to the student as to the accuracy of his or her responses to individual questions, and often as to the degree of mastery demonstrated within a given content area.

Such systems generally also support "branched" structures, in which the student's performance on one question, or degree of mastery of one content area, determines the sequence, and in some cases, the level of difficulty, of the instructional material and questions that follow. Additional time can then be spent on material with which the student is having difficulty, while avoiding needless repetition of subject matter that has already been mastered.

More "intelligent" CAI systems may be capable of inferring a more detailed picture of what the student does and does not yet understand, and of actively helping to diagnose and "debug" the student's misapprehensions and erroneous conceptual models. If a student is having difficulty learning to subtract, for example, the computer may recognize that he or she is systematically failing to "borrow a one," making it possible to offer specific coaching rather than a simple repetition of the original instructional material.

While promising early examples of such systems have already been demonstrated in such content areas as mathematics and computer programming, realization of the full potential of this approach will require significant research progress in several areas. In the absence of such progress, it is not clear that highly intelligent tutorial systems will be available for wide deployment within the schools for some time.

Although some of the more recent work on computer-based tutorial systems may well prove useful within a constructivist framework, conventional CAI systems have historically been employed primarily for individual instruction in isolated basic skills, most often in a "drill-and-practice" mode. Instructional sessions have generally focused on a single content area rather than on the integration of a wide range of skills to solve complex problems, and have been limited in duration to the traditional 50-minute class period.

The conventional approach to CAI is often embodied in network-based systems known as integrated learning systems (ILSs), which have typically incorporated computing and networking hardware, systems software, tutorial content, and student record management programs, all provided by the same vendor. As of 1990, approximately 10,000 such systems had been installed in the United States, and penetration is currently estimated at some 30 percent of all American schools.

In recent years, however, many have argued that the use of new technologies to improve the efficiency of traditional instructional methods will result in limited progress at best. This view holds that the real promise of technology in education lies in its potential to facilitate fundamental, qualitative changes in the nature of teaching and learning. While the educational research community has by no means reached consensus on the best way to educate children, a large part of that community has in recent years converged on a core set of pedagogic principles that form the basis of the constructivist paradigm.

By contrast with the more traditional view of instruction as a process involving the transmission of facts from an active teacher to a passive student, constructivists believe that learning occurs through a process in which the student plays an active role in constructing the set of conceptual structures that constitute his or her own knowledge base. Although the intellectual roots of constructivism considerably predate the current educational reform movement, contemporary constructivist thought has been strongly influenced by models of the learning process that have evolved over the past few decades within the cognitive science research community, and which differ in significant ways from those which arose within the theoretical framework of behaviorism.

Constructivist theory has given rise to an approach to educational practice that places the locus of initiative and control largely within the student, who typically undertakes substantial, "authentic" tasks, presented in a realistic context, that require the self-directed application of various sorts of knowledge and skills for their successful execution.

Such activities often involve student-initiated inquiries driven at least in part by the student's own curiosity, and are designed to motivate students in a more immediate way than is typical of traditional curricula based largely on the transmission of isolated facts. Constructivist curricula often emphasize group activities designed in part to facilitate the acquisition of collaborative skills of the sort that are often required within contemporary work environments.

Such group activities may offer students of varying ages and ability levels, and having different interests and prior experience, the opportunity to teach each other -- a mode of interaction that has been found to offer significant benefits to both tutor and tutee. Explicit attention is also given to the cultivation of higher-order thinking skills, including "meta-level" learning -- the acquisition of knowledge about how to learn, and how to recognize and "debug" faulty mental models. It would be misleading to suggest that the educational research community is unanimous and unambivalent in endorsing the principles and practice of constructivism without qualification.

For example, that project-based learning techniques may be best suited to highly qualified, highly motivated teachers, and that the extensive use of these techniques by other educators may prove disappointing. Others have raised concerns about the elimination or profound de-emphasis of externally assigned, linearly sequenced instructional content, pointing out that the authors and conveyors of such content have often devoted considerable attention to the choice of a presentation order they believe is likely to facilitate understanding.

While the foundations of constructivism provide a rich source of plausible and theoretically compelling hypotheses, the fact remains that the question of how best to teach children remains an empirical question that has not yet been fully answered.

While the Panel is thus unable to make a confident and definitive statement regarding the superiority of the constructivist approach, it believes there to be a higher likelihood that many or all of the essential elements of this approach could play a major role in improving the quality of nation's elementary and secondary schools.

Although technology is likely to find use within a number of more traditional instructional roles as well, it seems likely (though not yet certain) that the student-centered constructivist paradigm may ultimately offer the most fertile ground for the application of technology to education. In order to optimally cultivate this ground, schools will need to make changes that extend far beyond the mere installation of a network of computers.

While some benefits may be obtained by using information technologies to pursue existing curricular objectives or by adding new material to an existing course, the richest harvest is likely to accrue from a fundamental restructuring -- at least at the level of the individual course, and ideally, across disciplinary boundaries as well.

Such fundamental restructuring, however, is likely to prove complex, difficult, expensive, and time-consuming, and may encounter resistance from parents, educators, and the general public, particularly to the extent that such changes conflict with commonly held beliefs about the nature of knowledge and learning.

Constructivist Applications of Technology

The constructivist paradigm, information technology is not typically used to orchestrate the instructional process in a strictly "top-down" manner, but rather serves largely to facilitate student-initiated and mixed-initiative projects, inquiries, explorations, and problem-solving activities.

By way of example (and without any attempt at comprehensiveness), computers and networks might be used within a constructivist framework to implement:

— an environment for the simulation of any of a wide range of devices and machines, physical systems, work environments, human and animal populations, industrial processes, or other natural or artificial systems.

— an information retrieval or database search engine capable of extracting information from a single system or from sites distributed across the global Internet

— a tool for the symbolic manipulation or graphical display of mathematical functions, equations, and proofs

— a facility for the collection, examination and analysis of statistical data (which might be used in connection with any of a wide range of experimental or survey applications)

— a word processing, document preparation, or outlining system

— an environment for domain-specific problem-solving

— a vehicle for various forms of interactive exhibits and demonstrations

— an environment for the facilitation of group collaboration

— a flexible laboratory instrument supporting the collection of scientific data from various physical sensors and the flexible manipulation of this data under student control

— a general or application-specific numerical spreadsheet

— a "digital workbench" for the creation of musical, artistic, and other creative works

— a user-friendly environment for the acquisition of basic programming and system design skills

— a computer-aided engineering workstation supporting the design of mechanical or electrical devices, architectural projects, or even organic molecules

— an interactive hypertext encyclopedia incorporating various forms of multi-media illustrations, and supporting the rapid traversal of cross-reference links, or

— a medium for communication with teachers, parents, community members, experts, and other students, both locally and over great distances, and for the organization and coordination of group projects

If computers are destined to play an increasingly important role in education over the next 20 years, it is natural to ask what roles will be played by human beings. Although it seems clear that the expanded use of technology in education will have significant implications for teachers, students, parents, and community members, there is reason to believe that interpersonal interactions among all these groups will be at least as important to the educational process of 2017 as they are in 1997.

The use of technology within the framework of the constructivist paradigm is likely to have important implications for the day-to-day role of the teacher. When a high school student using the Internet to complete a self-directed project is able to quickly gain greater familiarity with the particular subject area in question than her teacher, for example, the teacher's traditional role as a font of knowledge is likely to become less relevant.

Because different students may be conducting different inquiries at any given point in time, this traditional role may be supplanted in part by one in which the teacher spends a considerable amount of time monitoring the activities of individual students (in part by wandering around the classroom and looking at their computer screens), helping them to "debug" their emerging "mental models," and providing encouragement, direction and assistance as needed.

Software can also be specifically designed to teach collaborative and cooperative skills, and to support group projects and learning exercises. In short, any fears we might have that the increasing use of computers in education will produce a generation of isolated nerds would seem to be unsupported by currently available evidence. In considering the human side of educational technology, it is also worth noting that elementary and secondary education takes place within a context that includes not only the student and teacher, but also the parents and other members of the surrounding community.

Substantial evidence now exists suggesting that parental and community involvement in the educational process has a significant positive effect on educational outcomes. If at least basic computing resources (perhaps based on television set-top boxes or a new generation of "network computers") and Internet connectivity could be made available within the homes of those with K-12 aged children, parents would be able to receive school announcements from teachers and administrators, to communicate more easily and frequently with teachers, and to otherwise involve themselves more actively in the education of their children.

The cultivation of such parental involvement may be particularly important for those students whose economic or environmental circumstances would otherwise place them at increased risk of educational failure. There is also a growing consensus that technology should be applied in such a way as to foster broader community-wide involvement in the educational process.

The linking of elementary and secondary schools with research universities, public libraries, and private companies, for example, could make valuable educational resources available to both students and teachers while simultaneously building awareness within each community of the needs of its local schools. "Real-world" projects initiated by outside organizations often generate considerable enthusiasm among students, and frequently prove unusually effective from an educational perspective.

Some educators have even discussed the possibility of instituting "tele-apprenticeship" or "tele-mentoring" programs involving brief, but relatively frequent interactions between students and other community members that would be impractical in the absence of networking technologies due to travel time considerations.

Conversely, high-tech schools could serve the broader community by making their computing and networking facilities available to local residents outside of school hours, or by offering state-of-the-art job training or lifelong learning programs tailored to community members, thus amortizing infrastructure costs over a larger effective user base while helping to foster intrinsically valuable community integration.

In examining the ways in which information technology is currently used within the schools, it is useful to distinguish between efforts that attempt to teach students about computers and those that use computers to teach things that may or may not have any relation to technology.

While basic "computer literacy" will indeed be important for twenty-first-century Americans, and while computer science, computer engineering, computer programming, and computer networking are all important areas of study, the Panel has concerned itself only incidentally with issues related to teaching about information technology. It should be noted, however, that "computer education" currently accounts for a substantial fraction of the current use of information technologies by elementary and secondary schools.

A 1992 IEA survey of school computer coordinators, for example, found that some 41 percent of the use of computers by American K-12 students involved the acquisition of keyboarding skills; instruction in the use of word processing, database management, spreadsheet, and other software tools; and the study of computer programming. Academic subjects (defined to exclude vocational instruction) accounted for 54 percent of all usage at the elementary school level, but only 31 percent within the nation's high schools. At the elementary school level, computers are often employed for teaching isolated basic skills and for playing educational games.

Word processing is used to a significant extent at all levels, but in most cases as part of an effort to teach computer skills, and not as a tool for writing in connection with English, social studies, or other academic classes. The situation would appear to be similar in the case of spreadsheet use, which is generally treated as an aspect of computer literacy, and less commonly integrated into, for example, the math or science curriculum. It should be noted that some schools have, in fact, integrated computers extensively and effectively within many aspects of the learning process, in many cases relying on information technology as an essential element of educational reform.

The 1995 NCES survey provides some interesting indications. Among schools with access to the Internet, the most popular application is electronic mail, which is available in 93 percent of all such schools. While e-mail is generally available to administrators and (to a somewhat lesser extent) teachers, however, the majority of all schools with Internet e-mail capabilities do not make this facility available to students.

A majority of such schools also have access to Internet news groups, resource location applications, and World Wide Web browsers (such as Mosaic, Netscape Navigator, or Microsoft's Internet Explorer). Once again, however, such applications are more commonly accessible to teachers and administrators than to students. Little quantitative data is available at present about the frequency with which the Internet is used by the schools to access different sorts of information resources stored on remote sites.

There is widespread agreement that one of the principal factors now limiting the extensive and effective use of technology within American schools is the relative dearth of high-quality computer software and digital content designed specifically for that purpose. While this problem is encountered by educators at all K-12 levels, it would appear to be particularly severe within nation's secondary schools, which typically demand a broader diversity of instructional content. Growth in the traditional ILS market, which has historically been quite robust, has recently begun to level off, leading to cutbacks in internal research and development spending by the manufacturers of such systems.

Unfortunately, these cutbacks are occurring at a time when changing educational goals and a reformist emphasis on higher-order thinking skills are posing new challenges for educational software manufacturers that will be difficult to meet without such R&D expenditures. A number of major ILS vendors have been unable to justify such expenditures in light of various problems that they perceive within the market. The commercial availability of software and information resources designed to support student-centered, constructivist approaches to education is even more limited, and there is little evidence to date of large-scale, well-funded efforts by either traditional educational software vendors, multimedia developers, or textbook publishers to develop such content.

Moreover, in spite of a general appreciation of the potential for long-term growth in the market for educational software, there has thus far been only limited activity within the venture capital community aimed at launching startup companies focused on the provision of software designed for such pedagogic approaches, and targeted specifically at the nation's elementary and secondary schools. A rather long and superficially disparate list of factors has been advanced to account for the current problems within the K-12 educational software market. Most of these problems may be best regarded as arising largely from one or more of the following five underlying factors:

— *Inadequate software acquisition budgets*: Estimates of 1995 school expenditures for instructional software range from $470 million to $724 million, representing between $10 and $16 per student-year, or less than one-third of one percent of all educational expenditures. If technology is to play a significant role in improving the quality of American education, this figure will have to be increased very substantially. Assuming no (inflation-adjusted) increase in total spending, priorities will have to be altered to allow funds now committed to other budget categories to be redeployed—a process that is complicated in many states and school districts by various statutory and procedural constraints. In the absence of such a reallocation, software developers may not find adequate incentives to justify the substantial research and development expenditures that will be required to produce a new generation of school-based educational software products.

— *Market fragmentation*: The market for school-based instructional software encompasses a wide range of academic subject areas (particularly at the secondary school level) and grade and skill levels. While this inherent diversity is arguably no greater (relative to the size of the potential market) than is found in various other software markets, the market for school-based educational software market (in contrast with the more robust market for home-based "edutainment" software) is further fragmented by idiosyncratic differences among the product specifications and other requirements imposed by the various states and school districts. Although it may not be feasible (for political reasons, among others) to eliminate these idiosyncratic requirements or to substitute a universally applicable set of national standards, federal guidance in the promulgation of standards could play a significant role in minimizing this potentially avoidable form of market fragmentation, providing incentives for private firms to develop software targeted toward a smaller set of more substantial submarkets.

— *Lack of modern hardware in schools*: Although America's roughly 50 million K-12 students would seem to represent a very attractive market for software developers, the effective size of this market is at present constrained by the limited size of the current installed base of hardware, and by the age of much of the equipment that is currently installed. Since effective market size is a critical determinant of private sector investment, the limited penetration of state-of-the-art hardware has thus far impeded research and development activities that might otherwise have led to more and better educational software products. Unfortunately, this leads to a certain circularity: While software vendors are reluctant to develop products in the absence of a substantial base of modern hardware on which to run them, educators and policy-makers are reluctant to appropriate additional funds for the acquisition, maintenance, and timely replacement of hardware in the absence of a demonstrably effective base of educational software.

—*Procurement-related problems*: The procedures used by various states to acquire textbooks and other educational materials are in many cases poorly suited to the acquisition of computer software and digital information resources. This is a particular problem in the 22 "adoption" states, in which textbooks and other instructional materials must be approved by the state prior to consideration for adoption by individual districts and schools. Such approvals are often granted only once every five or more years—a considerable period within the rapidly changing software industry. Applying for approval within all adoption states can also be quite expensive. Each such state may charge an application fee of as much as $5,000 for each product to be considered for adoption, and many require that a number of computers be made available at the expense of the developer for state-level testing. In some states, the procurement process is further complicated by unusual (by private sector standards) mandated payment terms, or by well-intentioned "equity pricing" rules that, when applied to computer software, compel the vendor to charge the same license fee to each school, regardless of the number of enrolled students.

— *Innovation-related economic externalities*: A substantial investment in research and development is likely to be necessary if effective educational software—and in particular, software supporting new pedagogic approaches of the sort recommended by many experts is to be made available to the schools. Economic theory predicts, however, that private firms will systematically underinvest (relative to an optimal aggregate industry-wide level) in research and development to the extent they are unable to capture the full benefit accruing from any such activities that might ultimately prove successful.

Because innovations in educational software constitute a form of intellectual property that cannot be fully appropriated by any one firm (since the marketing and use of innovative software inevitably results in the dissemination of information of value to competitors), an economically optimal level of research is likely to be conducted only in the presence of public funding at the highest level of taxing authority (the federal government, in the case of the United States).

While federal funding (especially in the form of grants provided by the National Science Foundation) has already been used to develop promising new types of software for use in math and science education, a considerably higher level of research will be required even in those subject areas to compensate for this form of market failure, while funding in the language arts, social studies, the creative arts, and other content areas has thus far been minimal.

Role of Teachers in Technology

As schools continue to acquire more and better hardware and software, the benefit to students increasingly will depend on the skill with which some three million teachers are able to use these new tools. In order to make effective use of educational technology, teachers will have to master a variety of powerful tools, redesign their lesson plans around technology-enhanced resources, solve the logistical problem of how to teach a class full of students with a smaller number of computers, and take on a complex new role in the technologically transformed classroom.

Yet teachers currently receive little technical, pedagogic or administrative support for these fundamental changes, and few colleges of education adequately prepare their graduates to use information technologies in their teaching. As a result, most teachers are left largely on their own as they struggle to integrate technology into their curricula.

Moreover, when teachers do make use of information technologies, they are often used for either teaching students about computers or for drill and practice sessions focusing on the acquisition of isolated basic skills. Most teachers report that computers initially make their job more difficult. Despite the daunting challenge of using computers and networks appropriately within an educational context, however, teachers commonly report that they have not received adequate preparation in the effective use of computers within the classroom. Part of the problem arises from the fact that school districts frequently purchase hardware and software without allocating sufficient funds to help teachers learn to use the new equipment within an educational context.

Although a consensus is emerging that school computers are likely to be underused or poorly used if less than 30 percent of the computer technology budget is allocated to professional development, a 1993 survey by Market Data Retrieval found that only 15 percent of the typical computer systems budget is in fact devoted to staff instruction. The State of Florida has addressed this disparity by requiring that recipients of its educational technology grants set aside at least 30 percent of all grant funds for staff development.

The Panel believes that similar provisions should be considered for incorporation in applicable federal programs, and that the Administration should assume a leadership role in encouraging other states and localities to do the same. When teachers do receive instruction on the use of new technology, the form and content of the courses leave much to be desired.

According to one survey, 46 percent of all educational technology courses are given as half-day workshops, and 79 percent of these courses focus on hardware, Internet usage, or a specific piece of software. Teachers often have a negative reaction to the narrowly technical orientation of most technology-related courses, which show them how to operate a computer, but not how to use computers to enhance their teaching.

Returning to the classroom from what are typically semi-annual encounters with such courses, they are generally unprepared to handle the diverse logistical and curricular challenges they encounter within a technology-rich environment. In the Panel's view, what teachers actually need is in-depth, sustained assistance as they work to integrate computer use into the curriculum and confront the tension between traditional methods of instruction and new pedagogic methods that make extensive use of technology.

Such assistance should include not only purely technical support, but pedagogic support as well, ideally including observation within the classrooms of successful technology-using teachers, periodic consultation with more experienced mentors, and ongoing communication with other teachers grappling with similar challenges.

Less than five percent of all schools, however, have such a full-time professional on staff. Moreover, computer coordinators spend over half their time teaching students and only twenty percent of their time helping teachers, selecting software, or writing lesson plans.

Most teachers, however, cannot use computers effectively unless someone is available to help not only with the technical problems that are likely to arise from time to time, but also with the deeper pedagogic challenges of choosing software, organizing projects that make use of technology, and learning how to guide students in the use of computer-based resources. If a school cannot afford to hire a full-time technology coordinator to assist its teachers, it may be possible to provide adequate (though perhaps suboptimal) technical and pedagogic support at the district level.

The 153 schools in Jefferson County, Kentucky, for example, are served by a Computer Education Support Unit staffed by 22 professionals who maintain a technical support hotline and work directly with teachers to encourage and improve the use of technology in the classroom. Another option is to intensively train several teachers at each school who can then function as a source of expertise for their colleagues.

It should be noted, however, that the provision of such training and assistance will take time away from the other responsibilities of these teachers—an implicit cost that should be realistically assessed in comparing the alternatives for providing technological support to the rest of the faculty. Cause for optimism, however, may be found in certain contributions that technology itself may ultimately make to the development of expertise in the educational applications of computers and networks.

Information technology may also help teachers to recover at least some of the time they have invested in deploying technology on behalf of their students. Some (though certainly not all) types of educational software, for example, may ultimately enable students to spend part of the school day learning with less continuous attention from a teacher.

Computing and networking technologies also have the potential to streamline many aspects of a teacher's daily responsibilities, facilitating the development of instructional materials, the recording and assessment of student progress, and access to various forms of information resources. Online seminars conducted over the Internet might prepare teachers to use technology at roughly half the cost of conventional courses for which the teachers must be physically present, and equally important, might make it feasible to provide opportunities for followup consultation and mentoring on an ongoing basis without the prohibitive travel expenses that would be associated with repeated face-to-face meetings. The Internet also provides an excellent medium for various forms of communication among teachers themselves, including the sharing not only of ideas, but of actual lesson plans and curricular materials as well. If teachers were given adequate instruction in the art of computer-enhanced pedagogy and had access to on-site assistance as needed, they would be in a better position to reap the benefits of educational technology, but one major obstacle would remain: a lack of sufficient time in their schedules to become familiar with available hardware, software, and content; to prepare technology-related material for use in the classroom; and to share ideas on technology use with other teachers.

On average, teachers have only ten minutes of scheduled preparation time for each hour they teach. Since this is generally insufficient to adequately prepare for their classroom responsibilities, they typically spend additional hours outside the school day preparing lessons and grading student work, resulting in an average of 47 hours of work per week. While some of the technology available to teachers—application packages designed to provide assistance with various administrative, record-keeping, and student assessment tasks, for example—may free up a certain amount of time, this effect is unlikely to offset the additional time required to effectively utilize computers on an ongoing basis.

The problem of insufficient teacher time encompasses both a logistical question and an economic question. To illustrate the magnitude of the latter challenge, if all of the nation's public K-12 schools were to set aside two hours per week for technology-related curriculum design, as is the case in Arizona's Agua Fria Union High School, technology-related educational expenditures would increase by about $9 billion per year—more than tripling by comparison with current spending levels.

Although technology itself may help to mitigate these problems, the (direct and/or opportunity) cost of the time that will be required for teachers to incorporate technology effectively within the curriculum will present a significant challenge—particularly during an initial transition period—to the effective utilization of educational technologies.

Over 200,000 new teachers enter the profession each year, and there is a 50 percent turnover in the teaching force approximately every 15 years. While advances in underlying technologies, educational software, and pedagogic methods will result in an ongoing need for in-service training, colleges of education have a valuable opportunity to introduce future teachers to the use of educational technology before the demands of an actual teaching position begin to impinge on the time available for such training. Judging solely from teacher certification requirements in the various states, it would at first appear that education students receive more technology-related instruction than do active teachers: Eighteen states require pre-service technology training, while only two require in-service technology training.

Pre-service requirements, however, can typically be satisfied by completing a course on how to operate a computer, or by taking a "methods" course in which educational technology is discussed, but never actually used by either the professor or the students. As a result, even in states with a technology-related certification requirement, new teachers typically graduate with no experience in using computers to teach, and little knowledge of available software and content. Colleges of education fail to instruct their students in the use of educational technology for reasons that mirror some of the major obstacles to the spread of technology at the K-12 level, including the inadequate allocation of funds for hardware and software, minimal technology-related professional development for the education school faculty, and a lack of time for professors of education to restructure their courses.

Education schools generally have the advantage of better technical support (often provided through the campus computer center) than elementary and secondary schools, but research, publishing, and other academic responsibilities place additional demands on the faculty, thus slowing the process of curricular reform. The Panel believes that the principal focus of an education school's technology program should be the ways in which elementary and secondary school teachers can use information technologies to facilitate thinking and learning by K-12 students. Nonetheless, given that K-12 teachers will find it difficult to help their students make effective use of computing and networking technologies if they have gained little experience doing so themselves, any element of the education school curriculum that affords prospective teachers the experience of making profitable use of information systems is likely to increase the probability of effective later use within a professional context.

Colleges of education should be encouraged to find ways to reward faculty members who include new technologies in the methods or content of their courses.

Specialized degree programs in educational technology should also be encouraged, both to address the need for computer coordinators capable of providing teachers with more than purely technical support and to foster the development of a nucleus of technological expertise within the education faculty. Education students should also be given the opportunity to observe the use of educational technology and to practice teaching with technology in K-12 schools.

If the elementary and secondary schools that are available for student teacher placement have not yet effectively integrated technology into their own curricula, education students may be able to obtain some (though certainly not all) of the same benefit by studying examples of technology-rich pedagogy on videotape or interactive videodiscs.

America's education schools are capable of producing teachers who are able to make effective use of educational technology. In the past, federal funding has not been available for pre-service teacher development at levels comparable to those associated with in-service training, and Federal support for technology-related teacher development in general has been described as "highly variable from year to year, piecemeal in nature, and lacking in clear strategy or consistent policy."

Current annual spending on educational technology is complicated by differences in the types of expenditures included within this category by different observers, the available data suggests that public elementary and secondary schools in the United States spent somewhere between $3.5 and $4 billion on computing and networking hardware, wiring and infrastructural enhancements, software and information resources, systems support, and technology-related professional development during the 1995-96 school year.

A 1995 study conducted by the RAND Corporation examined six "technology leader" schools and attempted to estimate the cost of providing similar capabilities within a typical American school.

Hardware and software investments were amortized over a five-year period to obtain annualized expenditure projections; equipment costs were based not on the historical cost of each school's actual inventory, but on the prices of roughly equivalent hardware as of the time of the study.

Infrastructure costs were amortized over a ten-year period, while staff costs, professional development, materials and supplies were treated as ordinary (non-capitalized) expenses. To facilitate the identification of an approximate consensus range for the projected cost of introducing technology into American elementary and secondary schools.

Moreover, the acquisition of computing and networking hardware—often the principal focus of efforts to bring technology into the schools—will in fact account for only a minority of the expense incurred over time. While special bond issues, private capital campaigns, and other one-time funding mechanisms may all have their place in helping schools to defray the costs of acquiring hardware, it is important that educators and policy-makers have realistic expectations regarding the ongoing operating expenditures that will be necessary if this hardware is in fact to be effectively used, and that they not base their planning on capital budgeting models of the sort used to analyze, for example, the acquisition of new school buildings.

In the absence of realistic budgetary planning, schools and school districts are prone to overspending on the initial acquisition of hardware, and may find themselves with inadequate funding for upgrading and replacement, software and content, hardware and software maintenance, professional development for teachers, and the hiring and retention of necessary technical support personnel.

If the promise of educational technology is to be realized, educators and policy-makers will thus unavoidably be faced with difficult decisions as they attempt to either control or justify a secular trend of increasing (inflation-adjusted) per capita educational spending within the constraints imposed by a number of well-entrenched claimants on current financial resources.

The potential role of technology in increasing educational productivity, it is worth noting that teachers are likely to play a critically important role within the sort of future classroom envisioned by most current researchers in the field of educational technology. While this may be a comfort to fearful teachers (and in some cases, parents), it may also be a disappointment to those who have looked to technology for a simplistic automation of the instructional function, accompanied by a wholesale reduction in nation's aggregate expenditures on teacher compensation.

The empirical validation of such an analysis is complicated by the fact that the return on an educational investment is determined in large part by such factors as lifetime earnings (which will generally not be known for many decades after the investment in question is made), along with a number of non-pecuniary factors even less amenable to straightforward quantification.

It seems quite possible, however, that in the presence of formidable global economic competition, a substantial nationwide investment in educational technology could be justified even if no value were placed on the direct (economic and non-economic) benefits accruing to the American people, using return calculations based solely on the additional tax revenues associated with an increase in their expected lifetime taxable earnings.

Equitable access to information technologies in education has been a central concern of educators and policy-makers since microcomputers first entered nation's schools some twenty years ago, but has gained special attention during a period in which powerful desktop computers and global Internet connectivity are rapidly becoming an integral part of the lives of some—but not all—American families.

On the one hand, it has been frequently noted that new computing and networking technologies have the potential to empower historically disadvantaged groups of Americans with greater access to the sorts of knowledge-building and communication tools that might help them to overcome at least some of their respective disadvantages.

While the Panel believes this potential can scarcely be overstated, it also believes that the ways in which educational technologies are actually deployed and used will determine whether they serve to narrow these historical disparities or widen them even further. The current accessibility of computing and networking technologies to various segments of the American student population is then reviewed, with special attention to differences associated with socioeconomic status, race and ethnicity, geographical factors, gender, and various types of special student needs.

Schools with higher computer densities typically provide greater access to other forms of educational technology (including local- and wide-area networks and peripherals supporting multimedia applications) as well, making computer density a useful (albeit imperfect) proxy for the level of overall technology deployment. While the ratio of computers to students varies widely from school to school, and while much of this variation is accounted for by other factors.

At present, computers are found in approximately half of all American households with children, and a large fraction of all children whose families do have computers at home use them regularly for school work. In addition, students having access to a computer at home appear to use it for about an hour each week for purposes that are at least broadly educational in nature, a figure roughly equal to the typical student's computer usage in school.

As information technologies begin to play an increasingly central role in K-12 education, a doubling in the time available for educational computer use can be expected to confer an increasingly significant advantage on those children whose families are able to provide them with computer (and in some cases, Internet) access at home. Because certain segments of the American population have a far lower level of computer ownership than others, home access may now be one of the most significant sources of educational inequity in the United States.

Specifically targeted federal programs have in recent years helped to substantially mitigate some of the disparities in access to educational technology that had earlier been associated with socioeconomic variables. Income-related differences in computer density, for example, have been reduced to a relatively modest level: During the 1994-95 school year, the poorest schools had one computer for every 11 students, while each computer in the richest schools was shared by 9.5 students. Students from families classified as low in socioeconomic status (SES) report 14 percent less usage of computers in school than do students from high-SES families.

Lower-SES high school students are also significantly more likely to be taught about computers than to use computers in the course of other learning. Moreover, when high-SES students are exposed to computers as a subject area, they are more likely to engage in computer programming (as opposed to lower-level computer-related tasks) than low-SES students. More generally, high-SES eighth- and eleventh-grade students were found to be 25 percent more likely to use computers primarily for "higher-order or mixed" activities (rather than drill-and-practice or other skill-building or knowledge acquisition activities) than low-SES students of the same grade levels.

To the extent that the sorts of higher-order computer activities in which high-SES students are disproportionately engaged in fact offer greater opportunities for learning, such SES-related disparities in the in-school use of computers may represent a form of inequity at least as important as (even if less obvious than) SES-related differences in computer density. Among the factors that may be contributing to the disadvantages experienced by low-SES students in both the amount and nature of computer use are (putative) differences in the degree to which teachers in wealthy and impoverished schools have acquired the knowledge and skills necessary to use technology effectively in their teaching.

While the Panel is aware of no research that explicitly compares the technology-related preparation of and ongoing support available to teachers in schools of different socioeconomic composition, anecdotal evidence suggests that significant differences may in fact prevail across socioeconomic lines. Wealthy school districts may be able to recruit teachers with greater expertise in the use of educational technologies by offering above-average salaries, or to offer their existing teachers more technology-related training and technical support.

Poorer schools, on the other hand, may have fewer teachers capable of making effective use of educational technologies, thus limiting both the quality and quantity of computer use by their students. The most significant disparities in SES-related access to technology, however, are currently found not in the schools, but in the homes of their students. As of June 1995, computers were present in only 14 percent of all households heade by adults who had completed no more than a high-school education, and in which annual household income was les than $30,000; the comparable figure for households h aded by college-educated adults having a combined incom of more than $50,000 per year was more than five times g eater, at 73 percent. At a time when U.S. income inequality has reached its highest level since 1947, the educational implications of SES-related disparities in home computer ownership should be regarded as a source of serious concern from a public policy viewpoint. While it will be difficult to eliminate all SES-based inequities in the accessibility of educational technology within the context of current efforts to restrain federal spending, a number of possible federal actions are worthy of consideration.

Consideration should also be given to the provision of various forms of private sector incentives for the expeditious wiring of impoverished rural and inner city schools to support local- and wide-area networking. Existing federal programs serving low-income students should be reviewed with an eye toward exploiting the opportunities provided by computing and networking technologies, while public policy related to the ownership and disposition of various forms of intellectual property should be examined with the aim of providing affordable access to a rich body of digital content that might not otherwise be accessible to less affluent schools. The substantially lower prevalence of computers within the homes of low-SES students may be among the most difficult forms of inequity to remedy. At the same time, it may prove difficult to provide the sort of educational opportunity that nation has striven to offer each American without addressing this disparity. The provision of modern computer systems and Internet connectivity in libraries, community centers, and other public institutions and spaces could represent an important first step in affording access to those students whose families are unable to provide such facilities at home, as would the provision of extended after-school and weekend access to technology within the schools themselves.

Geographical Factors in Education Technology

When the United States is divided into four regions—West, Midwest, Northeast, and South—for comparative purposes, students in these regions are found to encounter an in-school computer density that differs by no more than ten percent from the national average. Certain regional differences do exist, however, in the use of technology. Students in the Southern region, for example, are 32 percent less likely to be heavy users of school computers, and 25 percent less likely to use computers for "higher-order or mixed" activities, than Western students.

Examining the density and use of computers along a different dimension, students in rural schools have been found to enjoy a 24 percent higher ratio of computers to students than those attending suburban schools, and fully 40 percent higher than students enrolled in city schools. These effects largely vanish, however, when school size is statistically controlled; it would appear that rural schools may have more computers per student only because they are smaller. Certain forms of access inequities are not evident when schools are coarsely categorized by region, but become apparent when other, finer-grained classificatory schemes are used to identify geographical groupings characterized by common problems.

Inner city students, for example, are clearly immersed in an environment that differs markedly from that of a wealthy urban neighborhood or a middle-class "edge city," and are likely to suffer special disadvantages, and to have special needs, that do not surface in surveys that treat all three as members of the single category "urban." Such studies may also miss the problems faced by certain rural schools located in areas lacking the local "points of presence" or affordable high-bandwidth telecommunication links that are typically required to provide cost-effective access to online services and Internet service providers.

Schools located within geographic areas in which there is little technology-oriented business activity may also be disadvantaged relative to those in high-tech areas. While individual states and school districts may well be in the best position to solve some of these problems, the Panel believes that the federal government has an important role to play in monitoring the use of educational technology throughout the country with an eye toward minimizing the extent to which the educational opportunities available to children are constrained by geographical happenstance.

On average, girls and boys differ only slightly in their use of computers at school. The 1992 IEA data set yields results that are typical of studies in this area, indicating that boys make three percent greater use of school computers than girls. Another survey, however, suggests that boys and girls differ significantly in the ways in which they use computers at school.

Although high school girls made 50 percent greater use of the computer for word processing than their male classmates, for example, they accounted for only 26 percent of all elective computer use before and after school, and for only 20 percent of all in-school computer-based game-playing activities. As in the school, overall gender differences in computer use within the home are small. In a 1994 survey, for example, 53 percent of all parents reporting use of a home computer by one or more children indicated that the most frequent user was a boy, while 47 percent said that a girl made heaviest use of the computer. Again, however, the nature of that use differed: Girls were more likely to use a home computer for school work and for word processing, while boys were nearly twice as likely to play (non-educational) computer-based games. A modest amount of research has attempted to identify factors that might account for gender-specific differences in the appeal and effectiveness of certain types of programs and of various environments and contexts for computer use.

The differential use of word processing software may well be related to other gender-specific differences in linguistic behavior, and gender-related social factors (aggressive contention for computer resources by boys in certain school environments, for example, which may intimidate their female classmates) may account for the lesser participation of girls in certain forms of unstructured, elective computer-based activities.

There is also some evidence that girls and boys engaging in computer-related learning activities may differ in their relative responses to cooperative, competitive, or individualistic reward structures. Much remains to be learned, however, about the technology-related proclivities and usage patterns of male and female students of various ages. Although neither boys nor girls would appear to suffer a clear disadvantage in the overall use of computers, the differential usage patterns observed both at school and within the home raise the question of whether further research might lead to software, content, and user environments that more effectively serve the needs of both. Available evidence suggests that educational technologies may be even more valuable to low-achieving students than to their higher-achieving peers.

Educationally disadvantaged students in another computer-based instruction program recorded a 90 percent average performance improvement in mathematics -- far higher than the gains typically realized by high-achieving students. In spite of the potential value of educational technology for low-achieving students, however, such students would appear to have less in-school access to computers than higher achievers, particularly at the high school level.

In the 1992 IEA Computers in Education survey, for example, 11th grade students whose grades fell in the bottom 32 percent of the sample reported using school computers for an average of 22 percent fewer hours than the 19 percent whose grades were highest. Another way in which underperforming students may be disadvantaged with respect to their higher-achieving classmates is in the different types of computer-based learning activities to which they are exposed.

While high achievers may be allowed to use computers in the performance of relatively complex, "authentic" tasks involving the acquisition and integration of a wide range of factual and procedural knowledge, low-achieving students are more likely to be assigned extensive drill and practice on isolated basic skills presumably on the assumption that remediation in these areas is a prerequisite to activities requiring higher-level thinking and problem-solving skills.

Technology may present special challenges to students with learning disabilities, behavioral disorders, emotional problems, or physical disabilities, but may also provide them with unique opportunities for more effective learning. In the case of such students, equal access may not imply equitable access; special measures must sometimes be taken to ensure that they are afforded the maximum possible benefit from the use of educational technology. Fortunately, technology itself may often prove instrumental in providing such special assistance. Children with certain mobility or sensory impairments, for example, may be able to use single-finger devices, joysticks, mouthsticks, or other specialized hardware to provide input to the computer.

Students unable to enter data on a conventional keyboard may be able to achieve the same effect through the use of "eye gaze" technology, or by using a "single switch" device together with special keyboard scanning software to select first a row, then a column, from a "virtual keyboard" depicted on the monitor. Those who are unable to use a mouse may be able to employ an alternative device together with a specialized screen display to emulate conventional point-and-click operations.

Shorthand (based on either the standard Gregg system or the expansion of user-defined abbreviations) or interactive word prediction software may be used to reduce the number of keystrokes required for keyboard input. Alternatively, Morse code interpretation software can be used to support the input of arbitrary characters using a single-switch device, or speech recognition algorithms may be used to provide voice recognition capabilities within certain educational applications. Assistive output technologies for students with disabilities include magnification programs for low-vision students and systems that use voice synthesis technology to read out screen information or the contents of printed documents to blind students.

The latter technology may also be incorporated in "augmentative communication systems" that allow non-speaking students to converse using digitally synthesized speech. Both local- and wide-area networks may be used to permit students with various forms of mobility limitations or communication impairments to access and exchange information, making available valuable learning resources that might otherwise be inaccessible.

Technology also has the potential to significantly expand the educational opportunities available to children with learning disabilities—currently the largest category of students with special needs—and may prove valuable for children with emotional problems or behavioral disorders as well, though further research will be necessary to characterize the ways in which technology might best be deployed on behalf of such students.

The essential role of the federal government in insuring access to educational technologies for students with special needs arises in part from the fact that, within a typical school district, the number of students with a given disability is likely to be too small to adequately amortize the cost of researching, developing, and effectively deploying the assistive technologies that would provide appropriate educational support for those students.

In the case of less common disabilities, even the typical state is unlikely to have the resources that would be necessary to independently provide the necessary support. Federal funding should thus be provided for research on the use of technology to support learning by students with various forms of disabilities, for the development of assistive hardware and software for use in the school, and for professional training in the use of such technologies.

5

E-learning Approaches

The rapid expansion of the Web as a potential course delivery platform, combined with the increasing interest in lifelong learning and budget constraints, has created a significant incentive for universities to develop online programs. As the technology is now available and relatively user-friendly, those universities which do not embrace it will be left behind in the race for globalization and technological development. Universities to make the utmost use of the Web, it is essential to identify and understand the critical success factors affecting the online delivery of education. Indeed, if we continue to re-implement traditional models borrowed from classroom-based or distance education focused on passive transmission, we can expect only marginal improvements and may well simply increased the costs.

Effective Web-based learning should include not just training in the use of technology. It must be integrated with pedagogical uses of technology to bring about learning for the development of lifelong learning skills and other emerging goals of education to meet the demands of the information age. Whenever Web technology is used in educational settings, it is vital to reflect on how this affects students, faculty members, courses and institutions.

Distance learners have increased rapidly in recent years due to demand of learning and the improvement of technology that makes distance learning easier through the Web. Web-based learning is seen by many as a transformative vehicle for increasing the pace of change and reform in higher education. For these and other reasons, analysis of quality assurance in Web-based learning is an essential topic for education policy makers.

The common problem now in the higher education sector is to identify an effective model to assure quality in the delivery of Web-based learning that can fit the various stakeholders' expectations. The first stage for doing this is to identify the critical success factors that would contribute to quality assurance in Web-based learning. As the use of technology to facilitate and deliver distance learning courses has increased, new challenges have emerged for the administration, faculty, staff and students of universities developing and implementing distance learning programs.

Many faculties fear distance learning is just a means of reducing their ranks, or a means to solve budget problems. Others fear the dehumanization and alienation of students as well as loss of critical thinking and social skills. On the other hand, rather than feeling threatened, faculty should embrace distance learning as a way for more students to access their courses, resulting in a greater intellectual audience and less chance of a course being cancelled due to low enrollment.

The Web profoundly influence society in general and universities in particular. One of the consequences of this tremendous surge in online communication has been the rapid growth of technology-mediated distance learning at the higher education level. This extraordinary growth of technology-mediated distance learning in higher education has prompted several different agencies to develop principles, guidelines, or benchmarks to ensure quality distance education.

The Web is a major technological advancement reshaping not only our society but also that of universities worldwide. In the light of this, universities have to capitalize on the Web for both teaching and learning, and one progressive development of this is the use of Web-based learning in distance education settings.

The benchmarks for quality assurance of Web-based learning were considered important and in general the participated institutions strove to incorporate them into their policies, practices and procedures. At the same time, there were few benchmarks that did not enjoy consensus among the academic members and in some instances were not even considered mandatory to ensure quality for Web-based learning.

In order to have an effective quality assurance model for Web-based learning, it will need to conduct study on student's perception on this issue and incorporate the results with the perception of academic staff to form a more complete picture of the whole quality assurance model. Each quality assurance system needs to be careful in analyzing the situation of the specific institution. It needs to be very flexible in its approach, and the combination of process and technology needs to be carefully considered, as unintended consequences in one area can originate from a bad choice in another. It may be worth noting that a firm adherence to an explicit view of what constitutes good Web-based learning, and an explicit view of issues of change and culture will furthermore influence the specific approach taken in assuring the quality Web-based learning.

Multimedia Learning Opportunities

For education, broadband access means the elimination of time and distance from the learning equation. Broadband carries with it powerful multimedia learning opportunities, the full interactivity of instructional content, and the quality and speed of communications. Broadband access today is 50 to several hundred times more powerful than its precursors. Broadband access tomorrow holds even greater promise. The promise of widely available, high quality web-based education is made possible by technological and communications trends that could lead to important educational applications over the next two to three years.

The first trend is toward greater broad-band access and better data packet handling capabilities resulting from the new "Internet2" programme. For learners this will mean a richer delivery of content than today's delivery of simple text. Tomorrow, higher "bandwidth" will enable richer interactive environments. The second trend is that of pervasive computing, in which computing, connectivity, and communications technologies connect small, multipurpose devices, linking them by wireless technologies. It is much cheaper to build cellular relay stations than lay miles of cable. Wireless solutions may enable underdeveloped and remote areas to quickly take advantage of the Web via wireless phones, two-way pagers, and hand-held devices. The third trend is digital convergence: merging the capabilities of telephone, radio, television, and other interactive devices.

The ubiquitous infrastructure of television will be significantly enhanced by conversion to digital transmission, which has been mandated by the Federal Communications Commission (FCC). Through this increased capability, stations can offer dramatically enhanced programming by 'datacasting' a wealth of supplemental information to accompany the regular broadcast. This may include course materials, software, and reference guides delivered via text, video, or audio formats. Direct satellite connections to the home offer another pathway for rich content. The fourth trend accelerating the pace of educational technology advances is the establishment of technical standards for content development and sharing. Groups involved in developing learning standards are working together under the umbrella of the federal Advanced Distributed Learning (ADL) initiative. Led by the US Department of Defense, with the cooperation of other federal agencies, academia, the private sector, and the technology industry. The influence of this initiative will reach far beyond the military, as have past initiatives including the development of the Internet.

Similarly, the Schools Interoperability Framework (SIF) is an industry initiative to develop an open specification to ensure that K-12 instructional and administrative software applications can work together. Close to 100 hardware and software companies and school districts are involved in this effort. Their objective is to "revolutionize" the management and accessibility of data within schools and school districts, enabling diverse applications to interact and share data efficiently, reliably, and securely, regardless of platform. Adopting standards such as these makes sharing of content and collaborative design more feasible. The fifth trend is the emergence of 'adaptive technology' technology that combines speech recognition, gesture recognition, text-to-speech conversion, language translation, and sensory immersion to change the very substance of network-enhanced human communication.

A final trend is the dramatic drop in the unit cost of broad-band. Bandwidth will decrease in cost and increase in power more rapidly than the advances in chip technology described by Moore's law. Ubiquitous Internet access can become a viable option for all, rather than a privileged few. These are promising trends. But to benefit fully from these trends, learners must have affordable, easy access to the computing power necessary to bring these resources to the desktop, the laptop, or the appropriate Internet-enabled handheld-or even wearable-device.

A number of surveys tracking the growth of computer connections in homes and schools provide a picture of what the U.S. Department of Commerce calls a growing trend toward 'digital inclusion.' But digital inclusion must work wherever the learner and learning opportunities come together-at home, at school, and on the college campus. In the last two years Internet access in households has grown dramatically. In just a year and a half the share of households with Internet access doubled, rising from 26.2 percent to 41.5 percent. Rural households are catching up. The data show a 75 percent increase in rural household access over this 18 month period, so that today 38.9 percent of rural households have Internet access. Broadband penetration is still greater in central cities (12.2 percent) and urban areas (11.8 percent) than in rural areas (7.3 percent). The national average for households with broadband access is 10.7 percent.

Home access is important for students doing research, taking online courses, and communicating with teachers and other learners. For parents, online access means new kinds of communication with their children's schools, with their children's teachers, and with other parents. For all households, Internet access is another way to connect with their communities and government services. Home access helps to advance economic opportunities: low-income users were the most likely to display using the Internet to look for jobs. Those learners without Internet access at home rely on schools, libraries, and other public places to provide this access. For households with incomes below $40,000, students are more likely to have Internet access at school.

For many economically disadvantaged and minority group youngsters, a computer at school or in the library after school is the only link to the wide world of the Internet. Educational institutions are struggling to provide students with Internet access, and great strides have been made in bringing schools, libraries, and postsecondary institutions online. But here again, there are gaps. The E-rate has been a major factor in providing school and library access. Enacted as a part of the Universal Service Program of the Telecommunications Act of 1996, the E-rate program provides discounts to public and private schools, libraries, and consortia on the costs of telecommunications services, Internet access, and internal networking. However, E-rate discounts do not reach places where many others could benefit from the learning opportunities of the Internet-from daycare centers to senior centers, and from adult literacy programs and community centers to museums, and other venues for both formal and informal learning.

The recent growth in Internet connectivity has been dramatic. School connectivity has grown from 65 percent in 1996 to 95 percent in 1999. But what counts most for instructional purposes is classroom connectivity, providing student access to Internet connections where they learn-in the classroom. Classroom connectivity has soared from 14 percent in 1996 to 63 percent in 1999. Classroom access is still greater for the wealthy. Wealthy school classroom access almost doubles that of poor schools. And per computer access is no better: schools with the highest percentage of students in poverty average 16 students per Internet-linked computer. For wealthy schools the ratio is 7 students per computer, while the national average is 9 to 1. Poor schools need a significant investment to reach the ratio of 4 students per classroom computer considered a minimum level of access for effective use.

Postsecondary education institutions are also rapidly expanding student access to the Internet. Yet, there are institutional disparities. For example, 58 percent of all postsecondary students own their own computer. This figure varies from a high of 79 percent of students at private universities, to 34 percent of those attending private two-year institutions, and 39.6 percent of those attending public two-year institutions. The lower figure for community colleges is particularly troubling because community colleges-with their tradition of low tuition, flexible programming, open door admissions, and customized services-enroll proportionately larger percentages of the postsecondary student population, and larger percentages of minority students.

One in five Americans aged 16 and over has a disability of some kind. As our population ages, the number of learners with vision, hearing, and physical limitations will continue to grow. The Internet is a double-edged sword for these learners-it can be a gateway to new opportunities, or a barrier that challenges them even further. Among Americans of all ages, nearly 60 percent of those with a disability have never used a personal computer, compared with 25 percent of those without a disability. Among those with a disability, people who have impaired vision and problems with manual dexterity have even lower rates of Internet access and are less likely to use a computer regularly than those with hearing and mobility problems.

Students with disabilities comprise 11 percent of preK-12 and 7.2 percent of beginning postsecondary students. Current laws mandate that recipients of federal funds cannot discriminate on the basis of disability. These laws have been extended to ban discrimination by any state or local government under the Americans with Disabilities Act. Educational institutions receiving federal funds must offer equitable access to technology for all students. With the advent of adaptive technology, equity of access for disabled students is possible. Speech synthesizers and screen access software allow the computer to speak whatever text appears on its monitor, facilitating use for blind users. Audio components and simulcasts can be accompanied by real-time captioning. But not all sites and not all distance-learning programs provide these capabilities.

Center for Applied Special Technology (CAST)

Currently, there are basic design and development guidelines that are widely available and accepted by industry and consumers, through the Web Accessibility Initiative of the World Wide Web Consortium. As a support for Web site developers, the Center for Applied

Special Technology (CAST) created Bobby, a Web-based tool that analyzes Web pages for their accessibility to people with disabilities. CAST offers Bobby as a free public service in order to expand opportunities for people with disabilities through the innovative uses of computer technology. CAST also maintains a database of Bobby-approved Web sites. Universal designs are those that eliminate 'gratuitous barriers' while adding functional equivalents.

They support what neuroscience and other learning research have shown us about learning—there is not one 'typical' learner, just as there is not one path to learning. Web-based learning environments can provide support and challenge through multiple means of:

— Representation (e.g., a math concept in both text and graphic modes; animated science simulations; poetry read aloud by the author; etc.)

— Expression (i.e., use of text; sound; images; video; and combinations of media as vehicles for expressive literacy through writing, illustrating, speaking, video-making, and drawing)

— Engagement to attract the easily bored or the easily distracted learner. Designing accessibility into an Internet site or a course at the beginning is far less expensive than after the fact. Designs that create barriers harm everyone, not just people with disabilities. In the final analysis, if the Internet is to raise the quality of education for some of our nation's learners, it should do so for all.

Just as the Internet was opening up the world, the members of the Havasupai Indian reservation in Arizona felt the walls closing in on them.

Living at the basin of the Grand Canyon, the Supai are isolated on all sides by high canyon walls that make even radio communications impossible. Cable, fiber, and ISDN Internet access, common in densely populated areas, are prohibitive luxuries for this remote reservation. In short, the "Information Age" gives the Supai reason to feel even more isolated. No group among them has suffered more from this isolation than the Supai children. It was bad enough that these children were left out of the revolution in web-based education. Even worse, they faced a cutoff in critical Head Start services, triggered by changes in the federal program. Head Start now requires teachers in every state to obtain an associate degree in early childhood development or a related field by 2003 and certification by 2005, or face disqualification from the program.

Center for Advanced Learning Technologies (CALT)

The Centre for Advanced Learning Technologies (CALT) is a research centre of The European Institute of Business Administration (INSEAD). Its mission is to identify/invent/explore new tendencies in the field of technology that are likely to transform radically the way people carry out management and business activities. In this context, CALT addresses the ways in which companies and individuals acquire and adopt these new ideas and put them into practice. As part of its mission, the Centre articulates standards for the next generation of management learning in schools and companies and of continuous education at the individual and organizational level. CALT is involved in the domains of Knowledge Management, Organization Learning, & E-Commerce.

CALT teaching on advanced technologies & methods for learning focuses on how virtual learning communities, experiential learning (in particular business simulation games in change management) and management of knowledge can support the learning process. CALT continuously monitors the different areas that are likely to have implications on its research work.

The primary objective of CALT is not the analysis of technological trends per se. Instead, the Center considers technology as a key enabler of the new management and business practices. The focus of CALT is therefore not so much on how these technologies are created but rather on how they can be applied to introduce radical social innovation. CALT research covers three different learning modes:

— Learning by elicitation and absorption of theories
— Learning by interacting with others
— Learning by doing.

Learning by elicitation and absorption of theories is the more traditional one and consists in presenting to the student (in lectures, in the classroom) a high level theory of the field. The students are then expected to solve problems by applying the theory to a specific context. The process underlying this approach is clearly top down. Learning by interacting with others consists for the 'students', and people in general, to acquire knowledge by interacting with others and sharing experiences. Virtual learning communities represent a typical illustration of this approach. This process is centred on the social process.

Learning by doing is a mode of learning in which the student is able to experiment, and progressively discover and/or construct (by trial and error) knowledge in a domain. Practically, the students may play a simulation, etc. The underlying process in this case is bottom-up. The different "pedagogical" methods (lectures, cases, simulation, learning communities, etc.) are positioned differently in this space of learning modes. Research on the mode of education based on Presentation and Absorption (Learning by absorbing knowledge) Traditional education methods rely to a large extent on the impregnation of the student with knowledge that is delivered in a relatively passive (and mainly theoretical) way. Examples of ways of delivering this knowledge include lectures, reading, courses delivered in a classroom, etc. CALT has therefore tried to explore and improve this pedagogical process, first by improving the presentation and interactivity of the existing materials (CALT research on multimedia case studies), then by going deeper into how the knowledge is managed (CALT research on Knowledge Management). An important part of this research is focused on how to better structure (organize, scenarize, etc.) information and knowledge to be delivered to the student.

CALT designed web-based multimedia cases which had the advantage of providing a much more practical delivery channel than CDROMs. For instance, the " Internet Challenge Interactive Case Study" was written to show students how companies could use the Internet as a new marketing & sales channel. Finally, CALT tried to systemise this experience with the design of a Web Authoring System, InteractKit. The objective was to develop and refine on an ongoing basis an authoring toolkit that enables the testing of a pedagogical methodology that is based on the logic of viewing learning experiences as a path through a series of individual "learning units". Each of these units has a number of "standard components" such as problems, hints, extra information, other responses, solutions and so on. The toolkit is currently built on standard HTML templates, but the architecture was defined so that it could evolve to take advantage of the latest technologies, such as Java or Macromedia Flash. The results of this research, although interesting, did not show sufficient benefits to justify any further efforts.

A second area of research originated from the idea that the new Internet economy would give the student (or indeed anyone) access to a huge amount of good (and not so good) quality sources of information and knowledge. The availability of these sources would transform radically the process of knowledge acquisition by the student (and the manager). The student would therefore have to dedicate more of his attention in the process of selection of relevant knowledge and in the process of aggregating it in a creative way. CALT research in the domain of knowledge management covers several dimensions such as:

— Knowledge structuring & wrapping

— Knowledge management methodology

— Knowledge delivery

Another reason for the interest of CALT in Knowledge Management is that managing knowledge efficiently (and setting up learning organizations), has become a key success factor for companies in the new economy. It is therefore important that CALT gains an in-depth understanding of an area so critical to companies. CALT, however, has focused its attention more on the management of tacit knowledge, exploring issues such as the dynamics of circulation of knowledge in virtual communities or knowledge management behaviour, rather than on the management of explicit knowledge (such as companies' documents). The research work on virtual communities and on knowledge management behaviour will be presented later.

The CALT Encyclopedia consists of a structured set of pages that reference all the Web resources related to research conducted within CALT and at INSEAD in general. Two elements in particular are addressed in this system: (1) The design of a web architecture representing information and knowledge that is able to scale well as the content of the system grows. (2) The identification of categories of sources of information & knowledge that provides a rich perspective of how knowledge and information is made available to the user.

KnowNet

The KnowNet, addresses the knowledge management needs of business entities by developing, applying, testing and evaluating an ICT-based Knowledge Tool and a set of methods that will enable the creation, retention, sharing and leveraging of knowledge assets and enhance the performance of knowledge operations and learning capabilities of business organizations.

BOPS (Back Office Performance Support)

The objective of BOPS is to propose an environment that fosters the dynamics of organizations and supports employees in improving best practices through continual learning. The approach promoted by BOPS for offering such an environment is to mingle back office processes with training, and to embed 'strategic analysis of business performance and customer satisfaction' in training management.

ONTO-Logging

The ONTO-Logging aims to develop a next generation distributed Knowledge Management system, able to support different independent ontology and knowledge bases and provide the basis for transparent inter-operability and knowledge exchange. Some lines of action:

— Developing an ontology formalisation distributed system.

— Developing and incorporating metrics, which would allow quantification of the relative success and merit of competing ontology.

— Incorporating recent developments in related fields, like intelligent category extraction from users' search activities or via intelligent agents, and authority/ directory convergent partition of knowledge creators.

Proposed CALT role:

— "User modelling issues in the context of Knowledge Management", ONTO-LOGGING user modelling tools, etc.

Research on Learning Communities (Learning by interacting with others) Exploiting the social dimension (and in particular interaction between people) to support knowledge dissemination and acquisition has been an important subject of interest for CALT for a long time.

For instance, before the advent of the web, pre-CALT members were using Lotus Notes as a way of supporting the learning process (by improving student to professor and student to student communication) inside communities of managers (LEAPNET). Then, acknowledging all the advantages of web-related technology, CALT decided to focus a lot of attention on web-based collaborative systems. These systems were used to enhance the INSEAD MBA and Executive programmes with the objective of facilitating the communication (anytime, anyplace) among the students, and between students and professors. This experience was later extended with virtual community external system is used to facilitate the dissemination of knowledge among groups of managers (such as STC and ABN AMRO). Finally, CALT also participated in the design of more sophisticated virtual community platforms (WCSN) before working on the design of its own platform (Alpha).

STC (Swedish Trade Council Communities)

Design and validate an innovative approach to Internet-based learning for a community of geographically distributed managers. It addresses specifically the needs of the community of Swedish managers working in SMEs and coordinated by the Swedish Trade Council (STC).The STC aims at identifying key shifts in the valorization process associated with the transition to the "new economy". More specifically, the main objective of the STC is to identify the changing parameters of value creation which prioritize the intangible assets of corporations, such as knowledge and the capacity to adjust to a changing economic ecology.

WCSN (World Class Standard Network)

The mission of WCSN was to create an electronic community of business people interested in exchanging best business practices. One important output of the design of a virtual community platform used for facilitating the interaction of professional organizations. CALT role: Mediation in virtual communities according to a CSCW, a CMC (Computer-Mediated Communication) and an agent perspective. Utilisation of a computer-supported platform for the work of a distributed consortium.

This is the virtual learning community platform that is being developed by CALT. This platform, developed using Lotus Notes Domino technology, relies on structuring a "community space" based on the ICDT model (ICDT: Information, Communication, Distribution & Transaction). Research on Learning through Action (Learning by doing) An active, highly cognitive and situated learning environment in which the student is able to learn by experimenting (trial/error) is an approach which has received a lot of attention from CALT. In fact, we can consider that this is the area in which CALT has some unique expertise. More specifically, this expertise consists in the design and the use of computer simulation games for teaching change management and organizational learning. SAM (Simulation And Multimedia) was the first (Delta programme) conducted by future CALT researchers (CALT did not exist at this time) following the learning by experimenting approach. The objective of the SAM was to define a framework for simulations for learning. However, the work that laid the foundation of the vision of CALT in experimental learning was the paper "Business Navigator".

Subsequently, a first implementation of this vision was the EIS change management computer simulation game. This simulation, which has gained considerable success, is now used by some of the most important business schools (Harvard, Wharton, etc.). Another area, which can be considered as related to learning through action, consists of entrepreneurship (such as the CyberEntrepreneurship MBA course) research which will be presented later.

EIS simulation (change management simulation software)

EIS is a computer-based multimedia business simulation involving the implementation of organizational change. During the simulation, participants can develop and implement change strategies, select among many different tactics to meet their goal and incrementally change the attitude of the EuroComm managers, influencing their willingness to adopt the proposed innovation. In the "EIS Simulation", participants working in groups are challenged to introduce an innovation in a division of the EuroComm Corporation. They have up to 6 months of (simulated) time to convince as many of the 22 members of the division's management team as possible to adopt an EIS (Executive Information System). This simulation relies on change management models that follow the four phases: awareness, interest, trial, and adoption. In addition, this simulation incorporates social network theories and teaches the importance of social factors for the adoption of change. Other related/derived details:

— Online Marketing Simulation with Brands (managing brand adoption by the market)

— Building and Managing sustainable relationship
— RAP

RAP (Reengineering Airline Critical Processes)

The aim of the RAP subjects is to enable airlines to efficiently and safely redesign their Flight Operations business processes. Most significant CALT contribution: FOCS Airline Critical Change Simulation, which is a (Java) adaptation of the EIS simulation for the airline industry. Holistic (next generation) approaches to Learning: agent-enhanced social virtual worlds Research in this domain represents the unifying work of CALT and to some extent the natural evolution of the vision that was introduced in the Business Navigator. CALT research has shown that a pedagogical process has to rely on three main learning modes to be really effective:

— Learning by elicitation and absorption of theories (traditional mode of education)
— Learning by interacting with others (virtual learning community work)
— Learning by doing.

In fact, many pedagogical processes include these three modes even if one of them is predominant. For instance, a business simulation session such as the EIS simulation does not only consist in running software. The context of this simulation is generally introduced at the beginning by a lecture. At the end of the session, the results are analysed in the classroom: the idea is to elicitate and generalise (theoretic) the knowledge generated in the simulation. In addition, the simulation is usually not played individually by each student, but by teams of (4 to 5) students. The idea is that the interaction between the students in groups will facilitate the creation and the sharing of knowledge. As a long-term perspective, CALT considers that the systems which will implement these ideas the most effectively will be agent-enhanced highly cognitive social virtual spaces since they provide in a powerful way the possibility to:

— present highly structured knowledge (such as theories) in a straightforward way (by wrapping it into highly cognitive entities)

— facilitate interaction between people (these spaces are multi-user and also agents can provide social mediation mechanisms)

— create active mock-ups of real systems in which the student is able to experiment.

In order to achieve this vision, CALT has worked on more basic (generic) research (such as research on technologies). This criticise includes:

— Research on Virtual reality (experimentation with active world technology, and application to the virtual university and to e-commerce)

— Research on agent technologies (AWJavaBot, agent psychology & personality, user modelling, etc.)

— Research on knowledge and collaborative platforms (community portals, etc.).

— Research on change management

— More directly this holistic approach are KInCA and EdComNet.

Xerox KinCA (Knowledge Intelligent Conversational Agent)

A new approach to enable managers at every level or function in an organization to effectively learn, understand, and then apply Knowledge Management concepts and techniques. The approach is based on the concept of a "Personal KM Agenda" and consists in providing managers access to an interactive, web-based system, helping them to identify knowledge management opportunities in their jobs, to achieve their targets and objectives, and in their business environment. Manager(s) are hence helped to understand better the key principles of Knowledge Management, to develop stepwise their own Personal KM Agenda, and then act upon it.

EDCOMNET

EDCOMNET is an educational communal net, a virtual learning community platform for adult citizens to be set up in many regions of the European Union and associated countries like Israel. The net will act as a portal stimulating the active learning of social skills by the citizen, thus enhancing the social integration of individuals within urban communities. It will empower the individual citizen to be a self-reliant part of society, fostering creativity and autonomous opinion forming as well as decision-making.

Virtual Reality

CALT has conducted quite a lot of research in the use of the Active Worlds multi-user 3D virtual reality technology in 2 main areas:

The Virtual University (or how to use 3D multi-user virtual worlds to enhance the Virtual University). An example of a prototype: the virtual INSEAD Days, which was an online (3D version) of the INSEAD event. In this space, the visitors were able to see a VR presentation of INSEAD activities such as the research centres and the executive programmes available, and were also able to access the videos of the presentation of the INSEAD days event.

Research on Electronic Commerce (or how to use 3D multi-user virtual worlds as a new space to conduct commercial activities). For instance, the T-IBM explored the idea of a 3D virtual shop, including issues such as shop representation (realistic or not), interaction modes (how does a sales person behave in such an environment), and the use of bots.

CALT research on agent technology originated from the desire to provide the 'Business Navigator', with stronger technical and conceptual foundations. For instance, in the EIS business simulation (an implementation of the business navigator), the operating of the game relies on the modelling and simulation of people in an organization. The idea is that the learning will take place through the interaction with those artificial characters. Agent technology research was useful first for identifying technologies and a technical approach for implementing the next generation of the Business Navigator model (more flexible, modular, multi-user, etc.).

Other research was useful to clarify the internal structure of the artificial characters, and in particular to make the connection with research in the fields of psychology. For instance, the traits of the Big Five Factor

Model of personality (openness to experience, agreeableness, conscientiousness, extroversion, emotional stability) may provide some better scientific foundation to the "traits" of personality chosen for the EIS agents (openness to innovation, helpfulness, competence, dynamism). Finally, advanced user modelling (a sub-area of agent research) may prove to be very useful in many of the fields in which CALT is conducting research: student model in education, personalisation in knowledge & information management, better relationship management in the domain of e-commerce.

AWSdkJava

This is a Java-based library for designing bots operating in the Active Worlds 3D multi-user environment. Active World AWSDKJava is a Java and JavaScript encapsulation of the Active World SDK toolkit. AWSDKJava consists in the development of a set of abstract Java Classes which allow one to model using Java, and, at a relatively high level of abstraction, bots (agents) for the active world environment. JavaScript, which has been wrapped into the library, can be used as an application/glue/macro language. Domain specific work: e-commerce and entrepreneurship, etc. Different domains, which represent a special interest for CALT, represent perfect areas of application for experimenting and deploying the knowledge generated by CALT in education. We have already mentioned the domains of knowledge management and change management. Another important domain is entrepreneurship, in particular for an application in e-commerce.

ECAMP

This ECAMP aims to develop innovative and dynamically networked virtual environments called "corporation modelling platforms." These "Merchant Corporations" will draw their revenue by obtaining memberships and interfacing with existent web affiliate programmes. The created system will provide interested parties with the platforms, technological resources, business guidance, and real-world environments necessary for the building, business development, maintenance and growth of their own on-line merchant corporations. These real-world market business development environments will lead to unique business-led consensus e-commerce model building between all the participants.

CyberEntrepreneurship

The CyberEntrepreneurship elective course aims to help MBA participants who are seriously considering starting their own E-Business to acquire the necessary skills and understand the management implications of Internet start-ups. In parallel to the whole process, the CyberEntrepreneurship website is the reference platform that hosts the knowledge base as well as the on-line discussion forum.

CALT is in the process of analysing complex e-commerce strategies in financial markets. It is currently advancing research in the domain of e-commerce in the fields of treasury and fixed income markets, customer relationship management, and e-procurement. A central preoccupation of this research is to identify knowledge and change management processes that are increasingly becoming critical for competitive success in the "new economy".

Professional Development and Technology

We must train the nation's teachers-and the principals and administrators who lead them- or investments in high tech educational resources will be wasted. Teachers are the key to effective use of web-based tools and applications, but first they must become skilled at using them.It is the teacher, after all, who guides instruction and shapes the instructional context in which the Internet and other technologies are used. It is a teacher's skill at this, more than any other factor, that determines the degree to which students learn from their Internet experiences. Teachers must be comfortable with technology, able to apply it appropriately, and conversant with new technological tools, resources, and approaches. If all the pieces are put into place, teachers should find that they are empowered to advance their own professional skills through these tools as well. This is how it should be. The far from this ideal today.

— Almost two-thirds of all teachers feel they are not at all prepared or only somewhat prepared to use technology in their teaching. For some teachers, especially those who are older and were educated "B.C."-before computers—technology seems a foreign element, far from necessary to them in their teaching. They grew up without computers, were educated without them, and have taught their entire careers without them.

— Almost two-thirds of teachers (65 percent) had never used a computer before being introduced to one in the classroom. These teachers need basic technology training, especially those who are receiving computers and using the Internet in their classrooms for the first time.

Basic technology training alone is not sufficient. A recent survey by the National Education Association (NEA) found that most teachers have some facility using computers. Ninety-four percent of NEA members, and 99 percent of those under, are able to surf the Web. However, familiarity does not equal proficiency. Most do not know how to apply these skills in classroom instruction.

Common sense holds that technology training for teachers will no longer be an issue if it can wait long enough for a new generation of younger teachers, raised on technology, to enter the profession. However, this is one common sense belief that simply does not hold up to close examination. Another recent survey found that young teachers' self-assessment of their ability to teach with technology was no different than that of their older colleagues. While younger teachers may have basic technology skills (e.g., the ability to use word-processing software, spread-sheets, presentation software, and Internet browsers) they realize that they, like their older colleagues, do not know how to apply these skills to teaching. The ability to use technology for non-instructional purposes does not necessarily translate into either the will or the capability to use technology to support student learning. Although they are not technophobes, these new teachers lack a clear conception of effective classroom uses of technology in their subject area.

Professional development is the critical ingredient for effective use of technology in the classroom. Seventy percent of educators polled regarding technology in instruction put professional development at the top of their list of technology challenges. They said what is needed is both the initial training for those just beginning to use technology and continuing education to support the growth of innovators. Three consecutive years of surveys in higher education showed the same thing: institutions ranked their greatest technological challenge as 'assisting faculty to integrate information technology into instruction.' Professional development is often called 'training,' but the term implies much more than just building basic technology skills. It means developing a vision built on the understanding that technology is a tool that can offer solutions to longstanding teaching and learning problems. It is more than knowing how to automate past practices. It is the growing understanding that comes with confidence to 'think with technology' in order to approach old problems in new ways.

Change is necessary on two fronts: in the preparatory (pre-service) education of teacher candidates, and in the continuing (in-service) education of those already in the education profession. Both groups need assistance and support in using the best tools technology offers to meet teaching goals and challenges. Some might wonder why past investments in technology training for K-12 classroom teachers have not had a greater impact. The reality is that the money spent on teacher training with technology is just a fraction of what is needed. In 1995, the Office of Technology Assessment sounded the alarm in a teachers and technology, urging that schools and districts devote at least 30 percent of technology budgets to teacher training and support.

The training teachers do receive is usually too little, too basic, and too generic to help them develop real facility in teaching with technology. Ninety-six percent, the most common training they received was on basic computer skills. Another national survey of public school teachers found that while most (78 percent) received some technology-related professional development in the 1998-99 school year, the training was basic and brief, lasting only 1 to 5 hours for 39 percent of teachers, and just 6 to 10 hours for another 19 percent of those trained. Teachers need more than a quick course in basic computer operations. They need guidance in using the best tools in the best ways to support the best kinds of instruction. And they need something more. They need time. When asked in a National Center for Education Statistics (NCES) survey to name the greatest barrier to their use of computers and the Internet in the classroom, most teachers (82 percent) cited lack of 'release time' (time outside classroom) to 'learn, practice, or plan ways to use computers or the Internet.' This factor outweighed their concern about too few computers (78 percent) or lack of time in the schedule for students to use computers in class (80 percent).

The overwhelming majority (90 percent) of all corporate and government training occurs on paid time. In public schools, teachers, just over a third (39 percent) of their professional development occurs on paid time. Professionals in other fields expect to be trained regularly. Motorola, long the standard for industry, provides every employee with at least 40 hours of training each year. Equally significant, professionals in other fields are provided with follow-up support needed for that training to take root-including immediate access to the hardware and software on which they are trained, Internet connections, and easy access to support personnel and follow-up skill building. Many teachers have been trained on systems not installed in their schools. Many do not receive follow-up support. Only 67 percent of teachers in the NCES, that follow-up or advanced training was available to them.

Most business professionals have personal computers provided to them at work and some industries give employees computers they can use at home (such as Ford Motor Company). But K-12 teachers rarely are provided these benefits. Although 62 percent of teachers have access to a desktop computer while at school, only 28 percent have the ability to borrow one for occasional use at home. Most teachers are not rewarded or reimbursed for the time they spend in training. Just as some teachers spend their own money for classroom supplies, some teachers pay for their own preparation. Many take classes on their own time and pay their own tuition or fees.

Technology training rarely translates directly into higher pay for teachers. In fact, a growing concern among schools is the lure of higher salaries offered in the private sector to teachers and administrators who do exhibit strong technical proficiencies or a desire to develop these. In sum, the message to teachers is a mixed one-expect to teach with technology, but will not help do so. There are other ways K-12 teachers are treated differently than professionals in business and industry. Intellectual support, as well as technical support, is rare. A recent study in USA found that only 13 percent of the nation's teachers work in what could be defined as a "high quality technology-supported environment." For most teachers, technical assistance is limited, if available at all. Another study measuring technology support for district technology coordinators in 27 states found that it took from 14 hours to more than 7 days to fix a technology problem in a school or classroom. The average response time was more than two days. While this would be unthinkable in most businesses, imagine what it means to a teacher who has developed a lesson around the Internet, only to discover that the whole class is disrupted for an unknown period of time. It is simply intolerable.

Fewer than 20 percent of all schools have a full-time technology coordinator. In most cases, technology coordinators are charged with training teachers and helping them integrate technology in their classes. In reality, they spend most of their time on technical support. On a weekly basis, full-time technology coordinators spend only 3 to 4 minutes per teacher assisting with technology integration. Part-time technology coordinators perform this kind of assistance only 1 to 2 minutes per week.

But the larger problem is one that is endemic to the K-12 teaching profession the isolation of the classroom teacher. Most of a teacher's day is spent separated from colleagues, with little time or opportunity to share in the give-and-take of problem-solving common in most office or work environments. For elementary and secondary education teachers, planning periods are few and often occur in isolation.

Group meetings are focused on issues that affect the institution as a whole or the department or grade level, but they don't offer the opportunity to express the concerns or share the wisdom of the individual teacher. Teachers rarely have the opportunity to work with others to share their questions, concerns, and successes. Most are isolated and, unlike other professionals, have little access to the resources they need to stay up to date in their fields. In contrast, teachers in other countries are provided far more paid time for planning: Japanese teachers spend about 40 percent of their paid time on professional development and collaboration compared with about 14 percent for their American counterparts.

Net-based Teacher Training

Fortunately, the Internet is making it possible to connect teachers to each other, giving opportunities for mentoring, collaboration, and formal and informal online learning. Traditional one-size-fits-all professional development workshops are giving way to a new, more teacher-centered, self-directed model of teacher learning. Through the Internet, teachers have access to high quality online professional development opportunities beyond what the local school or district is able to offer. Online courses and seminars, follow-up consultations and mentoring, and collaborations with experts and peers can take place without the expense and classroom disruption created by repeated absences for face-to-face meetings. And, in working in online environments, teachers obtain a collateral benefit: they learn important technological skills. A supportive social structure is one of the key elements for successful online learning.

But unless new teachers enter the classroom ready to teach with technology, never catch up. If teacher education programs do not address this issue head on, lose the opportunity to get it right with a whole generation of new teachers—and the students they teach. The size of the challenge is staggering. There are three million teachers in K-12 schools today. In the next decade alone, must recruit and train two million more new teachers just to replace retirees and to meet expected growth in enrollment. Put another way, one-third of today's teachers have 20 years or more of teaching experience; two-thirds are in mid-career. As the teacher population ages, moving into retirement, 54.2 million students are expected in K-12 education by 2009, up 2 million from 1997. A fundamental change in recruiting new teachers, and giving them the tools to do a more effective job.

In the midst of this crisis, teacher education has yet to come to grips with the immediacy preparing a new generation of teachers to use technology as a teaching tool. Teacher education programs tend to be profit centers for colleges and universities—they pay for themselves with strong and steady student enrollments and have few of the expenses associated with equipping science laboratories, engineering, or other professional programs. Expect a college of education to provide, at a minimum, a high tech teaching laboratory that models instructional use of technology for the entire campus. Expect college and university presidents and trustees to make the necessary adjustments. Yet this rarely the case. As noted in a 1999, on teacher preparation by the CEO Forum on Education and Technology, many teacher education programs "receive less attention than the higher status professional programs in the university such as law, engineering, business, and medicine... (Furthermore, they) have a less affluent alumni base, meaning that large gifts from donors (as well as industry) are harder to obtain."

Chief technology officers (CTOs) of higher education institutions to compare the information technology components in departmental programs across their campuses. Overall, the CTOs ranked their campus' education programs eighth of 10 in use of the Internet and Web resources, seventh the use of technology for instruction, and tied for sixth in preparing their students with technology skills needed over the next decade. Most teacher education institutions now offer what is called 'the course' in information technology. But providing a stand-alone course about technology is not the same as ensuring that courses in teaching methods integrate technology as a way of building understanding or assessing learning.

Faculty in teacher education programs, many of whom were educated and taught in schools before computers were a part of the educational landscape, are not comfortable or skilled in teaching with technology. This problem extends across the college experience of teacher candidates. If they do not see their faculty use technology in the courses they take outside their teaching major (whether in science, literature, math, and history departments), tomorrow's teachers will not have a full understanding of how technology advances understanding in each academic area. It is clear that the need for professional development in technology among higher education faculty parallels that required by educators in K-12 schools. It is also clear that our campus higher education leaders have a deep responsibility for modernizing their colleges of education and incorporating a priority on teaching and learning with technology.

There are, of course, exceptions and promising new practices that suggest change is coming. These include leadership initiatives undertaken by Congress, the states, universities, professional organizations, and the business community.

— The Higher Education Act Amendments, passed by Congress and signed into law in 1998, provide a gateway for technology integration in college teacher education programs. A major objective within the section of the Act focusing on enhancing the quality of teaching in the US is to "hold institutions of higher education accountable for preparing teachers who have the necessary teaching skills and are highly competent in the academic content areas in which the teachers plan to teach, such as mathematics, science, English, foreign languages, history, economics, art, civics, Government, and geography, including training in the effective uses of technology in the classroom.

— An increasing number of states now require teachers to demonstrate proficiency in technology as one component for receiving certification. However, only 4 require technology training for re-certification.

— The National Council for Accreditation of Teacher Education (NCATE), the largest accreditation association of schools, colleges, and departments of education, has made technology an area of accreditation focus. While this is an important leadership message, only 38 percent of the nation's 1,300 teacher preparation programs are accredited by NCATE. Many schools, colleges, and departments of education choose not to apply to NCATE; others have been unable to meet its standards.

— The CEO Forum developed a special STaR (School Technology and Readiness) self-assessment tool for schools and colleges of education.

At the urging of Education Secretary Richard Riley and President Bill Clinton in May 2000, 243 institutions have 'taken the pledge' to conduct self-assessments as a first step for turning their programs around and moving from 'early tech' or 'developing tech' to 'advanced tech' or 'target tech.' New funding initiatives have also led to promising practices. The National Science Foundation-supported "Inquiry Learning Forum" is a model of using the Internet for teacher growth. The US Department of Education's Preparing Tomorrow's Teachers with Technology (PT3) Program, begun in 1999, is bringing new ideas, new collaborations, and new models to teacher education. The PT3 program has made $150 million in federal funding available to 352 teacher preparation institutions to help them develop capacity, implement new programs, and provide innovative catalysts for broader change. These programmes are just beginning to take root, but they offer promise for the future.

Many teachers lack connections to colleagues with similar interests, responsibilities, and challenges. Imagine being the only physics teacher in a school. Under normal school conditions, could go for weeks or months without contact with another physics teacher. Sharing teaching strategies and content with colleagues or even getting outside advice or constructive criticism-this just isn't a part of the world.

Four hundred teachers in Indiana are turning to a new online environment, the Inquiry Learning Forum (ILF), to establish connections with other teachers, as well as to expand access to classroom resources. They are acting to end the isolation of teachers. The ILF is a video centered, web-based learning forum designed to support an online community of current and future science and mathematics teachers interested in "inquiry-based" teaching. The ILF provides opportunities to virtually "visit" classrooms across Indiana. It features a large video library of classroom episodes and enables teachers to discuss, annotate, reflect upon, and replay these classroom episodes as needed.

The home screen of the ILF, shown here, displays which of the classrooms are available through the Visit

Classrooms space. When ILF members select a specific classroom lesson, they can view a videotape of that lesson being implemented. They can also review a lesson overview, reflective commentary, descriptions of teaching activity, lesson plans, students' examples, and connections with both state and national standards. In addition to the Visit Classroom spaces, there are also 5 other virtual spaces designed to support professional development needs. The ILF Office is the place where new participants can secure a password, get help with technology, or make suggestions. The Workroom provides groups with an online space to form working circles, or sub-communities, that facilitate collaboration on a particular programme, product, or goal.

The Lounge hosts general conferences that are not tied to a particular classroom as well as a space for real-time chat to allow users to communicate with others. The Auditorium is the place where special events can occur. These usually involve chat discussions with a white board and resources. It also provides the opportunity for video-casting live or recorded presentations for discussion. Any member of the community can hold a workshop, experts can be brought in, or there may be simultaneous discussion of specific issues.

The Library is a place where teachers can go to access reference materials of interest, including references on teaching resource materials (software, other classroom artifacts like the graphing calculator, manipulatives, sensory probes), state and national standards, grants, applied research and theory, state initiatives, and other materials the teachers identify as relevant. Finally, Desk is the place where a teacher can store bookmarks to resources and classrooms of personal interest. Not only do teachers have the opportunity to share lesson plans, unit plans, and other resources through the ILF, they are also able to watch other teachers implement these resources in their classrooms, read the personal reflections of these teachers, and discuss what they have seen, heard, or read. Every classroom resource available in the ILF community is 'attached' to a videotaped segment of a lesson or a particular discussion thread. This enables teachers to not only find resources, but also to read or hear about how they might be used in a particular classroom.

Research and Development

Compare research in medicine and sports with research in education. In medical research, cumulative, aggregated protocols, involving practitioners and patients, together with well-coordinated and publicized clinical trials, have led to treatments that enhance the health and extend the life span of many people. Technology has been central to studying diseases, to finding new solutions that address them, and to disseminating research results to medical practitioners and the public. Increasingly, technology has empowered an educated patient population to demand the best treatments. In short, research has made it possible to enhance health. Sports research offers another example. Research employing new technologies has made it possible to enhance performance in athletics. Research on new designs and materials in golf clubs, skis, and bicycles, as well as new training feedback mechanisms (e.g., video replay), allows professional athletes and weekend sports enthusiasts to attain new levels of performance. Research using the latest technologies has made it possible to enhance athletic performance.

Educational research, focused on using long-term, longitudinal studies as well as aggregated short-term trials supported by technology, should be directed at enhancing performance in learning. Technology offers both the impetus and the opportunity to vastly improve learning performance. Without a vigorous, dynamic research base, however, will miss the opportunity to advance the state of the art and science of education. Educational research suffers from three major problems-

Not enough money is spent on educational research Educational research often does not support enhanced learning performance Educational research often is not accessible to teachers or easily translated into practice. In its 1997 landmark, the Panel on Educational Technology of the President's Committee of Advisors on Science and Technology (PCAST) recommended that "the federal government initiate a large-scale program of rigorous empirical research aimed at improving both the effectiveness and the cost-effectiveness of elementary and secondary education in the United States at a level equal to at least 0.5 percent of the nation's aggregate K-12 educational spending, or approximately $1.5 billion per year at present expenditure levels." A long way from this goal. Consider the following:

— The current budget for the office of educational research and improvement, the major research arm of the U.S. Department of Education, is $540 million. Even adding the $60 million spent by the Research, Evaluation, and Communication Division of the National Science Foundation's Education and Human Resources Directorate, best estimates suggest total spending for education research is in the $600 million range.

— The federal government invests more than $75 billion a year in research in science and technology development in military, health, aerospace, agriculture, and other areas. Added to this are equivalent industry investments. It is obvious that R & D in these fields are mature. By comparison, the learning R & D field is in its infancy.

A critical moment of discovery in the quest to "unlock the mysteries of learning." In recent National Academy of Sciences, learning sciences have made substantial progress in the past 30 years, more than most people realize. This expanding knowledge base about how learn has important implications for improving education at all levels. And it is telling us something important: what goes on in schools is far from optimal for learning.

Learning environments should be centered around knowledge, learners, social interactions, and assessment. Instead, learning environments in school often:

— Focus on the short-term recall of facts, rather than opportunities for deeper building of knowledge

— Organize around the top-down, teacher-and-textbook centred instruction, rather than the need of the individual learner

— Limit social interaction to occasional times with peers in the classroom encouraging solo study, rather than collaboration

— Allow current assessment to influence instruction in ways that may not match the goals of 21st Century learning

— Schools often use technology to mimic this pattern of a top-down, lecture or text-driven model of instruction. Similarly, used the Internet in a narrow fashion, like vast textbooks or lectures online, instead of exploring its interactive potential. Technology can support what now know to be more effective learning environments. Interactive applications linked to the Internet can provide environments better matched to support learner-centered, knowledge-centered, community-centered, and assessment-centered conditions for learning.

New technological tools and applications allow for expanded forms of communication, analysis, and expression by students and teachers. These innovations support new forms of teaching and understanding built on the early findings of learning research.

6

Assessment of Quality Education

Traditionally, the assessment of educational entities—school systems, individual schools, and teachers—has evoked strong and sometimes violent emotions from the educational community, the general public, and their legislative representatives. In spite of attempts to codify standards for the evaluation of these entities, assessment experts remain denominationalized—often religiously so. Methods of assessment based on the use of standardized tests have come under intense fire in recent years with some critics going so far as to call for their complete elimination. Those who advocate alternative methods of assessment have become increasingly outspoken in establishing exclusive rights to the legitimate assessment paradigm. However, some of the most respected advocates of alternative assessment have taken a more moderate view, warning against an "either-or" mentality. No responsible person claims that any form of assessment can appraise the totality of a student's school experience or even the entirety of the learning that is a part of that experience. However, it is possible to develop indicators to measure learning along important dimensions, closely related to the curriculum, both in standardized assessment instruments and in alternative forms of assessment.

The real issue is not whether standardized assessment or alternative assessment is the better model in every case for the evaluation of educational outcomes. Rather, the issue is choosing the most appropriate indicator variables for the specific purpose at hand, whatever that may be. Non-standardized assessment is the traditional form of assessment within classrooms. Teachers construct questions, evaluate student responses, assign and check homework, monitor projects, and informally assess student progress hundreds of times a day. These assessments may be accurate or they may be faulty, depending upon the teacher's skill as a judge of various indicators and their applicability to the question at hand.

However, unrelated factors can affect this type of assessment. For instance, research has shown that good handwriting can influence grading on essays. Student behavior and appearance can likewise prejudice assessment. On the other hand, careful attention to the information provided by student actions and products can lead to a deep and revealing understanding of students' comprehension and skill attainment. Standardized tests, whether the ubiquitous multiple choice test or other forms of standardized assessment, vary in their ability to fairly assess student knowledge, just as teacher assessments do. But current construction practices insure that standardized tests are subjected to rigorous validation criteria, reliability testing, and standardization procedures.

The tests are open to review by experts and to criticism by anyone with credible grounds from which to argue. In the past, standardized tests have proved useful in comparing, generalizing, and indicating levels of attainment based on set standards. In current practice, they serve many additional functions including the assessment of higher-order reasoning skills and academic growth over time. Non-standardized alternative assessment, has yet to demonstrate the ability to provide generalizable information for comparison purposes over time on a large-scale basis without proving more costly in time and resources than standardized testing and without itself falling prey to the "teaching to the test" syndrome so often cited as a major deleterious result of standardized testing.

The strengths of alternative assessment lie in its ability to individualize assessment, to mimic good teaching practices, and to involve teachers more deeply in the assessment process. Currently, attempts are being made to improve the generalizability and reliability of alternative assessments in order to use them for the evaluation of school and school system efficacy. Ignoring the strident voices of those who deny that effective educational practices can be examined at all, in hopes that it will be possible to reach a more useful conclusion, it must be acknowledged that the assumptions underpinning many of the evaluation schemes of the 70's and 80's were spurious. Of the doubtful assumptions, the most obvious were these two:

1) there is a right way to teach and
2) good educational practice can be identified independent of any demonstrated relationship to student learning.

Although the public bought into the first assumption, they were never convinced of the second, and rightfully so. The major indicator that distinguishes effective from ineffective educational practice is whether students learn that which is purportedly taught.

However, student achievement data have rarely been incorporated in models for teacher and school evaluation, primarily because of the difficulty of delineating teacher and school effects on student learning from demographic effects--those effects that are embodied in the individual child-life of each student, independent of formal education. Informally, however, the public, through the media, assesses the success or failure of the schools by how well students perform on standardized tests. The media uses test scores to compare one educational entity to another, and, in a comparison, someone always loses.

The teacher-made assessment which forms the bulk of student evaluation does not figure at all into the media's analysis of school success, and educators are unconvinced that group-administered tests provide an accurate indication of what a student knows or has learned under their tutelage. Therefore, educators have come to view standardized tests as the root of the public's disenchantment with the schools and the prime reason for the denigration of the teaching profession. It's no wonder there has been such an outcry against their use.

The negative perception of standardized testing as a measure of educational efficacy is, as stated above, partially a result of the way the results have been interpreted by the media and the general public. This problem is only indirectly associated with standardized testing. Possibly, with time and effort, the media can be educated as to the proper use and interpretation of the data derived from test scores. Regardless, this aspect of the debate must be relegated to the realm of societal problems rather than problems with the tests themselves.

However, the perception that standardized scores can tell us very little about anything other than the status of a given student at a given time in regard only to the items on a specific test may derive directly from the historical uses of standardized data. This criticism is understandable in light of the past, but there have been a great many changes in recent years in the development of tests, the analysis of the data they render, and the uses to which they are put. Modern standardized tests reflect a response to past criticism. Item response theory informs the construction of tests that are equivalent but non-redundant, thereby addressing the question of the score inflation that results from administering the same test, year after year.

Test makers have also proved responsive to the need to assess higher-order thinking skills, so tests that contain items requiring application, analysis, synthesis, and evaluation are now readily available. Standardized test data is ubiquitous. It is readily available, cheap, and abundant. Most often, the scale scores, percentiles, and stanines provided by those who score the tests are duly recorded by the receiving school or system, precisely as received. No further analysis is attempted. The usefulness of the data is severely limited, and so it is used for very little other than placement and, occasionally, a crude form of program evaluation that is, as critics have rightfully stated, biased by extraneous factors such as socio-economic level, past achievement, and percent of minority students. The reasons for the misuse and lack of use of standardized test data are readily discernible.

— Performing the operations necessary to analyze test data beyond the provided measures required an inordinate amount of time and expertise prior to the recent advent of powerful and inexpensive computers. It simply wasn't feasible for schools or systems or even states to proceed beyond the basic measures provided to them by the normal scoring algorithms. Merely constructing and maintaining a data base of schools, teachers, and students used to be an impossible task for all but the smallest systems. Constructing such a data base for a state was altogether unthinkable. Today, none of these obstacles are insurmountable.

— There were enormous statistical problems involved in the use of test scores for evaluative purposes. Among these were the regression to the mean and the problem of missing data. There was also the problem of delineating educational influences from the influences of extraneous factors. Now, there are statistical models that can deal effectively with all of these difficulties.

The refinement of test construction techniques, the widespread use of powerful computer technologies, and the application of sophisticated statistical methodologies in education is producing a revolution in the use of standardized test data in educational assessment, but the misuse and under-utilization of test data in the past haunts the present. Standardized test scores, when subjected to appropriate methodologies and utilized for appropriate purposes, provide rich data for educational assessment. It would be lamentable if the perspective these data can afford were obscured by arguments no longer valid.

The answer as to what is happening in any situation is dependent upon the questions asked—not just what is asked but also how it is asked. The answer will be more or less precise depending upon the means used to gather data and the extent of the data gathered on the subject of the assessment. A meaningful evaluation depends to a large degree upon the quality of the indicators utilized. By knowing the capacity of the indicators to assess the subject and the correlation between various indicators, it is possible to form inferences from one indicator to another. If the indicators are highly correlated, then it is no longer a question of which is best but which is least costly in time and/or resources.

On the other hand, a total lack of correlation between indicators indicates one of two things: they are not measuring the same things, or at least one of them is a poor measure of the subject. Here is a simple example of the concept of multiple indicators. There is a multitude of ways to determine the body fat percentage of a given person. One way is to simply derive the ratio of height to weight and apply the result to a table. If the gender of the person is known, the indicator is considerably more precise. If the circumference of the wrist is then added to the equation, the estimate is further refined. Including a skin fold measurement brings the estimate even closer to the actual body fat percentage of the subject. If the subject is weighed while immersed in a pool of water, the best possible approximation achievable without endangering the subject will be attained. The correlation between these measures can easily be determined, and if each indicator is tested against the actual percentage of body fat as determined by the most accurate means available, it is possible to estimate the error of measurement of each of the less precise means. Once each indicator is optimized within the constraints of its own format, a decision can be made as to which single measure or group of measures best addresses the problem at hand.

If the best indicator is 99.1% accurate, the second best is 97% accurate, the third best is 93% accurate, and the fourth is 86% accurate, and they are all highly correlated, the decision as to which indicator to use is a function of needed accuracy versus cost/feasibility. Absolute accuracy in any type of measurement is impossible. Disregard of cost—time, resources, impact upon our subject—is irresponsible. Responsible assessment entails careful consideration of these factors in light of the purpose of the assessment at hand. In education, the assessment of learning is generally built around the demonstration of competence in certain domains. These domains and the goals and objectives that address them are codified in curricular frameworks and course outlines.

Teachers design a course ofinstruction based upon these guidelines and, generally, even though teaching may take any of a number of forms, there is a high correlation between what is taught and the formal curriculum. It is this correlation that makes large-scale assessment possible. Indicators can be developed that measure learning along the articulated curriculum, and, because of the correlation between instruction and the stated curriculum, inferences can be drawn about the effectiveness of instructional strategies in school systems, schools, and classrooms along curricular lines. The means used to determine whether students have achieved the goals set for them range from the results of simple observation to group-administered standardized tests; from a short homework assignment to the performance and analysis of a complex laboratory experiment. Test scores, performance, and artifacts are all indicators of learning. Determining which indicators are best suited to specific purposes is the core of the assessment debate.

Advocates of alternative assessment assume that standardized tests provide a limited and shallow description of what an individual knows. In fact, multiple-choice tests cover a broad range of questions in each field surveyed, thereby providing a more detailed picture of student learning than is implied by the previous statement. Even though a student's understanding of the tasks assessed can be examined in great detail with some alternative assessment techniques, the scope of the assessment is limited by the very constraints that comprise its raison d'etre. Alternative assessment, because of time constraints and, in the case of performance assessments, the complexity of the exercises, is generally limited to only a few tasks.

The limited generalizability from task to task is consistent with research in learning and cognition that emphasizes the situation and context-specific nature of thinking". Achieving a "substantial number of tasks" in alternative assessment is often impossible, making a generalization from the performance tasks to the larger realm of the subject area being assessed problematic. As Wiggins points out, "unpiloted, one-event testing in the performance area is even more dangerous than one-shot multiple-choice testing, because multiple-choice tests have many different but related items, which makes reliability easier to get and measure".

In Britain, where an assessment system based on students' performance on "standard assessment tasks" (SATs), a series of individually administered, performance-based measures, has been piloted in the areas of English, math, and science, "it has been estimated that the SATs took two to five weeks out of the school year". In fact, the number of tasks students are expected to perform will be only about a third of the number originally proposed, and there is a possibility that multiple-choice questions will be used to further speed up the assessment. The cost of the fourth grade math portion of the National Assessment of Educational Progress (NAEP) at $150 per pupil.

George Madaus has estimates that using performance assessment in most subjects in American schools would cost between $2.5 and $3 billion annually. Despite several advantages of the broad use of performance assessment in England, its financial and personnel costs are so immense as to threaten its continuation. For his estimate, Arthur Wise used the College Entrance Examination Board's fee for Advanced Placement (AP) tests: $65 per test. His projection of costs for five tests at three grade levels comes to between $2 billion and $3 billion a year. Keep in mind that the AP tests for the most part are scored by machine. In several [European] countries it is estimated that to score essay-on-demand exam papers in four to five subject fields at ages 16+ and 18+ costs $135 per student.

To mitigate the cost of alternative assessment, the use of a sampling of students and grades in key subjects through the use of "a few exemplary assessments" as opposed to the universal testing of most students in several subjects and in several grades through many assessment items, as is normally the case with standardized testing. This trade-off places severe limitations on the uses to which the assessment results can be put. If Shepard's suggestion was implemented, the resulting assessment data would be practically useless for assessment of educational entities. As Madaus and Kellaghan tell us, "matrix sampling offers one way to reduce costs—but only at the expense of information on individual performance. It is difficult to imagine that parents will be satisfied with the assurance that 'everything is progressing nicely although we don't know exactly how your child is doing'". Furthermore, whereas deducing the progress of a cohort of students on the basis of limited data can be logically accomplished through time-honored statistical means, it cannot be done unless the information is generalizable. Discerning the effectiveness of any individual teacher, school, or program would be nearly impossible due to the inadequacy of the non-standardized data to provide generalizable information. For these reasons, unless the cost of alternative assessment can be mitigated to allow for much more wide-spread implementation, its use as a model for large-scale educational assessment is problematic, at best.

The British Educational Research Association has concluded that the validity of the Standard Assessment Tasks, a performance-based assessment system by which student achievement is assessed in Britain, may be compromised by teachers coaching their students because of the high stakes consequences of the results. Standardized tests may be compromised in the same manner. In either case, the instructional process itself is subverted when assessment results become the goal of instruction. Fresh, non-redundant, equivalent tests, regardless of the format, are the simplest means to discourage "teaching to the test." Revising standardized tests by drawing from item banks that have been constructed based on item response theory is a simple and inexpensive matter. In Tennessee and in a growing number of other states, such revisions are now mandated for tests administered state-wide.

For alternative assessment schemes, which require that criteria for acceptable performance, articulation of performance levels, and training of assessors be revised in addition to devising a new problem or performance task, revision is clearly more difficult, time-consuming, and expensive. Furthermore, the complex task assessments are themselves difficult to devise. For these reasons, alternative assessment tasks are often administered unchanged, year after year.

In New York, where it is the case that the same tasks have been used to assess fourth-grade science manipulative skills for at least three years, the teachers are fully aware of what their students will be asked to do, so their students' performance on these tasks may actually reflect the results of practice rather than any higher-level cognition, thereby subverting the very purpose of alternative assessment. The case of a New York geometry teacher who had been recognized for superior teaching on the basis of performance of his students on the Regents geometry exam. Unfortunately, the superior performance of his students was achieved by having them memorize the 12 proofs that might appear on the Regents exam. It is apparent from cases such as these that we cannot assume that basing high-stakes assessment on alternative assessment would alleviate "teaching to the test." Rather, unless continual revision were an integral aspect of the process, the complexity of revising assessment tasks could exacerbate the problem.

In England in the late 1980s, when the assessments that make up the General Certificate of Secondary Education were changed to put more emphasis on performance tasks and less on written answers, the gaps between the average scores of various ethnic groups increased rather than narrowed. Teachers in Irish primary schools were quite biased in the evaluation of their students at the time of their study. They speculate that the reason such bias existed was due to the lack of standardized testing in Ireland. Bias in standardized testing can be detected and, when it cannot be eliminated, its effects can be measured so that scores can be fairly interpreted. Bias in alternative assessment is much more difficult to articulate. Because this is the case, the effects of biased non-standardized assessments may not be recognized as such and may, therefore, be attributed to the subject rather than to the assessment.

Perhaps the most common argument proponents of alternative assessment bring against the use of standardized tests is this: standardized tests measure only recall and other lower-order thinking skills whereas alternative methods of assessment require students to exhibit the higher-order skills such as critical thinking, analysis, synthesis, reasoning, and problem solving. If this were true, it would be a very damning argument indeed, but neither assertion is altogether accurate. The development of assessments that require the demonstration of complex problem-solving strategies is an essential component of the alternative assessment movement. Proponents of alternative assessment cite the ability of alternative assessment problems to elicit the use of higher-order thinking skills and to assess the quality of those skills as its primary advantage over standardized methods of assessment. While it is true that alternative assessment techniques certainly have the capacity to fulfill these high aspirations, it does not necessarily follow that they always do. Proponents of alternative assessment cannot assume that students are using such skills just because they are performing a hands-on task.

Performance assessments may show how students solve problems or how much they have practiced the skill being assessed. Essays may indicate the ability to organize thoughts and communicate them in writing or nothing more than the acquisition of a formula for writing essays, assiduously taught in preparation for the assessment.

Discerning the difference is another hurdle alternative assessment must surmount. As to the assertion that standardized, multiple-choice tests assess only recall of specific and isolated bits of knowledge, it is appropriate to admit that some do. Some criterion-referenced tests of basic skills are little more than recitations of factoids. But this is not a function of standardized tests: this is a function of the purpose for which a particular test was devised. Educational Leadership, there was a high correlation between aptitude and achievement test scores and the scores on special reasoning tests.

Standardization is of little importance if the results of assessment are to be used in isolation from all other factors. In other words, if the purpose is simply to learn about the state of a single subject, a unique assessment might be devised to furnish the information desired. However, if the assessment is to be used for the purpose of comparison, generalization, or decision-making, standardization is essential. Standardized testing achieves standardization by norming practices, machine scoring of multiple-choice questions, precise instructions for administration, and standard formats for tests and recording of responses. The results can then be used to draw inferences about the state of cohorts or individuals as compared to an established standard. The task of standardization is far more complex in the matter of alternative assessment.

The judgment of performance of designated tasks is a matter of interpretation and is carried out by any number of individuals who may have different understandings of what an appropriate response entails. The presentation of the task may take place in vastly different circumstances and contexts. The lack of comparable, reliable, and robust data is a function of a lack of standardization in the administration of the SATs, problems in making judgments about students' performance, and of wide variations between schools in the support received for testing and in the amount of changes in practices and routines occasioned by the assessments. Furthermore, those who are assessed may also have difficulty in understanding what response is needed. Maeroff cites problems in portfolio assessment of elementary students' work. In one case, when a student chose her "best" math work, it was all from the beginning of the school year.

The evaluator had nothing from which to judge the child's progress. It is not necessary that alternative assessment measures exhibit the same level of standardization as achievement tests do in order to be of value, but the appropriate use of alternative assessment may be limited by the very characteristics that make it a good indicator of individual achievement from being a valid indicator of how that progress compares to the progress of others. It may be that an alternative assessment that is a marvelous indicator of an individual child's academic progress will prove fairly useless for other purposes.

A combination of the alternative assessments correlates about the same with aptitude as does the standardized science achievement test. Aptitude, then, is a major factor in generalizing performance across assessment tasks". What this means is that students score at a comparable level on the battery of performance assessments on aptitude and a standardized science achievement test.

According to a new study, the same thing is true on the free-response and multiple-choice parts of the

Advanced Placement computer science exam. More work examining the correlation between alternative assessment ratings and standardized measures of learning must be done, but there is evidence that such a correlation exists. Since this is the case, the question becomes which form of assessment is most appropriate to a given purpose.

The Tennessee Value-Added Assessment System (TVAAS) is a process that measures the influence that systems, schools, and teachers have on the rate of academic growth for populations of students. To accomplish this, TVAAS uses statistical mixed-model methodology and student scale scores from the norm-referenced component of the Tennessee Comprehensive Assessment Program (TCAP). However, any reliable linear measure of academic growth with a strong relationship to the curriculum could be used as input into the process. Pilot studies revealed and subsequent research has confirmed that the statistical mixed model theory and methodology upon which TVAAS is based alleviates the problems associated in the past with the use of student data in educational assessment. When extraneous factors are identified that would bias the estimates, this methodology readily allows the incorporation of exogenous variables to insure unbiased results.

However, the research to date indicates that this has not been necessary. For example, the effects attributable to individual systems and schools have been shown to be unrelated to socio-economic indicators such as number of reduced-cost or free lunch students, racial composition of the student body, or location--rural, urban, suburban. Each child's own academic history incorporates socio-economic status, ability, past achievement, and many other factors. By modeling a learning profile for each student as part of the mixed-model equations, children serve as their own controls or "blocking factors" in TVAAS. Assessment should be a tool for educational improvement, providing information that allows educators to determine which practices result in desired outcomes and which do not. TVAAS is an outcomes-based assessment system. By focusing on outcomes rather than the processes by which they are achieved, teachers and schools are free to use whatever methods prove practical in achieving student academic progress. TVAAS does not assume a "perfect teacher" or a 'best way to teach.' Rather, the assumption is that effective teaching, whatever form it assumes, will lead to student gains.

The advantage TVAAS offers in this regard is that those teachers and methods that lead to greater student achievement can be identified. In other words, teachers can try something new and actually see the effects, at least insofar as they are reflected in student academic gains. In several ways, this is an entirely new approach to using normed data. One criticism of the use of normed data is that it is often used to place students somewhere on a distribution for the purpose of comparison with others. TVAAS, to the contrary, uses scale scores to establish where a child is academically and to determine how much progress that child makes in a subject year. Where s/he is in relation to other students is irrelevant. Whether s/he progresses normally from whatever point s/he begins is what matters. TVAAS concentrates on gains because student gains provide information on educational effects that measures of ability cannot.

High achievement scores do not necessarily indicate progress, but high gains do. By focusing on the gains that all students make from year to year, regardless of where they start, the school systems and the individual schools deemed to be most effective by TVAAS are those that provide educational opportunities for all students--the advanced learner as well as the slower learner. The basic argument underlying the value-added approach is that true excellence resides in the ability of the school or college to affect its students favorably, to enhance their intellectual development, and to make a positive difference in their lives. TVAAS was developed on the premise that society has a right to expect that schools will provide students with the opportunity for academic growth regardless of the level at which the students enter the educational venue. In other words, all students can and should learn commensurate with their abilities. This very brief description of TVAAS is provided simply to illustrate one viable model for utilizing standardized scores in assessing educational entities. For a far more detailed description of TVAAS, its development, methodology, and application.

Standardized testing renders viable, inexpensive, reliable, and valid indicators of student learning useful in the assessment of educational entities and student achievement. Standardized testing is already in place in most states of the union, so the data are readily available. Standardization makes it possible to generalize and to draw conclusions about the data and their implications. Alternative forms of assessment are also viable tools for the assessment of student progress and attainment, so long as care is taken to assure their validity and reliability. Because they are expensive and difficult to develop, administer and score, their usefulness for large-scale assessment is questionable. Should such assessment models achieve comparable reliability and validity as standard measures now possess, they would in effect have become standardized, also. There is a question as to whether this is a desirable result. If it is determined that this is the course that should be attempted, the results of assessments of any type that exhibit an appropriate degree of reliability and validity can be used for large-scale assessment.

However, if alternative forms of assessment are used, instead, for the assessment of individual students by in-house assessors, many of the problems listed above may be avoided and the strengths of alternative assessment modes may have the impact desired on the quality of instruction in the classroom. The issue is not whether one form of assessment is intrinsically better than another. No assessment model is suited for every purpose. The real issue is choosing appropriately among indicator variables and applying the most suitable model to render them. It is necessary to determine what information is sufficient to each purpose before deciding upon the form of assessment to be used. When a variety of valid and reliable assessment methods exist, it is parochial and ineffectual to adhere to only one, asserting that it is in all instances superior.

Teacher Quality and Student Achievement

Despite conventional wisdom that school inputs make little difference in student learning, a growing body of research suggests that schools can make a difference, and a substantial portion of that difference is attributable to teachers. Recent studies of teacher effects at the classroom level using the Tennessee Value-Added Assessment System and a similar data base in Dallas, Texas, have found that differential teacher effectiveness is a strong determinant of differences in student learning, far outweighing the effects of differences in class size and heterogenity. Students who are assigned to several ineffective teachers in a row have significantly lower achievement and gains in achievement than those who are assigned to several highly effective teachers in sequence.

Teacher effects appear to be additive and cumulative, and generally not compensatory. These studies also find troubling indicators for educational equity, noting evidence of strong bias in assignment of students to teachers of different effectiveness levels, including indications that African American students are nearly twice as likely to be assigned to the most ineffective teachers and half as likely to be assigned to the most effective teachers. These studies did not, however, examine the characteristics or practices of more and less effective teachers. These issues have been the topic of much other research over the last 50 years. Variables presumed to be indicative of teachers' competence which have been examined for their relationship to student learning include measures of academic ability, years of education, years of teaching experience, measures of subject matter and teaching knowledge, certification status, and teaching behaviors in the classroom.

The results of these studies have been mixed; however, some trends have emerged in recent years. General Academic Ability and Intelligence While studies as long ago as the 1940s have found positive correlations between teaching performance and measures of teachers' intelligence or general academic ability, most relationships are small and statistically insignificant. Two reviews of such studies concluded that there is little or no relationship between teachers' measured intelligence and their students' achievement. Explanations for the lack of strong relationship between measures of IQ and teacher effectiveness have included the lack of variability among teachers in this measure and its tenuous relationship to actual performance. However, other studies have suggested that teachers' verbal ability is related to student achievement, and that this relationship may be differentially strong for teachers of different types of students. Verbal ability, it is hypothesized, may be a more sensitive measure of teachers' abilities to convey ideas in clear and convincing ways.

Subject Matter Knowledge Subject matter knowledge is another variable that one might think could be related to teacher effectiveness. While there is some support for this assumption, the findings are not as strong and consistent as one might suppose. Studies of teachers' scores on the subject matter tests of the National Teacher Examinations (NTE) have found no consistent relationship between this measure of subject matter knowledge and teacher performance as measured by student outcomes or supervisory ratings. Most studies show small, statistically insignificant relationships, both positive and negative. The results of thirty studies relating teachers' subject matter knowledge to student achievement.

The teacher knowledge measures were either a subject knowledge test or number of college courses taken within the subject area. The results of these studies were mixed, with 17 showing a positive relationship and 14 showing no relationship. However, many of the 'no relationship' studies, had so little variability in the teacher knowledge measure that insignificant findings were almost inevitable. Only 5 of 14 studies they reviewed exhibited a positive relationship between measures of subject matter knowledge and teacher performance. It may be that these results are mixed because subject matter knowledge is a positive influence up to some level of basic competence in the subject but is less important thereafter. For example, a controlled study of middle school mathematics teachers, matched by years of experience and school setting, found that students of fully certified mathematics teachers experienced significantly larger gains in achievement than those taught by teachers not certified in mathematics.

The differences in student gains were greater for algebra classes than general mathematics. However, a review of mathematics teaching that the absolute number of course credits in mathematics was not linearly related to teacher performance. It makes sense that knowledge of the material to be taught is essential to good teaching, but also that returns to subject matter expertise would grow smaller beyond some minimal essential level which exceeds the demands of the curriculum being taught. This interpretation is supported more recent study of mathematics and science achievement. Using data on 2,829 students from the Longitudinal Study of American Youth, teachers' content preparation, as measured by coursework in the subject field, is positively related to student achievement in mathematics and science but that the relationship is curvilinear, with diminishing returns to student achievement of teachers' subject matter courses above a threshold level. In a multilevel analysis of the same data set, both positive and negative, generally insignificant effects of teachers' subject matter preparation on student achievement. They did find some evidence of cumulative effects of prior as well as proximate teachers' subject matter preparation on student performance in mathematics.

Effects differed for high- and low-achieving students and for different grade levels. In a review of 65 studies of science teachers' characteristics and behaviors, students' science achievement was positively related to the teachers' course taking background in both education and in science. The relationship between teachers' training in science and student achievement was greater in higher level science courses, a result similar to that in mathematics. It may also be that the measure of subject matter knowledge makes a difference in the findings. Measures of course-taking in a subject area have more frequently been found to be related to teacher performance than have scores on tests of subject matter knowledge. This might be because tests necessarily capture a narrower slice of any domain. Furthermore, in the United States, most teacher tests have used multiple-choice measures that are not very useful for assessing teachers' ability to analyze and apply knowledge. More authentic measures may capture more of the influence of subject matter knowledge on student learning. For example, a test of French language teachers' speaking skill was found to have significant correlation to students' achievement in speaking and listening.

Despite concerns that education majors may be less well prepared in their subject areas than are academic majors, comparisons of teachers with degrees in education vs. those with degrees in disciplinary fields have found no relationship between degree type and teacher performance. This may be because certification requirements reduce the variability in course backgrounds found for teachers with different degree types. For example, many states require the equivalent of an academic major or minor in the field to be taught as part of the education degree for high school teachers, regardless of the department granting the degree. Given the standardizing influences of licensing requirements within states but substantial differences in licensing requirements across states, within-state studies are likely to find less variation in teachers' education backgrounds than might be found in cross-state studies. Knowledge of Teaching and Learning Studies have found a somewhat stronger and more consistently positive influence of education coursework on teachers' effectiveness. Significant positive relationships between education coursework and teacher performance in four of seven studies they reviewed—a larger share than those showing subject matter relationships.

A consistent positive effect of teachers' formal education training on supervisory ratings and student learning, with 11 of 13 studies showing greater effectiveness for fully prepared and certified vs. uncertified or provisionally certified teachers. With respect to subject matter coursework, 5 of 8 studies they reviewed found no relationship and the other three found small associations. Reviewing findings of the National Longitudinal Study of Mathematical Abilities, the number of credits a teacher had in mathematics methods courses was a stronger correlate of student performance than was the number of credits in mathematics courses or other indicators of preparation. Similarly, study of student's mathematics and science achievement found that teacher education coursework had a positive effect on student learning and was sometimes more influential than additional subject matter preparation. In an analysis of science teaching, teachers' coursework credits in science were not significantly related to student learning, but coursework in science education was significantly related to students' achievement on tasks requiring problem solving and applications of science knowledge.

Teachers with greater training in science teaching were more likely to use laboratory techniques and discussions and to emphasize conceptual applications of ideas, while those with less education training placed more emphasis on memorization. In a study of more than

200 graduates of a single teacher education program, the influences on 13 dimensions of teaching performance of education and subject matter coursework, NTE subject matter test scores, and GPA in the student's major. They found that the amount of education coursework completed by teachers explained more than four times the variance in teacher performance than did measures of content knowledge,which explained less than 4 percent. In a similar study which compared relative influences of different kinds of knowledge on 12 dimensions of teacher performance for more than 270 teachers, consistent strong, positive relationships between teacher education coursework performance and teacher performance in the classroom as measured through a standardized observation instrument, while relationships between classroom performance and subject matter test scores were positive but insignificant and relationships between classroom performance and basic skill scores were almost nonexistent.

Another program-based study, positive relationships between the extent of teachers' professional education coursework and their teaching performance, including their students' achievement. It may be that the positive effects of subject matter knowledge are augmented or offset by knowledge of how to teach the subject to various kinds of students. That is, the degree of pedagogical skill may interact with subject matter knowledge to bolster or reduce teacher performance.

The kind and quality of in-service professional development as well as pre-service education may make a difference in developing this knowledge. Several recent studies have found that higher levels of student achievement are associated with mathematics teachers' opportunities to participate in sustained professional development grounded in content-specific pedagogy linked to the new curriculum they are learning to teach. In these studies, both the kind and extent of professional development mattered for teaching practice and for student achievement.

The National Assessment of Educational Progress has also documented how specific kinds of teacher learning opportunities correlate with their students' reading achievement. On average, in the 1992 and 1994 assessments, 4th grade students of teachers who were fully certified, who had master's degrees, and who had had professional coursework in literature-based instruction did better than other students on reading assessments. While these relationships were modest, the relationships between specific teaching practices and student achievement were often quite pronounced, and these practices were in turn related to teacher learning opportunities. NAEP analyses found that teachers who had had more professional training were more likely to use teaching practices that are associated with higher reading achievement on the NAEP tests--use of trade books and literature, integration of reading and writing, and frequent visits to the library--and were less likely to engage in extensive of use of reading kits, basal readers, workbooks, and multiple choice tests for assessing reading, practices that the NAEP analyses found to be associated with lower levels of student achievement.

Interestingly, students of teachers who had more training in phonics instruction did noticeably less well than other students in both years. Often, this kind of training, narrowly cast, is focused heavily on the use of basal readers and workbooks rather than an integrated approach that teaches decoding skills in the context of other important reading skills and language development strategies. Other studies have found that students achieve at higher levels and are less likely to drop out when they are taught by teachers with certification in their teaching field, by those with master's degrees, and by those enrolled in graduate studies. However, like the NAEP analyses described above, these are simple correlational analyses that do not take into account other school resources or student characteristics like poverty or language background that may affect student performance. Continuity of teachers' learning may also matter. In earlier work, demonstrated that the recency of voluntary educational experience was related to teacher performance.

Teachers in exemplary science programs had higher levels of education and more recent educational experiences than others, even though they were older than the average science teacher. These findings may indicate that it is not only the knowledge acquired with ongoing professional development but also the teacher's enthusiasm for learning that relates to increased student achievement. Teaching Experience Other studies of the effects of teacher experience on student learning have found a relationship between teachers' effectiveness and their years of experience, but not always a significant one or an entirely linear one. While many studies have established that inexperienced teachers are typically less effective than more senior teachers, the benefits of experience appear to level off after about five years, especially in non-collegial work settings.

A possible cause of this curvilinear trend in experience effects is that older teachers do not always continue to grow and learn and may grow tired in their jobs. Furthermore, the benefits of experience may interact with educational opportunities. Veteran teachers in settings that emphasize continual learning and collaboration continue to improve their performance. Similarly, very well-prepared beginning teachers can be highly effective. For example, some recent studies of 5-year teacher education programs—programs that include a bachelor's degree in the discipline and master's in education as well as a year-long student teaching placement—have found graduates to be more confident than graduates of 4-year programs and as effective as more senior teachers. It is also possible that uneven effects of experience in cross-sectional studies can be the result of cohort effects or of attrition effects. Presumably, the direction of this effect would change if retention policies kept the most able beginning teachers in the profession. Since experience is also correlated with teacher education and certification status, these variables may be confounded in some analyses. Certification Status Certification or licensing status is a measure of teacher qualifications that combines aspects of knowledge about subject matter and about teaching and learning. Its meaning varies across the states because of differences in licensing requirements, but a standard certificate generally means that a teacher has been prepared in a state-approved teacher education program at the undergraduate or graduate level and has completed either a major or a minor in the fields to be taught plus anywhere from 18 to 40 education credits, depending on the state and the certificate area, including between 8 and 18 weeks of student teaching.

There are only a few states that have requirements outside these parameters; however, individual teacher education programs often require more preparation than the state demands in education, in clinical practice, and in the content areas to be taught. Most states now also require one or more tests of basic skills, subject matter knowledge, and/or teaching knowledge or skills as the basis for the initial or continuing license or for admission to teacher education. While most states have been increasing their standards since the 1980s, more than 30 states still allow the hiring of teachers who have not met their licensing standards, a practice that has been on the increase in some states as demand has grown in recent years. Some allow the hiring of teachers with no license. Others issue emergency, temporary, or provisional licenses to candidates who, depending on the state, may or may not have met varying requirements. More than 40 states have also initiated alternate route provisions for candidates who enter through postbaccalaureate programs.

Most of these are master's degree programs which offer an education degree that meets all of the normal state requirements but does so in a fashion tailored to individuals, like mid-career entrants, who already have a bachelor's degree. Some states allow candidates to complete a short summer course of study and assume full teaching responsibilities, with or without completing additional coursework. In times of relatively low demand, like most of the 1980s, virtually all teachers were certified and there was too little variability to find effects of this variable in large-scale studies. Most studies of the influence of training and certification on teacher performance are from the high-demand era of the 1960s and 1970s and from the 1990s when demand increased again. Studies in different subject matter fields that compare teachers with and without preparation have typically found higher ratings and greater student learning gains for teachers who have more formal preparation for teaching. In addition to the studies of science and mathematics teachers cited earlier, these include reading and elementary education, gifted education, and vocational education.

Other studies point out the differences in the perceptions and practices of teachers with differing amounts and kinds of preparation. A number of studies suggest that the typical problems of beginning teachers are lessened for those who have had adequate preparation prior to entry. Studies of teachers admitted with less than full preparation—with no teacher preparation or through very short alternate routes—have found that such recruits tend to be less satisfied with their training, and they tend to have greater difficulties planning curriculum, teaching, managing the classroom, and diagnosing students' learning needs. Principals, supervisors, and colleagues tend to rate them less highly on their instructional skills, and they tend to leave teaching at higher-than- average rates. These findings are reflected in performance of alternate route candidates in Dallas, who receive a few weeks of summer training from the district before they assume full teaching responsibilities. Although these candidates were rated near the average on some aspects of teaching, they were rated lower on such factors as their knowledge of instructional techniques and instructional models. The performance of alternate route candidates was also much more uneven than that of trained teachers, with a much greater proportion of them—from 2 to 16 times as many—rated 'poor' on each of the teaching factors evaluated.

The strongest effects of this unevenness were seen in students' achievement in language arts, where the achievement gains of students of alternate route teachers, adjusted for initial student scores, were significantly lower than those of students of traditionally trained teachers. Two studies of alternative certification in Texas have failed to find such gaps in the performance of students of alternative and traditionally licensed teachers. No evidence of differential student outcomes and little evidence of teacher effects.

Some recent multivariate studies of student achievement at the school and district level have found a substantial influence of teachers' qualifications on what students learn, especially when scores on licensing examinations are included. In an analysis of nearly 900 Texas school districts that evaluated the effects of many school input variables and controlled for student background and district characteristics, combined measures of teachers' expertise—scores on a licensing examination, master's degrees, and experience—accounted for more of the inter-district variation in students' reading and mathematics achievement in grades 1 through 11 than student socioeconomic status. An additional, smaller contribution to student achievement was made by lower pupil-teacher ratios and smaller schools in the elementary grades. Of the teacher qualifications variables, the strongest relationship was found for scores on the state licensing examination, a test that measures both basic skills and teaching knowledge.

The effects were so strong, and the variations in teacher expertise so great, that after controlling for socioeconomic status, the large disparities in achievement between black and white students were almost entirely accounted for by differences in the qualifications of their teachers. Ferguson also found that every additional dollar spent on more highly qualified teachers netted greater increases in student achievement than did less instructionally focused uses of school resources. Another study found that North Carolina's teachers' average scores on the National Teacher Examinations had a strong influence on average school district test performance. Taking into account per-capita income, student race, district capital assets, student plans to attend college, and pupil/teacher ratios, teachers' test scores had a strikingly large effect on students' failure rates on the state competency examinations: a 1% increase in teacher quality was associated with a 3 to 5% decline in the percentage of students failing the exam.

Together, teachers' academic ability, education, and experience, when combined with class sizes, accounted for 31.5% of the predicted difference in reading and mathematics student achievement gains between districts scoring in the top and bottom quartiles in mathematics, while 29.5% was explained by poverty, race, and parent education. When student characteristics are held constant, the relationship of teachers' qualifications to student achievement is even more pronounced. A study of high- and low-achieving schools with demographically similar student populations in New York City found that differences in teacher qualifications accounted for approximately 90% of the total variation in average school-level student achievement in reading and mathematics at all grade levels tested. A study of high school students' performance in mathematics and science using data from the National Educational Longitudinal Studies of 1988 (NELS) found that fully certified teachers have a statistically significant positive impact on student test scores relative to teachers who are not certified in their subject area, as do teachers who hold a degree in mathematics or mathematics education.

Furthermore, in states with licensing examinations, newly trained teachers have a strong positive influence on student achievement. In an unusual finding, the study indicated that teachers with emergency certificates in science had higher-scoring students after other teacher education and student demographic variables were controlled. However, because there were only 23 such teachers in the sample of more than 2900 and more than 20 variables simultaneously tested in the equations, many of them highly correlated with certification status, it is difficult to know what to make of this finding. In cases like this, small cell sizes and multicollinearity problems often combine to produce sign changes and poor estimates of effects. A more recent Texas study found that students in districts with greater proportions of licensed teachers were significantly more likely to pass the Texas state achievement tests, after controlling for student socioeconomic status, school wealth, and teacher experience.

Teacher licensing was especially influential on the test performance of elementary students. In a recent school level analysis of mathematics test performance in California high schools, a strong negative relationship between average student scores and the percentage of teachers on emergency certificates, as well as a smaller positive relationship between student scores and teacher experience levels, after controlling for student poverty rates. These findings about the influences and relative contributions of teacher training and experience levels are reinforced by those of a recent review of 60 production function studies, which found that teacher education, ability, and experience, along with small schools and lower teacher-pupil ratios, are associated with increases in student achievement across schools and districts. In their estimate of the achievement gains associated with expenditure increments on various resources, spending on teacher education was found to be the most productive investment for schools, outstripping the effect of teacher experience and reduced pupil/teacher ratios.

There are aspects of teaching effectiveness that may be related to teacher education, certification status, and experience, they do not reveal much about what it is about teachers' behaviors or abilities that makes the difference in how their students perform. Research on teachers' personality traits and behaviors has produced few consistent findings, with the exception of studies finding a recurring positive relationship between student learning and teachers' "flexibility," "creativity," or "adaptability". Successful teachers tend to be those who are able to use a range of teaching strategies and who use a range of interaction styles, rather than a single, rigid approach.

Effective teachers adjust their teaching to fit the needs of different students and the demands of different instructional goals, topics, and methods. In addition to the ability to create and adapt instructional strategies, strong research support has linked student learning to variables such as teacher clarity, enthusiasm, task-oriented behavior, variability of lesson approaches, and student opportunity to learn criterion material. Teachers' abilities to structure material, ask higher order questions, use student ideas, and probe student comments have also been found to be important variables in what students learn. No single instructional strategy has been found to be unvaryingly successful; instead, teachers who are able to use a broad repertoire of approaches skillfully are typically most successful. The use of different strategies occurs in the context of "active teaching" that is purposeful and diagnostic rather than random or laissez faire and that responds to students' needs as well as curriculum goals.

Teacher education appears to influence the use of these practices. Teachers who have had formal preparation have been found to be better able to use teaching strategies that respond to students' needs and learning styles and that encourage higher order learning hypothesizes that since the novel tasks required for problem-solving are more difficult to manage than the routine tasks associated with rote learning, lack of knowledge about how to manage an active, inquiry-oriented classroom can lead teachers to turn to passive tactics that 'dumb down' the curriculum, busying students with workbooks rather than complex tasks that require more skill to orchestrate.

Teachers' abilities to handle the complex tasks of teaching for higher-level learning are likely to be associated, to varying extents, with each of the variables reviewed above: verbal ability, adaptability and creativity, subject matter knowledge, understanding of teaching and learning, specific teaching skills, and experience in the classroom, as well as interactions among these variables. In addition, considerations of fit between the teaching assignment and the teacher's knowledge and experience are likely to influence teachers' effectiveness, as are conditions that support teachers' individual teaching and the additive effect of teaching across classrooms, such as class sizes and pupil loads, planning time, opportunities to plan and problem solve with colleagues, and curricular supports including appropriate materials and equipment.

Despite logical presumptions and research evidence that student learning depends substantially on what teachers know and can do, states differ greatly in the extent to which they invest in teachers' learning as a key policy lever. At the front end of the career, there is wide variation in the standards to which entering teachers and teacher education institutions are held. Licensing standards are noticeably different from state to state, as are state commitments to enforcing these standards. Later access to professional development is also widely disparate. In high-standards states like Wisconsin or

Minnesota, for example, a prospective high school teacher must complete a bachelor's degree that includes a full major in the subject area to be taught plus coursework covering learning theory, child and adolescent development, subject matter teaching methods, curriculum, effective teaching strategies, uses of technology, classroom management, behavior and motivation, human relations, and the education of students with special needs. In the course of this work, the teacher must complete at least 18 weeks of student teaching in Wisconsin under the supervision of a cooperating teacher who meets minimum standards. In Minnesota, this experience must include work in a multicultural setting and with special needs students. If teachers are asked to teach outside the field of their major for part of the day, they must already be licensed with at least a minor in that field, and can receive a temporary license in the new field only briefly while completing a major. By contrast, in Louisiana, prospective high school teachers can be licensed without even a minor in the field they will be teaching.

The state does not require them to have studied curriculum, teaching strategies, classroom management, uses of technology, or the needs of special education students, and they can receive a license with only six weeks of student teaching. In addition to differences in the standards themselves, there are great differences in the extent to which they are enforced. Whereas some states do not allow districts to hire unqualified teachers, others routinely allow the hiring of candidates who have not met their standards, even when qualified teachers are available. In Wisconsin and eleven other states, for example, no new elementary or secondary teachers were hired without a license in their field in 1994. By contrast, in Louisiana, 31% of new entrants were unlicensed and another 15% were hired on substandard licenses. At least six other states allowed 20% or more of new public school teachers to be hired without a license in their field.

Studies of teacher hiring show that even when there are an adequate number of qualified teachers in the labor market--which was the case nationally and in most states from the early 1980s through the mid-1990s--some districts hire unlicensed teachers because of cumbersome and poorly managed hiring procedures that discourage qualified entrants, perennially late hiring, patronage hiring, preferences for hiring lower salaried staff, and inequalities in salary schedules caused by state funding formulas and by local decisions to use budgets for purposes other than teacher salaries. More than 30 states allow teachers to be hired on temporary or emergency licenses without having completed preparation or having met other licensing requirements. During the late 1980s and early 1990s, at least 50,000 emergency or substandard licenses were issued annually by states. In 1994, 27% of those who were new entrants into public school teaching held no license or a substandard license in their main teaching field. Even the rigor of these restricted licenses varies. States such as Minnesota will issue a restricted license only to a teacher who has already been fully prepared in a teaching field but who needs to complete additional coursework in order to enter from out-of-state or switch to a new field or teaching level. Such a license is only good for one year, while the necessary coursework is completed. Others, including Louisiana, will issue an emergency license to a person who does not even hold a bachelor's degree and will allow it to be renewed for several years while the candidate makes little progress toward becoming licensed. It is certainly true that differences in student enrollment growth, coupled with teacher production rates and attrition, construct different levels of teacher demand that can affect the ease or difficulty of hiring within states.

While incentives to enter and stay in teaching are affected by policies governing salaries, working conditions, and teacher education funding, student enrollments are less amenable to policy control. It is reasonable to ask whether these differences in operational teaching standards are mostly a function of demographic trends beyond the control of state policymakers. In examining state variations in hiring practices, however, it is clear that a number of high-growth states have enacted and maintained high standards for entry to teaching while many low-growth states have not. Policies appear to be at least as important as demographics in determining the qualifications of teachers hired and retained. Because of these differences in licensing standards and enforcement, in 1994, more than 80% of high school teachers of academic courses in Wisconsin and Minnesota had fully met state certification requirements and had at least a college major in the field they teach. Four other states—Connecticut, Iowa, Montana, and North Dakota—reported similarly well-qualified teaching forces in that year. The comparable proportion of teachers with full state certification and a major in their field in Louisiana was only 64%. Interestingly, students in Minnesota and Wisconsin have typically scored at the top of the distribution on national assessments of reading and mathematics, along with the four other states who share similarly well-qualified teachers.

Together these states held six of the top ten spots in the national rankings in reading and mathematics in 1994 and 1996. Students in Louisiana have typically scored near the bottom of the NAEP distributions—no higher than

47th of 51 states in any of the assessments in 1996. The other six states with similar proportions of teachers holding a license and a major in their field all fall in the bottom quartile of states in the national rankings of average student achievement scores. Some have quipped that state-level student achievement in the U.S. can be best predicted by proximity to Canada—which in turn may be a proxy for variations among states in factors ranging from demographics to political culture and spending on education. States also differ greatly in the levels of funding they allocate to preservice and inservice teacher education, in the standards they apply to teacher education institutions and to schools, in the types and extent of professional learning opportunities and the incentives for professional study they make available to educators, and the extent to which they require or fund induction supports for beginning teachers. To illustrate these differences, in 1997 only three states required professional accreditation for schools of education and only nine funded induction programs that provided a structured program of mentoring for beginning teachers, including trained, state-funded mentors. Student teaching requirements ranged from 5 weeks in Massachusetts to 18 weeks in Wisconsin. As of 1994, the proportions of academic high school teachers teaching with both a license and a major in their field ranged from a low of 52% to a high of 85% across states.

The proportions of mathematics teachers teaching with less than a minor in the field ranged from a low of 9% to a high of 56%. This means that a student in one state might have only one chance in ten of being taught by an out-of-field teacher, while a student in another state might have more than a 50% chance of being taught a subject by a teacher who is not adequately prepared in that subject. In every category of possible investment in teachers' knowledge and in every area in which standards for teaching are set, there are substantial differences in the policies and practices employed by states. States with some of the highest, most consistently enforced standards for teachers have tended to cluster in the upper Midwest. States with the lowest and least well-enforced standards have tended to include many in the southeast and in remote locations. Some states have developed relatively ambitious standards for teaching but do not enforce them for large numbers of candidates. Others have made major investments in preservice and inservice teacher development in recent years that have affected a substantial share of the teaching force.

Trends in Student Achievement

The US secondary school students tend to score below the median in international assessments of mathematics and science, students in some states score as high as those in the top-ranked countries in the world while students in others score among the bottom-ranked. U.S. students also perform relatively better in some fields than others. For example, U.S. students have compared favorably with students in other countries in reading and at about the median in general science. However, in mathematics and physical science, U.S. students do much more poorly: In the most recent international assessments, 8th graders ranked 18th out of 25 countries that met the TIMSS guidelines in mathematics and 17th out of 25 countries in physics. Twelfth graders did even more poorly. Although it may be purely coincidental, these differences in rankings are similar to the differences in teacher qualifications across these fields. Since the early 1980s, the U.S. has made major investments in teacher preparation in the area of reading.

Not only are almost all elementary school teachers fully certified an increasing number have been prepared in programs that have a strong emphasis on training to teach reading; there has also been a large increase in the number of reading specialists throughout the 1980s. In general science and biology, where US middle and high school students scored at about the median on the most recent international assessments, there are relatively few uncertified or out-of-field secondary teachers. By contrast, in mathematics and physical science, where US students fall well below the international norms, teacher qualifications are much weaker. In addition to the fact that most US elementary teachers have had little background in mathematics, about 30% of US mathematics teachers and 50% of physical science teachers at the high school level have been teaching with less than a minor in the field, many of them uncertified. While these are only casual observations, other evidence point in similar directions.

Not only do U.S. students appear to perform least well in the fields in which U.S. teachers are least well prepared, the states that repeatedly lead the nation in student achievement in mathematics and reading have among the most highly qualified teachers in the country and have made longstanding investments in the quality of teaching. The three long-time leaders—Minnesota, North Dakota, and Iowa—have all had a long history of professional teacher policy and are among the 12 states that have state professional standards boards which have enacted high standards for persons entering the teaching profession. They are recently joined at the top of the achievement distribution by Wisconsin, Maine, and

Montana, states that have also enacted rigorous standards for teaching and that are among the few which rarely hire unqualified teachers on substandard licenses. Iowa, Minnesota, Montana, North Dakota, and Wisconsin have among the lowest rates of out-of-field teaching in US and among the highest proportions of teachers holding both certification and a major in the field they teach. Maine joined these states in requiring certification plus a disciplinary major when it revised its licensing standards in 1988. These states have also been leaders in redefining teacher education and licensing. Minnesota was the first state to develop performance-based standards for licensing teachers and approving schools of education during the mid-1980s and has developed a beginning teacher mentoring program in the years since.

Wisconsin was one of the first states to require high school teachers to earn a major in their subject area in addition to completing extensive coursework in a teacher preparation program. Thus, teacher education in Wisconsin is typically a four-and-a- half to five year process. Maine, Wisconsin, Iowa, and Minnesota have all incorporated the rigorous new standards developed by the Interstate New Teacher Assessment and Support Consortium (INTASC) into their licensing standards and have encouraged universities to pilot performance-based assessments of teaching using these standards.

The state was recognized in the recent National Education Goals Panel, for having made among the greatest gains in teacher mentoring of beginning teachers as well as the greatest achievement gains for students. These extensive investments in teaching occurred alongside sizable investments in early childhood education and general K-12 spending increases which lowered pupil/teacher ratios slightly. In the early 1990s, new curriculum standards were introduced and accompanied by an extensive program of professional development for teachers statewide. In 1993, the state enacted an assessment system linked to the curriculum standards and substantially aligned to the NAEP tests. This assessment program, which was implemented in 1994-95, occurred too late to account for most of the gains in achievement. Its effects would require several years to appear, but it may have had some modest influence on the gains after 1994.

A recent analysis of student achievement gains on the National Assessment of Educational Progress attributed much of the NAEP score increase in North Carolina between 1990 and 1996 to the test-based accountability system. However, the new standards and assessments were not on-line until 1995, and the rewards and sanctions component of the accountability system was not enacted until 1997, so it was clearly not a factor in these trends. Grissmer and Flanagan also note the state's large-scale investments during the 1980s in early childhood education, reduced class sizes, teacher salary increases, teacher education upgrades, and extensive professional development. All of these factors could have influenced the achievement gains observed during this time period. North Carolina's 1997 Educational Excellence Act furthered efforts to upgrade the quality of teacher preparation and teaching quality, pouring hundreds of millions of dollars into a new set of reforms.

The Act created a professional standards board for teaching and required that all colleges of education create professional development school partnerships to provide the sites for year-long student teaching practicums. It also funded a more intensive beginning teacher mentoring program, further upgraded licensing standards, created pay incentives for teachers who pursue master's degrees and National Board certification, and authorized funds to raise teacher salaries to the national average. It will be useful to watch future trends in the state. The state's 1986 Educational Enhancement Act spent over $300 million to boost minimum beginning teacher salaries in an equalizing fashion that made it possible for low-wealth districts to compete in the market for qualified teachers. At the same time, the state raised licensing standards by requiring a major in the discipline to be taught plus extensive knowledge of teaching and learning as part of preparation; instituted performance-based examinations in subject matter and knowledge of teaching as a basis for receiving a license; created a state-funded mentoring program which supported trained mentors for beginning teachers in their first year on the job; and created a sophisticated assessment program using state-trained assessors to determine which first-year teachers could continue in teaching.

An analysis of the outcomes of this initiative found that it eliminated teacher shortages and emergency hiring, even in the cities, and created surpluses of teachers within three years of its passage. Connecticut also required teachers to earn a master's degree in education for a continuing license and supported new, content- based professional development strategies in universities and school districts. In a National Education Goals Panel, highlighting Connecticut's strong performance and large gains in mathematics, state officials pointed to the salary increases and teacher education investments as central to their progress. These investments include an intensive professional development program in mathematics, science, and technology which, since 1983, has offered 4-week institutes with follow-up support to elementary, middle, and high school teachers. The state has more recently invested in new curriculum frameworks and a statewide assessment system for students using extended performance tasks and constructed response items intended to measure higher order thinking and performance skills. Launched in 1995, this system, which is tied to statewide of scores and substantial new professional development, may support future gains in student achievement. In addition, the state has further extended its performance-based teacher licensing system to incorporate the new INTASC standards and to develop portfolio assessments modeled on those of the National Board for Professional Teaching Standards (NBPTS). The new teacher assessments, which are tightly linked to the student standards, require beginning teachers to demonstrate that they can implement content-based teaching standards within their subject matter field and can analyze student work and learning.

Finally, as part of ongoing teacher education reforms, the state agency is supporting the creation of professional development schools linked to local universities as sites for clinical training of entering teachers. The Connecticut and North Carolina reforms both featured substantial investments in pre-service and in-service education for teachers linked to standards that incorporate much of the current knowledge base about teaching and learning. While the reforms also included salary increases, the dollars were linked to improved quality via heightened licensing standards. Both states sought to increase not only the quality of preparation for teachers, but also the consistency with which they enforced their standards, sharply reducing the hiring of unlicensed and under-prepared staff. Kentucky also realized substantial achievement gains during the 1990s, after undertaking perhaps the most extensive systemic education reforms of any state in the 1980s.

These included major equalization of school funding along with large increases in teacher salaries and overall spending; changes in school organization, including multi-age primary grade classrooms; investments in early childhood education; the introduction of standards and curriculum frameworks, along with portfolios and performance assessments. Changes in teacher education and licensing accompanied these reforms, including the adoption of the INTASC licensing standards developed by a consortium of more than 30 states, the introduction of new licensing tests and teacher education requirements, incentives for colleges of education to meet national professional accreditation standards; and massive investments in professional development. All of these efforts undoubtedly combined to produce the steep gains in achievement experienced in Kentucky. By 1994, data from the Schools and Staffing Surveys showed that Kentucky teachers were much better prepared in terms of their content and teaching coursework background than in 1988 and had experienced more extensive professional development than teachers in any other state.

A recent survey of Kentucky teachers also found that more than 80% of beginners who graduated from Kentucky colleges of education felt well-prepared for virtually all aspects of their jobs, in contrast to teacher education from previous studies elsewhere. Although somewhat less ambitious in their reforms, Arkansas and West Virginia also raised teacher salaries and licensing requirements and required national accreditation of education schools during the late 1980s or early 1990s, while investing in more professional development for in-service teachers. These states also realized steeper gains in student achievement than the national average. They attributed Texas' gains primarily to the state's accountability system, although they also mention its shifts of resources to more disadvantaged students through school finance equalization, class size reductions, and the creation of full day kindergarten.

The school funding investments that occurred in the 1980s and were continued into the following decade may indeed have made some difference in Texas students' achievement in the 1990s. However, the state's new assessment and accountability system was not initiated until 1994 and not fully implemented until 1995-96, so it could not have accounted for gains between 1990 and 1996. Texas was not included in the above analysis of state test score gains because it was not one of the states that made large comprehensive investments in teaching during the 1980s. In addition, however, there are questions about the stability of scores in Texas and the extent to which the posted gains are real. First, Texas included fewer than 45% of its students with disabilities in the testing pool, a much smaller share than most states. Excessive exclusions of low-scoring students from the testing pool can cause gain scores to appear much larger than they would otherwise be. In addition, recent studies in Texas have raised concerns that much of the ostensible gain registered by African American and Latino students has been a function of grade retentions and dropouts or pushouts, which have increased substantially in recent years. These practices also make average test scores look higher by eliminating lower scoring students from the testing pool.

Assuming that some of the gains in Texas are not spurious, however, it is worth noting that, in addition to the equalization of funding and investments in kindergarten and reduced class sizes, Texas was among the few states recognized by the National Education Goals Panel for large gains since the early 1990s in the proportion of beginning teachers receiving mentoring from expert veterans. Texas has also had a growing number of 5-year teacher education programs in response to an earlier reform eliminating teacher education majors at the undergraduate level. State reform strategies during the 1980s that did not include substantial efforts to improve the nature and quality of classroom work have shown little success in raising student achievement, especially if the reforms relied primarily on student testing rather than investments in teaching. For example, the first two states to organize their reforms around new student testing systems were Georgia, with its Quality Basic Education Act (QBE) of 1985, and South Carolina, with its Education Improvement Act of 1984. These states developed extensive testing systems coupled with rewards and sanctions for students, teachers, and schools. Although both states also mandated tests for teachers, they did not link these assessments to emerging knowledge about teaching or to new learning standards, nor did they invest in improving schools of education or ongoing professional development.

Few districts in either state require teachers to hold a degree in the field to be taught and full state certification as a condition of hiring. Student achievement in mathematics has been flat in these states while achievement in reading has declined. Since 1996, Georgia has launched an ambitious series of reforms through its P-16 Council to upgrade the quality of teacher preparation and professional development and to raise licensing standards, as well as to recruit high ability students to teaching. Future analyses might examine whether these moves have made a difference. There are competing hypotheses that could explain these across-state differences in achievement trajectories. One could speculate that student testing and curriculum changes are not in themselves powerful enough reforms to overcome the depressing effects on teaching quality of low standards for teacher education, licensing, and hiring, and the resulting large numbers of under-prepared teachers.

On the other hand, one can argue that variables like student poverty and language background, rather than conditions that might influence the quality of teaching, are the determining factors in student achievement and that the critical differences between high- and low-achieving states are differences in their student populations. It is interesting to compare the student achievement levels and trajectories for some of these states in comparison to geographically proximate states with similar student populations that have taken very different approaches to teaching policy. Although the states that have aggressively pursued investments in teacher knowledge and skills have equal or higher levels of student poverty than nearby states that pursued other, distinctively different reform strategies, their students now achieve at higher levels. Even though all of these states increased teacher salaries during the 1990s, those that insisted on higher standards for teacher education and licensing realized gains that were not realized by states that maintained or lowered their standards for entering teaching.

Finally, the level of aggregation necessarily influences the interpretations of results. Aggregating data to the state level produces different results than one would find if one looked at similar kinds of data at the individual student, teacher, school, or district level. The direction of the differences cannot be predicted with certainty. While, on one hand, the possibility of greater variability or noise exists in disaggregated analyses, it is possible that omitted variables may bias the coefficients of school input variables upward when the data are aggregated to the district or state level. Although the results of more and less aggregated specifications can be consistent Alabama analysis found comparable influences of teacher quality and class sizes on student achievement when measured at the student and the district levels, this may not always occur. In particular, the size of relationships found between variables measured at the state level cannot be assumed to represent the effect sizes one would find in a classroom level analysis. For the purposes of assessing broad policy influences at the state level, it is nonetheless reasonable to examine state-level data as a gauge of major trends when other confirming and disconfirming evidence is available to supplement the analysis.

Student characteristics such as poverty, non-English language status, and minority status are negatively correlated with student outcomes, and usually significantly so. These student characteristics are also significantly and negatively correlated with the qualifications of teachers; that is the less socially advantaged the students, the less likely teachers are to hold full certification and a degree in their field and the more likely they are to have entered teaching without certification. Student characteristics are generally not significantly correlated with state per-pupil spending or with teachers' salary schedules, with the exception that salary schedules are higher in states with larger percentages of minority and LEP students. Salary levels show an insignificant, negative relationship with levels of student poverty. Teacher quality characteristics such as certification status and degree in the field to be taught are very significantly and positively correlated with student outcomes.

Characteristics such as education level show positive but less strong relationships with education outcomes. Per pupil spending shows a significant positive relationship with student outcomes in 4th grade reading in both years, but no relationship with student outcomes in mathematics. This may be because the spending measure incorporates resources spent not only on teacher salaries and professional development but also on class sizes and other resources that may especially support students in the early grades as they are learning to read. Although salaries and spending are strongly related to one another, teacher salary levels, unadjusted for cost of living differences, are not correlated with student outcomes when aggregated to the state level. Other school resources, such as pupil-teacher ratios, class sizes, and the proportion of all school staff who are teachers, show very weak and rarely significant relationships to student achievement when they are aggregated to the state level.

Partial correlations confirm a strong, significant relationship of teacher quality variables to student achievement even after controlling for student poverty and for student language background in. The most consistent highly significant predictor of student achievement in reading and mathematics in each year tested is the proportion of well-qualified teachers in a state: those with full certification and a major in the field they teach. The strongest, consistently negative predictors of student achievement, also significant in almost all cases, are the proportions of new teachers who are uncertified and the proportions of teachers who hold less than a minor in the field they teach. General spending and salary variables, along with class sizes, are not significantly related to achievement once student characteristics are taken into account. It should be noted, however, that this analysis did not take into account cost-of-living differentials that may affect both salaries and spending levels; controlling for such differentials could produce a different set of results with respect to these variables.

Ordinary least squares regression analyses were performed to create the most parsimonious specification of a hyperplane of best fit with student achievement data. Because of the small sample size, the number of independent variables in each equation was minimized to preserve the necessary degrees of freedom. Variables were selected according to three criteria: to examine relationships often tested in other studies, to maximize explanatory power, and to avoid problems of multicollinearity. Teacher quality variables included the percentage of all teachers with full certification and a major in the field and the percentage of uncertified newly hired teachers, because these exhibit large influences on achievement, and the percentage of teachers with master's degrees, because this is a frequently examined teacher quality variable. Class size was also included because it is commonly found to influence achievement. Spending and salary variables were not included in the final estimations because they showed little relationship to student achievement in preliminary estimates. Because the percentage of minority students is highly correlated with both poverty rates and LEP status, while poverty rates and LEP status are not as highly related to each other, the equations were estimated with poverty rates and LEP status as key student characteristics to avoid multicollinearity.

Other teacher quality variables contribute modestly to explaining student achievement. The proportion of teachers with master's degrees exerts a small, generally positive effect on achievement, while the proportion of uncertified new teachers exerts a small, generally negative effect. Together, these three teacher quality variables account for between 40 percent and 60 percent of the total variance in student achievement in reading and mathematics in each of the years and grade levels assessed, once student characteristics are taken into account. Smaller class sizes are moderately associated with higher achievement in five of the six equations, with the largest effects visible in 4th grade reading. Student poverty rate exerts a negative influence on achievement, although it is not significant in four of the six equations. In mathematics, the proportion of LEP students exerts a positive effect on achievement after controlling for poverty status. In reading, LEP status exerts an insignificant negative effect on achievement when poverty is controlled.

Clearly, in any analysis such as this, the variables that can be measured are only proxies for the actual conditions or traits that may matter to student learning. In this case, a large number of variables associated with teacher quality appear to bear a significant relationship to student achievement. These include various ways of measuring state certification status and disciplinary preparation. Given the differences in licensing standards and teacher education programs across states, these proxies are fairly crude ones; nonetheless, they seem to indicate that teachers' knowledge, skills, and preparation matter for student achievement.

The findings are similar to those of several other studies described earlier in finding much stronger influences on student achievement of variables measuring teacher knowledge and skills than of variables like teacher experience, class sizes, or pupil-teacher ratios, which are generally found to have noticeable but smaller effects on student achievement where data are aggregated to the school or district levels. The strength of the "well-qualified teacher" variable may be partly due to the fact that it is a proxy for both strong disciplinary knowledge and substantial knowledge of education. If the two kinds of knowledge are interdependent as suggested in much of the literature, it makes sense that this variable would be more powerful than either subject matter knowledge or teaching knowledge alone. It is also possible that this variable captures other features of the state policy environment including general investments in, and commitment to, education, as well as aspects of the regulatory system for education, such as the extent to which standards are rigorous and the extent to which they are enforced. Recall that some states require teachers to acquire a subject matter major as well as extensive education training in human development and learning and in the methods of teaching in their field, while other states require much less extensive preparation in the content area as well as teaching and learning. In addition, some states are vigilant in enforcing their certification standards while others are not.

There may be unmeasured correlations between the extent to which states enact and enforce high standards for teachers and the extent to which they have enacted other policies that are supportive of public schools. Although it does not appear that teaching standards are strongly related to investments regarding class sizes or to overall education spending, it is possible that there are other factors influencing student achievement which generally co-exist with teacher quality and which were unmeasured in these estimates. Since most of the states which ranked among the highest-scoring on the NAEP examinations are strong local control states that have traditionally not exerted much control over school decision making, there are relatively few policy areas in which they have been active. Perhaps the relative lack of policy intervention is itself a support for student learning, leaving educators free of regulations that might force greater attention to procedures than learning.

Another possibility is the influence of these states' small school and district sizes, a factor that has been identified in much research as contributing to student learning. In another analysis, most of the top-scoring states on NAEP have very small average school sizes relative to national norms. One area in which policies have not been positively correlated, however, is the extent to which states engaged in statewide student testing in the 1980s and the extent to which they enacted high standards for teachers. Among the 12 highest- scoring states in 8th grade mathematics in 1996, none had mandatory statewide testing programs in place during the 1980s or early 1990s. Only two of the top 12 states in 4th grade mathematics had statewide testing programs in place prior to 1995. By contrast, among the 12 lowest-scoring states, 10 had extensive student testing programs in place prior to 1990, some of which were associated with highly specified state curricula and an extensive menu of rewards and sanctions. There are several possible interpretations of the almost inverse relationship between statewide testing policies and both teaching standards and student performance: It may be that states with low student performance and less qualified teachers were more likely to seek education improvements through student testing strategies and curriculum controls. It may also be that states have tended toward different theories of reform, with some investing more in testing and others in teaching. It is possible that regional differences in education investments and centralization happen to be correlated with policies regarding both testing and teacher investments. The lack of apparent relationship between testing programs and student achievement might be because, without other investments to improve teaching and schooling, tests alone do not transform learning.

Another possibility is that the kinds of basic skills tests and curricula enacted in many states during the 1980s were at odds with the NAEP assessments which increasingly seek to measure higher-order skills and performance abilities. It may be worth noting that most of the high-scoring and fast-gaining states discussed earlier instituted curriculum and testing reforms in the mid-1990s that were linked to the national student standards that guide NAEP and were much more performance-oriented than the basic skills tests that predominated in state assessment systems of the 1980s. While there is little evidence yet of the effects of these assessment programs on student learning, policy analysts may want to watch to see whether the types of tests matter for broad student outcomes as well as whether and how the supports that do or do not accompany testing programs make a difference.

There are particular policy strategies used by states or districts that are associated with the preparation and hiring of better qualified teachers. The SASS data set and additional data collected directly from states provides several policies in this regard. Teacher education accreditation National data from the National Association of State Directors of Teacher Education and Certification and from the National Council for the Accreditation of Teacher Education provided the percentage of teacher education institutions that were accredited by NCATE. NCATE-accreditation might lead to higher overall standards for teachers because NCATE standards revisions in 1988 and 1993 required higher admissions standards, evidence of greater subject matter preparation, and stronger rationales for the content of education coursework than those often emphasized by state approval systems. Standard setting and enforcement mechanisms The state survey tracked the presence of a state professional standards board for teaching, analogous to the boards that govern other professions, which might enact and enforce higher standards.

Since any policies for teacher education adopted by such a board would require several years to take broad effect, the enactment of a standards board prior to 1990 is the measure we used for examining influences on teacher qualifications in 1994. District hiring standards SASS data provided the percentage of school districts in each state requiring each of the following as conditions for hiring: full state certification, graduation from an approved teacher education program, and a college major or minor in the field to be taught. There was wide variation across the states in the degree to which districts looked for evidence of these kinds of teacher qualifications as part of the hiring process. Many more fine-grained variables, such as the content of licensing standards and the nature of teacher education programs, could not be tested with these data. Nonetheless, the results suggest some interesting associations. The strongest predictor of the percentage of well-qualified teachers is the percentage of teacher education institutions in a state that meet national accreditation standards through NCATE.

The proportion of NCATE-accredited institutions is also significantly and negatively correlated with the proportion of English and mathematics teachers who are "out-of-field". This may be because institutions that are NCATE-accredited must demonstrate that their students have the opportunity to acquire a base of content knowledge deemed acceptable by the subject matter associations that review applications as well as pedagogical knowledge in their field. Thus, these institutions may, as a group, have less variability than others in establishing reasonably high standards for disciplinary knowledge as well as knowledge of how to teach the discipline. It may also be that states in which professional accreditation is more widespread also happen to have other policies or practices in effect that support the preparation and hiring of well-qualified teachers.

Since teachers' certification status is also related to state demographics, these variables were regressed against hiring standards along with student poverty, percent minority, and percent LEP students. The relationship between hiring standards and teacher certification status continues to be highly significant after controlling for student poverty, race, and language status. This analysis triangulates data from surveys of state policies, case study analyses of state policymaking, and quantitative examination of the distribution of state achievement scores and resources, taking student characteristics into account. Some findings are particularly noteworthy. First, while student demographic characteristics are strongly related to student outcomes at the state level, they are less influential in predicting achievement levels than variables assessing the quality of the teaching force. Second, when aggregated at the state level, teacher quality variables appear to be more strongly related to student achievement than class sizes, overall spending levels, teacher salaries, or such factors as the statewide proportion of staff who are teachers. Among variables assessing teacher "quality," the percentage of teachers with full certification and a major in the field is a more powerful predictor of student achievement than teachers' education levels. This finding concurs with those of other studies cited earlier. It is not surprising that masters degrees would be relatively weaker measures of teacher knowledge, given the wide range of content they can include, ranging from specialist degrees in reading or special education that are directly related to teaching to fields like administration and others that have little to do with teaching.

Other measures of certification status are also strong correlates of student achievement. Finally, certain policy strategies associated with standard-setting at the state and local level—NCATE-accreditation of teacher education institutions, district hiring standards, and, to a lesser extent, state professional standards boards--appear to be related to teacher qualifications in the field. While the triangulation of data from several sources lends some confidence to these findings, they should be viewed with caution. Like all studies that draw inferences from broad state trends and correlational data, there are many variables in play at any given time and many possible explanations for any phenomenon observed.

Because the state data on average class sizes and other school resources ignore wide variations in teaching and learning conditions that may be very important at the district, school, and classroom levels, these estimates cannot fully capture the effects of such variables. Average class sizes, for example, vary relatively little across states but vary substantially within states and districts. Thus, effects of this variable are much more likely to be perceived with more disaggregated data. By merging district, school, and teacher files, the SASS data can allow for the use of Hierarchical Linear Modeling techniques, which would be a useful tool for further exploring relationships between teaching and schooling variables at the school, district, and state levels. Nonetheless, in conjunction with a number of other studies in recent years, suggest that states interested in improving student achievement may be well-advised to attend, at least in part, to the preparation and qualifications of the teachers they hire and retain in the profession. It stands to reason that student learning should be enhanced by the efforts of teachers who are more knowledgeable in their field and are skillful at teaching it to others. Substantial evidence from prior reform efforts indicates that changes in course taking, curriculum content, testing, or textbooks make little difference if teachers do not know how to use these tools well and how to diagnose their students' learning needs.

The effects of well-prepared teachers on student achievement can be stronger than the influences of student background factors, such as poverty, language background, and minority status. And while smaller class sizes appear to contribute to student learning, particularly in fields like elementary reading, the gains occasioned by smaller classes are most likely to be realized, as they were in the Tennessee experiment, when they are accompanied by the hiring of well-qualified teachers. States may impact the qualifications of the teachers through policies that influence the hiring standards of school districts, the accreditation of teacher education institutions, and the bodies that establish and enforce teaching standards. Reforms underway to create more thoughtful licensing systems, more productive teacher education programs, and more effective professional development strategies are producing evidence of the stronger effects on teaching and learning of approaches that strengthen teachers' abilities to teach diverse learners with a keen diagnostic eye and a wide repertoire of strategies supporting mastery of challenging content.

7

Ethical Issues of Infoage Education

Information Technology can be used to simply automate the procedures currently used in organisations; but existing activities are much more likely to be at least rationalised, in order to take advantage of new possibilities that the technology creates; and in some cases they need to be substantially re-invented.

The impacts on organisational processes are therefore generally noticeable, and can be quite profound. The expectation is that the changes will have considerable benefits, but these will often be felt only in the medium-term. Commonly, the short-term impact on the organisation and its profit is negative, as investment is undertaken, once-off expenditure is written-off, and disruption occurs to the existing routine. The impacts on employees are almost inevitably significant.

Many people currently in the workforce have not been well conditioned for change by their education and training, and are not mentally well-prepared for it. Quite commonly, those workplaces most in need of radical re-design are those in which the employees have been in a settled (and increasingly inefficient) mode of operation; and hence the shock of change is all the greater.

People's work-patterns, and the skills required of them, may be quite different from those that have, until recently, been conventional. Capabilities in relation to computers and communications are vital. The conventional approach of deferring particular kinds of transactions, and processing them occasionally in batches, may be replaced by on-demand handling of clients' needs.

There may also be impacts on working-hours, such as customer support extended beyond the traditional 9am-5pm time-frame. The location at which the work is performed may also change, with more performed on client's sites, or at home. These changes can result in major impacts on organisational structure as well. Increasingly, the primary focus is on business processes, and the hierarchy of managers and supervisors is being regarded as less important. Organisational units that run as mini-empires are often inefficient because they are resistant to change for extended periods.

When IT is implemented, such units are likely to be dis-established. The looser workgroups which replace them, rather than being associated with other, similar groups are more likely to be linked along the business chain by which value is added to the organisation's raw materials to produce its finished products. Beyond the workplace, communities are functioning differently because of I.T. Some of the more important impacts are in the following areas:

— changes within existing communities;

— the emergence of electronic communities.

One of the tendencies of 'successful' I.T. applications is that they deliver a great deal of what each individual needs at a workstation or playstation. So there is less reason for each individual to get up and walk around. Apart from being physically unhealthy, this also reduces people's direct interactions with one another, which is the cornerstone of existing communities. Another negative impact is the reduced need for humans to work, arising from the productivity in white-collar work which I.T. is delivering.

For many people, this results in lowered self-respect, and reduces their commitment to themselves, their community and their society. New forms of communities are emerging, based on USENET, Fidonet and the Internet during the last 20 years, and the explosion in popular use of the Internet during the last 3-5 years. Electronic communities have quite different characteristics from traditional communities based on physical proximity, and on cultural, ethnic, religious and professional commonalities.

Society as a whole, and individuals within society, are being significantly affected by IT. Some of the more important impacts are in the following areas:

- equity of access to information;
- pricing;
- regulation;
- consumer rights;
- privacy; and
- electronic freedoms.

In a society that claims to offer equality of opportunity, there is a need for equity of access to information, and hence to the infrastructure whereby information is accessed. Currently, the Internet and the world-wide web are accessible for relatively low costs. A related issue is that of pricing, particularly of information gathered and made available by government. The information infrastructure comprises many components, including high-bandwidth backbones, regional capacity, 'tail-ends' out to user sites, and workstations in public institutions such as schools and libraries.

The cabling, network hardware and software, and communications protocols need to respect a sufficiently common set of sufficiently advanced standards and protocols that inter-operability can be achieved; and yet the whole undertaking must incorporate sufficient flexibility and adaptability that future advances can be exploited. It is also important to appreciate that the scheme is intrinsically supra-national, or global rather than just regional, national or local. Many difficulties must be confronted, however. One which has attracted attention is the question of regulation of the information infrastructure.

A great deal of attention has been focussed on sexually explicit material, particularly that which would be refused classification by the Censor, and which would accordingly be illegal to possess or distribute in printed or filmed form. Other risks exist, however, such as incitements to violence, including extreme forms of racist behaviour, and instructions on how to prepare explosives, commit crimes and perform terrorist acts. Concerns also arise about the impact of IT on consumer rights.

The challenge for governments is to impose controls in support of the public interest, without destroying the free, open and self-regulatory nature of the Internet. The 'equity of access to information' issue was discussed earlier. The other side of the same coin is the question of the privacy of personal data and personal communications.

In general, activities on the Internet and the world-wide web are identified: the postings individuals read, the goods and services they enquire about or purchase can be monitored and recorded. The growth rate in traffic on the information infrastructure has been so great that its impacts on privacy have so far been more theoretical than real.

But both commercial, marketing interests, and government agencies whose functions include data surveillance, are taking an increasing interest in the information that can be gleaned about individuals from their behaviour on the Internet. Many people are arguing for considerable electronic freedoms for individuals. One example is the movement to ensure that any individual is free to use any form of cryptography.

This means, on the one hand, that individuals will have the same rights in cyberspace as they do in the real world, to obscure their conversations from people who may be listening. On the other hand, it makes the tasks of national security and law enforcement agencies in combating organised crime and terrorist groups more difficult than it otherwise would be.

At a more general level, IT is affecting aspects of the national economy, in particular in the following areas:

— employment levels;

— the distribution of income; and

— access to education and training.

Productivity tools of many different kinds are enabling organisations to perform functions with fewer resources, and in many industries this means that fewer humans are being employed. The rate of new job creation by emergent industries appears not to be high enough to take up the slack. The result is that, even when the economy is improving, unemployment levels are staying high, participation rates are falling, and more people are in part-time employment than was the case in the past.

Some people are fairly well-adapted to part-time pay for part-time work, especially at particular stages of their lives, such as the period when young children are at home or needing care after school, and in the years preceding full retirement from the workforce.

Unfortunately, many of the people out of work in Australia at present are recent school-leavers, many of them matriculants, and in some cases even tertiary-trained graduates. In the past, people who had never been employed, and had therefore never had an occupation, were rare exceptions; but we may be seeing the emergence of a whole class of permanently unemployed and unemployable.

Many others among the currently unemployed are people who have not only an economic, but also a psychological, need to be in employment. IT is succeeding for the organisations that use it, and may do so for the customers of those organisations. It may also do so for the people who continue to be employed. There is therefore a need for society to deal fairly with the people who don't have jobs as a result, at least in part, of IT's success. Measures of several kinds are needed:

— to ensure that the distribution of income is equitable;

— to enable the unemployed to achieve individual quality of life; and

— to address the problem of whole communities within which few members are employed.

The law establishes the framework within which people's rights and responsibilities exist, and can be enforced. IT is having an impact on some aspects of the law, including:

— evidentiary questions;

— intellectual property, especially copyright; and

— unintended contingent liabilities.

Another legal issue is that of intellectual property law in general, and copyright in digital materials in particular. Similar concerns arose with the widespread use of photocopiers, and of audio and video tape recorders.

Digital technologies are much more complex, and their impacts more profound. Copyright statements accompany many on-line databases, but it is not entirely clear how enforceable these statements are, and what steps governments need to take to protect the rights of the authors. Another matter of concern is whether organisations providing electronic services to other corporations and the general public may be incurring unintended contingent liabilities.

For example, the contents of some web-pages might be interpreted by the courts as representing advice, and a person who relied on it and suffered because of that reliance, might have a case in negligence against the publisher. Alternatively, a page might breach another person's copyright, or contain material whose display is illegal in some other jurisdiction.

Some people are concerned about the cultural integrity of their regional or lingual groups. The President of France has expressed concern about the predominance of english on the Internet, despite the fact that 47 countries in the world speak french. Critics suggest that the use of english is a convenience, and not an attempt by the U.S.A. and other english-speaking countries to dominate the world and destroy local cultures.

On the other hand, equity and freedom of speech and information may be considered to be basic rights within the so-called 'advanced western world', but this is not the case in all cultures, particularly those in which a particular religion plays a major role. There are also ways in which national sovereignty is threatened by the global information infrastructure.

The law can be difficult enough to impose within a geographical jurisdiction; but when data storage, information communication, and funds, all flow freely across national borders, the ability to enforce the law, and to collect the taxes on which government agencies depend, may be greatly reduced.

Many people are sceptical about the ability of nations to survive the challenges that the global information infrastructure represents, and anticipate breakup of large countries into smaller communities. An important part of the national sovereignty question is the integrity of the currency.

During most of the twentieth century, currency has been mainly issued by national governments. Things approaching supra-national currencies have emerged (such as Eurodollar bonds and the forthcoming common European currency), but these have been subject to considerable influence by national governments. Now new forms of currency are beginning to appear that may within a few decades completely undermine the ability of central banks to provide a framework within which all flows of funds take place, and to influence the level of activity within the national economy through the instrument of monetary policy.

Stored value schemes using 'smart' chip-cards, of which several variants were launched in Australia during 1995-96, are one threat. A much larger one is electronic cash, also referred to as E-cash, or digital cash. Electronic cash is based on cryptographic techniques, and enables organisations and individuals to make payments in a secure manner, directly over the information infrastructure. It performs several functions, including that of:

— a medium of exchange, which is immediate, convenient, cheap, and relatively difficult to trace; and

— a store of value, which is no more intangible than existing deposit balances recorded on a remote computer, but is much more readily spirited across national borders.

Electronic cash is capable of subverting traditional monetary controls. And it is technically proven, and in the course of being implemented. Rather than just listing problems, we need to work out what to do about them. The key terms that are used in this regard are:

— risk analysis;

— risk management; and

— controls and audit.

Risk Management Strategies encompass the following alternatives:

— Proactive Measures

— Avoidance (don't use risky forms of IT, e.g. neural networks)

— Deterrence (motivate people not to do risky things with IT, e.g. make people liable in criminal and civil law)

— Prevention (put barriers in the way of people who might do risky things with IT, e.g. ban client-side scripting products like Java, install firewalls, avoid connecting company networks to the Internet)

— Reactive Measures

— Detection (have means of knowing when people make risky uses of IT, e.g. install virus-testing software on all workstations)

— Recovery (have means of repairing the damage, e.g. data backup and recovery procedures)

— Insurance (share the risks around, e.g. compulsory computer centre fire and earthquake insurance policies, duplicated processors, uninterruptable power supplies)

— Non-Reactive Measures

— Tolerance

In Australia, Information technology students played a significant role in ethics education and shaping their perceptions and deliberation of situations involving ethical considerations. The effects of cumulative ethics education with regard to students' ethical behaviour when dealing with various computer oriented situations.

A study shows that students' perceptions of the amount of training they received in computer ethics differ from one student to the next, regardless of their level of education. The burgeoning information technology sector has placed greater on the ability of its professionals to deal with a range of situations which have ethical implications. Educators must take responsibility for providing effective training that identifies and stresses the importance of appropriate ethical behavior especially as it relates to the use of computers.

The information technology revolution we are now facing affects all aspects of our daily life. The issues that arise from such rapid changes include the impact on our social values as well code of ethics. While the motives of unethical behaviour are not new, the manifestations in the IT (information technology) context present a challenge to our society.

As more and more people are now employed in the IT industry and society depends more and more on IT, it is important that IT professionals graduating from Universities have the right ethical attitude and understand the conflicts they are facing when tempted to carry out unethical behaviour.

The Cognitive Dissonance theory is based on a few assumptions. The central assumption is that human beings cannot tolerate cognitive inconsistency. The theory states that dissonance (psychological inconsistency) exists whenever one cognitive element conflicts with another cognitive element. The magnitude of dissonance is a function of the importance of each cognitive element and the number of dissonant and cognitive elements that exist at that time. Once dissonance is aroused, there will be a need to reduce dissonance.

Dissonance may be reduced in many ways, including revoking the decision that causes the dissonance, lowering the importance of the decision and adding consonant elements. Thus, from the Cognitive Dissonance Theory perspective, when a person who believes he/she is a good person is tempted to commit or has committed an act of unethical behaviour, cognitive disssonance arises.

The belief that one is a nice and honest person and the thought that one is about to commit or has committed an act of unethical behaviour (such as copying software illegally) causes conflict, dissonance or psychological discomfort. After the theory is introduced, the students are given scenarios of unethical behaviour and requested to analyse the unethical behaviour from the perspective of the theory.

In United States, the fair use doctrine has been called "the most significant and perhaps murky of the limitations on the copyright owner's exclusive rights. This limitation becomes even more murky when applied to the educational use of copyrighted material on the global Internet, either in the form of downloaded material or material that has been "uploaded" for use by others.

A study of United States university deans revealed that the deans had a very limited understanding of what the act entailed and the relationship between the law and the guidelines. As a result, American educators tend to err on the side of conservatism, while other countries interpret simple accessability as unlimited license.

Section 107 of the United States Copyright Act of 1976 provides four statutory factors for the court to consider in determining whether the alleged infringement was "fair use", namely 1) the purpose and character of the use, 2) the nature of the copyrighted work, 3) the amount used and 4) the effect of the use on the potential market. Many courts have attempted to address "fair use", often leaving confusing and sometimes seemingly contradictory decisions for academicians.

The global nature of the Internet has further complicated the issue of fair use of Internet material. Cultural differences and social cohesion are examined as key variables in examining the international implications of copyright. One of the biggest challenges to intellectual property right protection is derived from the global access of the Internet and the varying, culturally based, perceptions of individual or community rights regarding knowledge products.

The copyright enforcement policies of countries should be expected to vary and this idea is explored using the values topology created by Hofstede. Specific examples of differences between countries are reviewed to provide insight into how the cultures perceive the protection of intellectual property.

Educators using the Internet to provide class materials need a clearer understanding of the implications and boundaries of "fair use". As the computer, the Internet, and multimedia become more involved in education, teachers need to be aware of the implications and limitations of fair use from both a legal and ethical perspective.

Guidelines for educators, based on the current law, are offered. Then, the authors suggest clearer guidelines which should be adopted either by way of international legislation or court decisions. Those guidelines suggest that any conflict between "fair use" as it is now defined and "educational fair use", should be resolved in favor of the educational fair use.

Internet Privacy

The new communication and computer technologies has generated a host of ethical problems, and some of the more pressing concern the moral notion of privacy. Some of these problems arise from new possibilities of data collections, and software for computer monitoring. For example, computers can now combine and integrate data bases provided by polling and other means to enable highly personalised detailed voter profiles. Another cluster of problems revolves around the threat to privacy posed by the new possibilities of monitoring and surveillance. For example, telephone tapping, interception of electronic mail messages, minute cameras and virtually undetectable listening and recording devices give unprecedented access to private conversations and other private communications and interactions.

Possibly the greatest threat to privacy is posed by the possibility of combining these new technologies, and specifically combining the use of monitoring and surveillance devices with certain computer software and computer networks, including the Internet. Provision of an adequate philosophical account of the notion of privacy is a necessary precursor to setting the proper limits of intrusion by the various new technologies.

Such an account of privacy would assist in defining the limits to be placed on unacceptably intrusive applications of new technologies. Moreover it would do so in such a way as to be sensitive to the forms of public space created by these technologies, and not unreasonably impede those new possibilities of communication and information acquisition which are in fact desirable. As always it is important to balance the rights of individuals against the needs of the community.

On the one hand there is a fundamental moral obligation to respect the individual's right to privacy, on the other hand there are the legitimate requirements of, for example, employers to monitor the performances of their employees, and law enforcement agencies to monitor the communications and financial transactions of organised crime. Moreover the working out of these ethical problems is relativised to a particular institutional and technological context.

Perhaps email messages sent on a company owned computer network ought to be regarded as public communications within the organisation however personal their content, since unlike ordinary mail, email messages are always stored somewhere in the backup system owned by the company and are therefore accessible to the dedicated company cybersleuth.

Cyberspace and Ethics

The most pervasive Internet metaphor is 'cyberspace'. It conjures sci-fi images of travel through an outer space. The freedom to go anywhere in next to no time and seek out new worlds of information is evident in the mythology of hackers and the explorations of web surfers. The other main Internet metaphor is the infobahn.

Cyberspace as a newly discovered wonder of the world. There are two ethical reasons:

— If cyberspace is considered a natural phenomenon, it should be explored respectfully, and the laws that govern it should be discovered, rather than imposed.

— If cyberspace is seen as a human environment, we are responsible for its (mis-)use and (un)sustainable development.

These points offer conditions of entry into cyberspace. We assert that any proposed regulations should be consistent with any properties of cyberspace that may be discovered. When observing cyberspace phenomenologically, the most important property that distinguishes it from 'realspace' - i.e. our physical reality - is its detachment from the space-time reference system and proceed to demonstrate the following contrasts exist: cyberspace: realspace:

— absolute relative

— unbounded bounded

— intangible material

— free governed

— dynamic static

— homogenous heterogeneous

The effects of these contrasting properties are not considered in the conventional method to decide an ethical issue in cyberspace. Instead, the cyberspace scenario is transplanted into an analogous situation in realspace.

The interpretation of the realspace issue in the external analogy is intended to clarify the cyberspace issue. However, it is often simplistic because contrasts between cyberspace and realspace are omitted. A cyberspace ethics methodology that explicitly considers cyberspace and realspace contrasts during analogical thinking. A reciprocal internal (cyberspace) analogy is devised in parallel with an external analogy. This focuses attention on the impact of cyberspace and realspace contrasts and avoids a simplistic external interpretation. The effectiveness of our methodology is demonstrated in the virtual rape issue.

Trials with introductory computer ethics students also showed they formulated more solution options to a given ethical issue than with the conventional method. This can indicate deeper understanding.

With the advent of appellate review concerning the Internet and similar systems of computer-mediated communication, jurists are increasingly called upon to define rights and duties within virtual environments. This task necessarily involves the use of some operative definition of the nature of digital interaction and of relationships to conventional situations. The term 'cyberspace' is often used within judicial decisions to describe virtual activities. Although ubiquitous, the word is not neutral.

The recent American appellate decisions which attempt to describe 'cyberspace' and its relationship to conventional legal paradigms. It will additionally investigate sources, both academic and popular which are invoked by courts to support their characterisations. As a result of these endeavours, proposes that because much of what transpires within electronic confines is resistant to direct empirical description, judicial treatment will necessarily be interpretative and heavily- reliant upon rhetorical characterisations.

Ethical Use of Information Technology

In the use of Information Technology (IT), ethical considerations have become a focus point for many practitioners and educators because of the rapid proliferation of this technology. Many issues, however, remain unresolved.

Information Systems (IS) curricula often fail to include a discussion of ethical considerations, and even when they do, fail to reach the relevant audience. Worse yet, studies have shown remarkably lax ethical standards among IS faculty and students. The situation has now become immensely more complex. In the very recent past, the capacity to place material on the World Wide Web has been acquired by a very large number of people.

As evolving software has gently hidden the complexities and frustrations that were involved in writing HTML in its rawest and most nasty form, more and more web sites are being created by people with a relatively modest amount of computer literacy. At the same time, once the initial reluctance to use the Internet and the World Wide Web for commercial purposes had been overcome, sites devoted to doing business on the Internet mushroomed and e-commerce became a term permanently to be considered part of common usage.

The assimilation of a new and sometimes revolutionary technology is almost never entirely smooth sailing. The employment of the Internet and the World

Wide Web for the many and diverse purposes that they are used for today is certainly no exception.

As the technology begins to grow out of its infancy, a multitude of new issues surface continually, and a large proportion of these issues remain unresolved. Many of these issues contain a strong ethics content. As the ability to reach millions of people instantly and simultaneously has passed into the hands of the average person, the rapid emergence of thorny ethical issues is likely to continue unabated. There is little argument regarding the power of the Internet to inform.

As a media, it has far more potential than radio or television ever did, and both of those have permanently changed the world we live in, although not always for the better. One enormous difference between traditional mass media radio, television, print) and the new media of the Internet is accessibility. The former were domains of the well heeled: a relatively small number of people controlled radio, television, or the print media.

Software piracy

Software piracy - which refers to the practice of 'pirating' or 'unauthorised copying' of a computer program that is neither site licensed nor in the public domain, has become a serious global problem. Software piracy occurs not only in industry, but it is equally prevalent in educational institutions. A normative model was also developed to identify those factors that are related to students' use of pirated software. The model ties together eight independent variables with the dependent variable - the use of pirated software. These independent variables are grouped into four categories: students' piracy attitude, demographics, computer exposure, and institution parameters.

Ethics of Visual Persuasion

In past twenty years, computer technology has allowed more sophisticated and mostly undetectable alteration of photographs, so that consumers and readers are intentionally deceived. The increasing tendency of the news media to use the photograph to illustrate preconceived editorial ideas, a development in photojournalism which has seen the profession's manipulation of photographs move beyond the conventional retouching techniques and simple cropping of extraneous details to the continual revision of photographs so that they more precisely illustrate the point of view expressed in the text.

Furthermore, photographs can be constructed to illustrate anyone's point of view in the publishing chain of command. Such practices have led critics to label this change a move from photojournalism to photofiction.

The realignment of the photographs of personalities has allowed misperceptions of closeness such as Margaret Thatcher appearing in debate with George Bush by the juxtaposition of their images, The advertising industry has also attracted criticism for misperceptions in consumers such as travel photographs showing non-existing natural features, and Beneton's use of the harrowing picture of a dying AIDS patient to advertise its products. The ethics of visual persuasion in advertising by the manipulation of images have been raised comprehensively by Messaris, 1997. Further image ethics issues are raised in respect of copyright and ownership of intellectual property. Whereas a book or painting may be seen as a whole, and where the copying of all or part is reasonably detectable, the easy and most often undetectable manipulation of photographs and clip art renders the ownership of this artwork impossible to protect. The ethical issues raised by the ease of image manipulation in the digital age require the estabishment of an ethical protocol.

Prominent in this protocol should be the definition of photographs under categories in the manner in which text is defined, such as fiction and non-fiction or editorializing and reportage. It may be necessary to employ a specific terminology such as 'photo-illustration' to differentiate physically manipulated photographs from others. Educators of students in computer subjects where the techniques of image manipulation are taught have a responsibility to establish an image ethics protocol for their students to follow in both their academic work and future professional activities.

Science to solve all the major problems faced by society, in the early 1950s . This was not surprising since the world had just emerged from a war that had essentially been won by the application of new technologies. Society gave scientists and other professionals the freedom to develop new innovation with little or no accountability.

For a decade or so, the quality of life steadily increased, people prospered and life was good. However, this period also saw the beginning of a steady increase in the diffusion of new technological innovation aimed at transforming the business world, with a subsequent impact on society in general. From the 1960s onward, this new innovation increasingly leap-frogged ahead of society's ability to accept and integrate it. Many of the problems that science promised to solve are still with us. Many new problems actually created by innovation have been added to the list. In our nation, increased access to education and rapidly expanding communication networks mean that most people are well informed.

They perceive that many of the problems they now face could have been moderated, or avoided, if technological innovation could have been scrutinised prior to wide spread adoption. Constant change means that it is practically impossible to plan for the future.

Many individuals face considerable uncertainty and fear for themselves and their children. Some feel betrayed, that the interests of business; the pursuit of favourable economic outcomes through technological innovation, has been at the expense of their quality of life.

Most people are now unwilling to give scientists and other professionals the same freedoms afforded their predecessors in the 1950s. During the past five decades, and especially in the last two, much of the technological innovation impacting on society has been computer-based. It is beyond question that computer-based technologies have had a most profound impact on people and society. With the rapid internationalisation of trade, many important industrial and commodity markets have adopted a global focus.

The business world has become dependent on computer and telecommunication sciences. The importance of the computing profession has rapidly grown, and competent specialists are in short supply, and high demand, around the world. Society's expectation is that computer professionals will produce systems that will enhance the human experience and not hinder it. They expect that they will not be injured, exploited or ignored.

To review the literature and identify professional and ethical issues of importance to society and the individuals within it. Care will be taken to rank these issues in order of significance. These issues will be reviewed against the framework of the various mechanisms through which society can exert an influence on the conduct of computer professionals:

— The Law, in its various forms

— The activities of the professional associations

— The expectations of employers

— The expectations of customers

— The collective will of society as a whole expressed through accepted practice, social taboos etc.

I.T. professionals in many ways enjoy powerful and privileged positions within society, as they are commonly at the forefront of the construction, interpretation and dissemination of knowledge. Because I.T. professionals enjoy the privileges , they should conversely be sensitive to the expectations of broader society, a task which inevitably involves a thorough and critical investigation of how the activities of I.T. professionals impact on the world around them.

Interface design and Ethical issues

Interface design is an important factor in determining how well a human can interact with a computer system.

However the issue of ethics in interface design seems to receive considerably less attention. Historically off-line processing and trained operators provided an environment where the lack of ethics in design did not cause major problems.

The environment of humans interacting with computers is changing rapidly and ethics should become increasingly important. We have moved to real-time online processing with a wide range of users interacting with computer systems.

Current interface design most often requires an interface that allows immediate interaction and feedback. Design of the interface can introduce bias and this in turn can disadvantage or offend users because of gender, age, culture and the workplace environment. The historical background of human computer interaction and the increasing relevance of ethical considerations at the interface. Global communication and interaction with its many cultures and conflicting norms highlights the need for a strong ethical foundation in interface design.

Codes of Professional Ethics

Computer science and related fields are comparatively recent professions. Following the example of many professional bodies, associations of computer professionals have developed and adopted codes of ethics for their members.

The Australian Computer Society has both a Code of Ethics and a Code of Professional Conduct and Practice. Like other professional codes, the ACS codes aim to provide guidelines for their members as to how to exercise their responsibilities to society, clients, the computing profession itself, and other stakeholders.

Teaching Ethics to Computing Students

The Australian Computer Society has identified a body of knowledge for computing professionals. This includes the teaching of ethics in computing courses as mandatory for professional level accreditation of a course.

The Division of Information Technology at La Trobe University Bendigo offers three entry-level courses in computing that are accredited by the ACS: a Bachelor of Business where students can elect to major in Information Technology (BBus(IT));

— a Bachelor of Computing, which includes a requirement for study in a different discipline of the student's choice (commonly accounting, electronics or psychology)(BComp);

— and a Graduate Diploma in Computing, with no non-computing components (GradDipComp).

Core subjects in the Information Systems streams of these courses introduce students to, for example, the ACS Code of Ethics. However, the only in-depth treatment of computer ethics is currently in an elective ("capstone") subject called Professional Environment, open only to final year students in all three courses.

The objectives of Professional Environment are to assist students to orientate themselves to the professional aspects of practising in the computing field, to learn about ethical and legal responsibilities, to consider social implications of their work, to do independent research, and to further develop oral and written communication skills. This subject has been taught in its present form since 1995.

The ACS core body of knowledge in its section entitled Ethics/Social Implications/Professional Practice states that students should be "encouraged to develop a personal ethical framework". Both the teaching methods and assessment in Professional Environment have been chosen specifically to encourage and assist students to do just this.

In teaching ethics a combination of methods are used: ethical theory via a lecture, tutorials using case studies and/or role plays, videos, and an assignment where students need to apply ethical theory to solve an ethical dilemma drawn from their personal experience. Some of the methods used have been more successful than others, from both a teaching and a student perspective. Student comments from the Professional Environment subject evaluations have singled out ethics as the most valuable component of the subject.

Many people would argue that ethics should be taught in every computing subject, and certainly there are some subjects in our courses where lecturers successfully weave ethics into the subject content. However, the reality is that many do not, and an elective capstone course for those students who are interested and motivated to learn about professional issues in computing has been our choice at La Trobe University Bendigo over the last four years.

The rapid advancement of computer technology has left the community sector in general and senior citizens in particular lagging behind. This generates issues involving social justice and equity for all. The social impact of computers in the life of an aging person is examined, particularly the impact of computer technology on senior lifestyles in the 1990's.

If computer technology in design and availability does discriminate against seniors then questions of social justice and the distribution of resources arise. As human individuals we are unique. This also is true for senior citizens. Thus, there is no one typical senior who we can use as a basis for examination. Therefore, in order to provide a balanced analysis, a number of variables characteristic of the senior citizen context need to be examined.

There are, for example, many ailments, disabilities and changes to lifestyle that occur or take place, as one grows older. On the health side a range of problems may generate special needs. For example, Alzheimer's and other forms of dementia in some degree are common among the aged.

Computers are functional machines. They are used to write letters, assignments, calculate the weather forecast and solve many other problems. Computer technology does have a bias, attributable to inherent features of the technology and to the social settings in which computers are developed and used.

This bias can be seen in the types of computer-based products and services available, in their locations and in their sources'. It may be the case that computers have been designed for a specific reason for a specific environment. When one takes these machines and tries to adapt them for personal use one finds that the design is not always compatible with the intended purpose.

This maladaptive aspect of computer technology, it is argued, is nowhere more evident than in groups of senior citizens. There is very little in the way of interface design and hardware that takes senior lifestyle into consideration. Yet, we see the increased marketing of computer technology within the senior context and thus, the ethics, or the lack of ethics, of the advertising industry is brought into focus.

In United States, Computer Based Information Systems (CBIS) is a "conversion" course for graduates from non-computing disciplines who have little or no computing experience. While our M.Sc. in the Management of Information Technology (MIT) is intended to assist graduates in computing, or others with an equivalent existing background, become hybrid managers. That is, managers who combine information technology and computing skills with business and organisational skills in order to ensure the effective deployment of information technology in their organisation.

Unemployment and the Internet

The new information technologies are universally blamed for the disappearance of many traditional jobs, they have at the same time opened new horizons, provided new opportunities and given new hopes. The Internet has already proven to be a major and most innovative tool/ resource in many important areas of human activity, i.e. business, education and entertainment among others.

These areas are of crucial importance for the unemployed since they often need to upgrade (refresh) their skills and knowledge (poor or insufficient skills/ educational background being usually the main reason for the unemployed not being able to join the workforce).

The Cybernation, a "nation whose communication of commonly held beliefs and philosophies is effected through the Internet", already exists and the unemployed are among its citizens. At the same time the processes of globalization, technological change and organizational restructuring in the past decade are forcing governments and institutions to redefine their concepts of work and (un)employment.

The latest trends of labour force mobility and flexibility and the frequent redundancies (downsizing) are a sign of the inevitable - during the new millenium many people will be without long-term secured jobs; immersed in an Information Age environment they will have more free time and hopefully access to the Information Superhighway. The Internet can benefit the short/long-term unemployed in various ways: through on-line educational and training programmes, non-residential learning centres, alternative schools and youth centres, job-search databases, ties to individuals in other unemployment settings, through creating and maintaining novel relationships that can lead overtime to new employment opportunities, etc.

However, unlike the use of television, radios and telephones, the individual use of network information services currently appears to be accelerating at higher income and education attainment levels. Unemployed people with poor education do not often find the way or the financial means to the Internet and its resources. Governments should implicitly encourage the use and development of Internet based educational programs. It should be noted that the relative cost of developing such educational programmes (reaching many people) can be significantly reduced.

Incentives should be provided to unemployed that would qualify for participation in Internet professional training programmes, varying from raising the unemployment benefits for the successful participants or alternatively directly subsidising the costs of Internet access on the participants' side.

The US administration's National and Global Information Infrastructure initiatives, providing a broad, modern concept of universal service and open access to the Internet can serve as an example of using the Internet as a generator of new employment opportunities. Governments should combine market incentives and individual tax credits to increase computer ownership among unemployed, provide free e-mail and fund educational programmes in order to avoid the emergence of a "two-tier" society of information haves and have-nots.

The ethical issues involved in the participative development of cultural heritage information systems for indigenous people, based on geographic information systems (GIS) technology. GIS are combinations of hardware, software, data, procedures and people assembled for the capture, storage, retrieval, analysis and display of spatially and temporally referenced information.

The key ethical issues for information systems practitioners and reviews some approaches for dealing with them. Ethical considerations are especially important where the system users may be vulnerable to exploitation, breaches of confidentiality and misrepresentation of concepts (e.g. GIS for indigenous communities).

The use of a highly participative system development methodology is critical in such circumstances, however this will not guarantee that all relevant ethical issues are appropriately addressed. A large number of ethical issues for cartographyand GIS related to indigenous peoples. He highlights so many potential pitfalls and ethical dilemmas that one could infer that such projects should never be attempted. However, there are strong reasons why at least some indigenous people want to use GIS.

Equally, in the era of information society the importance of ethical dimensions encompassing ordinary end-users (henceforward referred as 'end-user ethics') are of crucial relevance e.g., for example because increasing amount of people (at least in Western societies) use computers for different purposes. Due to certain differences between teaching matters of end-users and professional users, albeit there are certain similarities in the most abstract level, the both groups are likely to need separate frameworks for ethics teaching in the area of computing.

This is simply because computer usage of professionals have, for example, a professional focus, such as planning and implementing of computer systems, etc. (there is, of course, advanced end-users that may use fourth generation languages, do macro programming and similar - that need to be taken into consideration). Also, professional codes of conducts, specially the most detailed ones, may not be fully appropriate at least per se for end-users.

Furthermore, irrespective of category of users, there is often argued to be a gray area, for instance people have difficulties to extend their moral reflection in cases where IT/computer are involved. There have been several reasons to describe this kind of problem, such as conceptual muddle by; moral distance by; a moral crisis by; people are under a spell of IT; problem related to conventional moral notion, etc.

End-users' education needs efforts to avoid the aforementioned problem - a facet that is not approached holistically. Also, the ethics of ethics teaching demands that we should avoid indoctrination and the teachers should act in the neutral way. However, in spite of such a demand, ethics teachers should promote commonly agreed ethical goals of computer usage, and notice the importance of an occurrence of moral responsibility as well as they should tell about dangers and problems related to computer usage.

Although teachers are not directly responsible of users' actions and their goals, teachers are responsible to tell facts and outcomes of computer usage - as far as it can be predicted. Components represent possibilities for moral failure in general, but they also give framework and goals for developing ethics teaching. The main research problem is to develop such a state of art framework that can be used providing end-user education in a university level. This furthermore includes certain restrictions and limits of our framework.

Conceptual analysis is used as a primary research method. Also qualitative research, mostly related to literature review and our earlier experiences, is used.

Analysis of computer usage Use of IT (excluded computer professionals' usage) for variety of purposes. The nature of IT, the dangers and pitfalls of computer usage and possible future usage are covered. The responsibilities of the usage of "universal tool". Moral Distance The distancing effect of IT creates gap between computer users and the people affected. Moral distance made known to students.

Practices which help the distance can be narrowed. Solving and avoiding conflicts and dilemmas By teaching theoretical virtues we may hope that students form good practical virtues.

Moral vacuum The absence of ethical traditions in IT. The applicability of our values in IT. Amorality in the area of IT. Forming solutions to new situations. Using ethical theories in problem solving. Use and usability of analogies. Ethics of ethics teaching The ethical problems and conflicts in ethics teaching. Free will, autonomy and weakness of will. Neutral teachers. Students make their own decision how they use IT. Practice of ethics teaching Organization matters of end-user ethics teaching.

The development and application of recent computer technology offers some revolutionary, complex and wide-ranging challenges in this area. The altering of images has up until recently been a largely manual process of editing and bringing together photos or film from various sources. Recently technology has enabled more adroit manipulation of images, by manipulating them in the very act of filming them in the first instance. It is possible, for instance, to superimpose an advertising image onto say the playing field at a sporting fixture. This has both advantages and disadvantages. It enables advertising material to be superimposed where traditional methods of applying it may be hazardous (eg material pained onto the road surface of a formula one race). However, it alters the point from which advertising content is controlled and hence the relationship between the event and the advertisers. This developing technology also enables material received from international sources to have local advertising superimposed onto it (often in real time), much as though that advertising had been there in the first instance. This enables material where the original may have been inappropriate for cultural or legal reasons to be superimposed with material more appropriate for a particular audience. There is however a more serious set of ethical questions to be faced. These relate to the fact that even the original source from which the image is later copied (be it photo, film, internet, or other) is already computer mediated.

The representation has already been purposefully altered or changed in the act of filming. Here is where a substantial debate arises. On the one hand it is typically the case that any image represents only a certain aspect of what 'was actually there' and in that sense any image "edits reality". On the other hand here is a tool which can be used by advertisers and others to add material (or edit or alter material) in almost any scene so as to make it appear that this particular material was part of the scene when the image was taken.

Bibliography

Anderson, J. R., and Skwarecki, E. (1986). *The automated tutoring of introductory computer programming, Communications of the ACM*, Vol. 29, 9, 842-849.

Anderson, J.R., Boyle, D.F., Farrell, R, and Reiser, B.J. (1987). *Cognitive principles in the design of design of computer tutors.* In P. Morris (Ed.), Modeling Cognition, Wiley.

Brown, J.S. and Duguid, P. (1993). *Stolen knowledge. Educational Technology*, March, 1993.

Bruneau, J. Chambreuil, A., Chambreuil, M, Chanier, M, Dulin, P, Lotin and Nehemie, P. (1991). *Cognitive science, artificial intelligence, new technologies: How to cooperate for a computer-assisted learning to read system.* In Proceedings of the International Conference on the Learning Sciences, Evanston, Il.

Burton, R. R., and Brown, J. S. (1982). *An investigation of computer coaching.* In D. H. Sleeman & J. S. Brown (Eds.), Intelligent Tutoring Systems (pp. 79-98). New York: Academic Press.

Cohen, D. K. (1988). *Educational technology and school organization.* In R. S. Nickerson & P. P. Zodhiates (Eds.), Technology in Education: Looking Toward 2020 (pp. 231-264). Hillsdale, NJ: Erlbaum.

Collins, A. (1991). *The role of technology in restructuring schools.* Phi Delta Kappan, September, 28-36.

Collins, A., and Brown J.S. (1987). *The computer as a tool for learning through reflection.* In H. Mandl and A. Lesgold (Eds.),

Learning issues for intelligent tutoring systems. New York: Springer-Verlag.

Cuban, L. (1993). *Computers meet the classroom; Classroom wins.* Education Week, November 11, pp 26-27.

Hunter, B. (1993). *Internetworking: Coordinating technology for systemic reform.* Communications of the ACM, 36(5), pp. 42-46.

Lesgold, A., Eggan, G., Katz, S., and Rao, G. (in press). *Possibilities for Assessment Using Computer-Based Apprenticeship Environments.* To appear in W. Regian and V. Shute (Eds.), Cognitive approaches to automated instruction. Hillsdale, NJ: Erlbaum.

Lewis, M., McArthur, D., Bishay, M., and Chou, J. (1992). *Object-Oriented Microworlds for Learning Mathematics through Inquiry: Preliminary Results and Directions.* Proceedings of the East-West Conference on Emerging Computer Technologies in Education, Moscow, April.

Robyn, A., Stasz, C., Ormseth, T., and McArthur, D. (1989). *Implementing computer-assisted instruction in first-year algebra classes.* Paper presented at the American Education Research Association National Conference, San Francisco, April.

Scardamalia, M, and Bereiter, C. (1993). *Technologies for knowledge-building discourse.* Communications of the ACM, 36(5), pp. 37-41.

Index